LIVING PALESTINE

Gender, Culture, and Politics in the Middle East
Leila Ahmed, Miriam Cooke, Simona Sharoni, and Suad Joseph
Series Editors

Other titles in Gender, Culture, and Politics in the Middle East:

Beyond the Exotic
Women's Histories in Islamic Societies
AMIRA EL-AZHARY SONBOL, ed.

The Dance of the Rose and the Nightingale
NESTA RAMAZANI

Faith and Freedom
Women's Human Rights in the Muslim World
MAHNAZ AFKHAMI, ed.

Gendering the Middle East
Emerging Perspectives
DENIZ KANDIYOTI, ed.

Intersections
Gender, Nation, and Community in Arab Women's Novels
LISA SUHAIR MAJAJ, PAULA W. SUNDERMAN, AND THERESE SALIBA, eds.

Intimate Selving in Arab Families
Gender, Self, and Identity
SUAD JOSEPH, ed.

Missing Persians
Discovering Voices in Iranian Cultural History
NASRIN RAHIMIEH

Muslim Women and the Politics of Participation
Implementing the Beijing Platform
MAHNAZ AFKHAMI AND ERIKA FRIEDL, eds.

No Shame for the Sun
Lives of Professional Pakistani Women
SHAHLA HAERI

LIVING
PALESTINE

Family Survival, Resistance,
and Mobility under Occupation

EDITED BY Lisa Taraki

 Syracuse University Press

First Edition 2006

06   07   08   09   10   11   6   5   4   3   2   1

Mohamad El-Hindi Books on Arab Culture and Islamic Civilization
are published with the assistance of a grant from the M.E.H. Foundation.

The paper used in this publication meets the minimum requirements
of American National Standard for Information Sciences — Permanence
of Paper for Printed Library Materials, ANSI Z39.48-1984.∞™

ISBN: 0-8156-3107-3 (cloth)
        0-8156-3134-0 (pbk.)

Library of Congress Cataloging-in-Publication Data
available from the publisher upon request.

Manufactured in the United States of America

CONTENTS

TABLES

CONTRIBUTORS

Lamis Abu Nahleh is assistant professor at the Institute of Women's Studies at Birzeit University. She has conducted research concerning gender and education, the Palestinian family and household, and women's microcredit projects. She is the author of *Gender Planning, Vocational Education, and Technical Training (VETT) in Palestine* (1996). She is actively involved in community outreach programs involving gender planning and empowerment at the Institute of Women's Studies. She is currently engaged in research on the Palestinian family.

Rita Giacaman is professor at the Institute of Community and Public Health at Birzeit University. She is a member of the Consultative Committee of the Reproductive Health Working Group, Arab World and Turkey, a network of researchers from the region. Her current research interests include mental/psychosocial health and urban health and policy studies. She has published in the areas of women and health, health policy, and health sector reform, as well as the impact of warlike conditions on the physical and mental health of civilians. She is the author of *Life and Health in Three Palestinian Villages* (1988).

Jamil Hilal is a Palestinian sociologist who has published several books and numerous articles on Palestinian society and politics. His recent publications include *Israel's Economic Strategy Towards the Middle East* (1996, in Arabic), *The Palestinian Political System after Oslo* (1998, in Arabic), *Towards a Palestinian Social Security System* (1999, in English and Arabic), and *The Formation of the Palestinian Elite* (2002, in Arabic). He is also one of the main contributors to *The Palestine Poverty Report* (1998, in English and Arabic). Hilal is senior research fellow at the Palestinian Institute for the Study of Democracy (Ramallah) and has participated in and supervised research at the

Law Institute, the Development Studies Program, and the Institute of Women's Studies, all at Birzeit University in the West Bank.

Penny Johnson is an associate researcher at the Institute of Women's Studies at Birzeit University. Her recent work has focused on gender, law, and citizenship; social policy; and families, gender, and war. She has contributed to the *Encyclopedia of Women and Islamic Cultures* and *The Encyclopedia of Social Policy*. She was a member of the National Poverty Commission and is on the editorial committee of the *Jerusalem Quarterly File*.

Eileen Kuttab is assistant professor of sociology at the Institute of Women's Studies at Birzeit University and serves as its director. As an activist, she has been involved with grassroots women's organizations and has served on boards of trustees of human rights and development research centers. Her main research interests center around the relation of feminism to nationalism, social movements and in particular the women's movement, gender and development and in particular women's work in the informal sector, and coping strategies. She has many publications in these areas. Her current work is on the new wave of internal displacement of Palestinians.

Lisa Taraki is associate professor of sociology at Birzeit University. She has published articles in books and professional journals on Palestinian mass organizations and the Palestinian national movement, Jordanian Islamists and gender relations, and various aspects of gender relations in Middle Eastern and Palestinian society. She has also contributed to several commissioned reports on socioeconomic and gender issues in Palestine. Her current work on urban life in Palestine is ongoing, and the chapter coauthored with Giacaman in this volume is part of this effort.

INTRODUCTION

Lisa Taraki

N o study of Palestine and the Palestinians can ignore the momentous impact, significance, and consequences of the two defining moments in modern Palestinian political history, the *Nakba* (literally, disaster) of 1948 and the military occupation of the rest of Palestine in 1967. Understandably, the bulk of scholarship on Palestine in the decades since 1948 has been devoted to documenting and analyzing the impact of wars, dispossession, and military occupation on Palestinian society. Dominated by a macro-level political-economy approach, much of this scholarship, especially that produced since 1967, has been notable for its preoccupation with structural transformations at the level of the economy, the class structure, and the polity. In the 1980s, and spurred by the widening of mass resistance to the occupation, a body of more anthropologically oriented works began to appear alongside the ever-expanding corpus of political studies. Much of this later scholarship, while attempting to understand Palestinians as they lived their lives, focused on Palestinian political agency and was more interested in understanding Palestinians as political actors who organized, resisted, and otherwise challenged the occupation.

The political-economy and political-agency approaches share a common shortcoming in that they do not render Palestinian lives very approachable or accessible. Even the voluminous literature on the first intifada (1987 to the early 1990s), with a few exceptions, treats Palestinians as one-dimensional political subjects. The internal dynamics, stresses, and contradictions of the social groups and communities within which people live out their lives, or the sensibilities and subjectivities of individuals as they negotiate their mundane existence away from the barricades have not received much serious attention from most researchers.

This volume is one product of a multifaceted research project launched by the contributors in 1999 with the broad task of studying the dynamics and modalities of social reproduction in Palestinian society in the West Bank and Gaza and, in particular, strategies of households and families for survival and social mobility. It considers how individuals, households, and families negotiate their lives and strategize to achieve their goals. It interrogates the proverbial elasticity of the Palestinian family as a "shock absorber" and is mindful of the limits of "coping" and endurance, whether of the household or the individual. It also raises critical questions about modernity and tradition, and about migration and its social and cultural consequences. The volume also explores the meaning of place for life choices, lifestyles, and life projects, and for the construction of identities and subjectivities.

But, like any work on Palestine, this volume recognizes that the political reality must be the basic backdrop against which we examine the routines of life and the small dramas of daily life; it thus foregrounds the salient aspects of the enduring and ubiquitous conditions of war, near-war, threat, instability, and vulnerability experienced by Palestinians for over five decades, especially in the latest phase of the confrontation with the Israeli occupation.

This volume was inspired by the collective experience of the contributors as we pondered the initial findings of a survey conducted in the summer of 1999 of over two thousand households in nineteen communities in the West Bank and Gaza. The survey, designed by the Institute of Women's Studies at Birzeit University,[1] aimed at going beyond prevailing macro-level analyses of Palestinian society by taking a look inside the "black box" of the Palestinian household. By compiling the "empirical" evidence and examining the internal dynamics of the Palestinian household, we hoped to find clues to many unanswered questions and to challenge what we believed were sweeping and unwarranted generalizations about Palestinian society, gender relations, and family and kinship networks. In particular, it appeared to us that scholarly, policy, and everyday discourses alike invested the family with too much agency in the matter of "absorbing shocks," as if the ability and capacity to adapt and adjust were infinitely elastic. In other words, the assumption that family networks have historically functioned as a sort of social safety net for

1. Hereafter also referred to as the IWS survey. The survey was based at the Institute of Women's Studies at Birzeit University (where most of the contributors work) and supported by a grant from the International Development Research Centre in Ottawa, Canada.

Palestinians ignored the issue of what kinds of households or which individuals within households and families bore the brunt of the shocks (Giacaman and Johnson 2002b).

The community household survey was conceived as an antidote to the standard national survey, which samples a limited number of households in a wide range of locations with varying economic structures, household compositions, and political features. Such sample surveys usually focus on broad definitions of national-level representation using basic demographic parameters such as age, sex, and locale (camp, rural, urban) or region (Gaza Strip, West Bank, south, north, center) and then generalize the results to the nation as a whole. While such data are indeed useful for all sorts of purposes, they are not useful for some analytical purposes because the inevitable homogenization they produce obscures important differences among locales and communities (Giacaman and Johnson 2002b). Thus, the survey started out by acknowledging the necessity of embedding households in their "natural" environment, that of a particular village, city, or refugee camp, chosen as prototypes representing different economies and modes of life (for example, villages that rely mainly on agriculture versus those that have a large proportion of the labor force working in Israel).

As is common in such undertakings, our understanding and appreciation of the complexities of studying Palestinian families and households have grown considerably since that hot summer when we struggled with the fieldwork training held at the Institute of Women's Studies at Birzeit University. Later, as we began to look at the data, it appeared that some of our own assumptions also needed to be reexamined and that to understand the data properly we had to be more versatile and methodologically eclectic. This volume is the product of the theoretical and methodological journeys traveled by the authors as they tried to make sense of the data and their relevance to the main research problem, which centered around social reproduction and in particular strategies of households and families for improving their chances for survival and social mobility. This volume is thus the initial outcome of the as-yet uncompleted journey from statistical analysis to a more nuanced analysis; we have deployed whatever tools seemed appropriate from the arsenal of sociologists, historians, and anthropologists, including, it should be noted, informed speculation and questions for further inquiry.

Household or Family?

Our investigation into the Palestinian household examined a wide range of issues, from the division of labor to parental preferences regarding whom their
children marry and the educational levels they should attain, with special attention to gender and generation. The focus on the household was inspired by
recent scholarship that stresses the centrality of the household in two senses:
as a site for mediating the relationship among individuals, local communities,
markets, and the state (Singerman and Hoodfar 1996) and as a terrain where
both conflict and cooperation characterize the relations among household
members (Sen 1990). The household was thus not conceived as an insular or
unitary construct, and many questions in the survey were designed to explore
the intersections of the private and the public as well as the local and the national, and sought to capture instances of cooperation and conflict, consensus
and dissent.

Being very much aware of the embeddedness of the household in wider
family and kin relations and networks, we built into the survey instrument
questions that would help us understand better the links between household
members and others in their kin universes (such as relations between household members and their migrant relatives, living arrangements, and economic ventures among kin). We were thus mindful of scholarly work on Arab
society that was critical of the concept of the household (whether it consisted
of the nuclear or extended family) as a discrete and autonomous social unit
(Barakat 1993; Altorki and Zurayk 1995; Farsoun 1970; McCann 1993).

It became apparent, however, that we had to foreground that embeddedness if we hoped to be able to interpret our findings in a meaningful and comprehensive fashion. Furthermore, it became apparent that we had to go
beyond the survey data in order to capture the workings of what we thought
was the heavy hand of family groups and kin networks in the lives of households and their members. Jamil Hilal and Penny Johnson explore the consequences and social meanings of the reconstitution and reconstruction of
extended-family and kin relations by marshaling data from other sources,
while Lamis Abu Nahleh unravels the thick web of kin relations in which
households find themselves entangled by using narratives recorded in urban,
rural, and camp households.

In short, just as it is clear that the lone individual cannot be used as the unit of social analysis, it is also clear that the lone household cannot be examined in a social void; the latter is firmly anchored in a larger universe of family (*'a'ila*), a construct that has significance and concrete resonance in the everyday experiences of individuals and households as they fashion their present realities and strategize for their futures. It is equally clear that survey data about the household, however rich or painstakingly collected, cannot answer all our questions about households and families, because the data capture phenomena at one moment in time and abstract from the dynamic relationships over time between individuals and their households and between households and their kin. Furthermore, because these relationships are shaped, in part, by prevailing political conditions, it is very important to contextualize our study of family and household dynamics. We can now say with the benefit of hindsight that the survey was conducted at what transpired to be the end of the short-lived era of optimism; prospects for "peace" were quickly receding, but more important, it was becoming evident that the Oslo process had ushered in a new social and political regime marked by tensions, fissures, and contradictions within the social order. Tales of rampant corruption in the Palestinian bureaucracy and the abuse of power circulated widely among the public. The strike of public school teachers in 1999 can be seen as one indicator of dissatisfaction with the Palestinian Authority, especially on the part of a sector widely recognized as being one of the most underprivileged segments of the burgeoning public sector.

Family and Household in a Colonial Context

Just as it is important to consider the intersections of the household with wider kin groups, so is it imperative that we ponder the larger political and social context, the most salient aspect of which is the reality of colonial rule with all its dynamics—not only of dispossession and repression but also of resistance, resilience, and survival. Indeed, as Johnson notes in her chapter, "it would be hard to argue that the dynamics of one of the most prolonged occupations in modern history have not affected most Palestinian households and families, including their internal dynamics, processes, and economies" (p. 60).

The overwhelming reality of dispossession and occupation looms large in the analyses contained in the chapters here. The consequences of the *Nakba* in 1948 and the military occupation in 1967 have been far-reaching and must be brought into the analysis of family and household dynamics. Statelessness, economic dependency on Israel, water and land confiscation, the marginalization of agriculture, migration to oil states and beyond, and arrested urbanization are only some of the more salient aspects of this condition. Resistance to colonial domination stands out as an important component of this lived reality, as Palestinians have struggled in many different ways, throughout most of the twentieth century and into the twenty-first, for freedom from domination.

The lives of individuals as well as households and the families they belong to have been affected in myriad ways by this overpowering reality. This volume is based on the premise that Palestinian households' and families' strategizing for survival, reproduction, and social mobility cannot be understood apart from the national traumas of the past and the deep uncertainties of the present. The precariousness of life for all Palestinians is compounded by the vulnerability experienced by poor peasants, the urban poor, and refugees, especially those who have been living in refugee camps for more than half a century. Thus, household-level dynamics such as decisions regarding children's education and marriage, living arrangements, the division of labor, and emigration can only be understood if we attempt to link them with the larger historical trajectory in which the Palestinians have been thrust, and within which they live, struggle, and resist as individuals and households, and as a society and nation.

Theoretical advances in the conceptualization of the household in Arab societies have special relevance to the Palestinian household and family. The French historical demographer Philippe Fargues (2003, 45), discussing the quite different case of mid-nineteenth-century Cairo, has remarked that while stable as an institution, the family unit was in fact extremely volatile as a grouping. He attributes this volatility to extremely high mortality rates entailing a rapid turnover of individuals living together and the rapid redistribution of household members related to state policies and labor requirements. One may posit a similar volatility for the Palestinian household and family group arising out of conditions of war, near-war, military occupation, and resistance to that occupation. For despite the active and determined efforts of Palestinians to maintain, constitute, and reconstitute "normal" and stable family relations and living arrangements, they are inevitably thwarted by the ubiquity of imprisonment, loss of income due to "security considerations" and restrictions on mobility, and a host of other impediments that are all part and parcel of the highly unstable political field. It is in these directions that some of our investigations have to move, to see what kind of imprint the turbulent history of the Palestinians has left on households and families.

We can take migration as an example. Emigration, both in the form of the violent and forced uprootings of 1948 and 1967 and the more gradual but steady pattern of exit to other lands and places in search of work and better lives, has no doubt left its mark on the stability of domestic and family groups, spawning all sorts of combinations of residential groups and arrangements of varying durability. Imprisonment by Israel, which has affected the lives of hundreds of thousands of Palestinians since the onset of the occupation in 1967, is another powerful factor in the volatility and instability of the Palestinian household. Even the most intimate aspects of people's lives, such as the spacing of children and thus household size and composition, have been affected by the reality of male imprisonment (see Abu Nahleh's chapter in this volume). How families arrange and rearrange their affairs to accommodate migration and imprisonment is part of the everyday lived reality of Palestinians in all communities and across classes, although the prison experience has affected the poor with greater force. Yet another example of the volatility of the household comes from the incessant disruptions of community life since 2000 as a result of Israeli assaults on neighborhoods, often accompanied by destruction of homes and the displacement of families. A survey conducted in May 2002 in five West Bank cities and towns just after the invasions of March and April revealed that many households in the five cities and towns reported hosting displaced family and friends whose homes were destroyed or who were fleeing unsafe neighborhoods (Giacaman et al. 2004b). With incursions and invasions of varying duration having become a routine feature of life for Palestinians since 2002, we can only speculate as to what this has meant for the stability of the domestic group, not to mention changes in the burden of care within the household.

The Limits of Coping

The Palestinian family has long been hailed for its ability to absorb shocks and to provide sustenance to its members. Like the silently suffering mother-heroine who bears the burden of her family's survival with stoicism and forti-tude, the family is also idealized as the privileged symbol of Palestinian re-silience in the face of occupation and its adversities. This idealization of the family is echoed in a range of discourses on Palestine, from scholarly works to art and literature, both popular and highbrow.

However, we cannot assume that all households and families are equally successful at juggling the requirements of social reproduction in the face of major disruptions of their lives, nor can we assume that the outcome and process are free of conflict and contention, especially concerning gender rela-tions within the household.[2] The family narratives examined by Abu Nahleh provide a window into these dynamics, as does the discussion by Eileen Kut-tab of the limits to the "coping mechanisms" used by families and especially by women who have to compensate for loss of income and opportunity.

One obvious issue is what has been called the "crisis of the male bread-winner" resulting from rampant male unemployment in recent years. This crisis, as Abu Nahleh shows, is not only economic. It has other important con-sequences for family life under patriarchy, where men who are vested with the power to protect their families find themselves severely compromised in the fulfillment of this duty. The erosion of men's ability to provide for and protect the family in the face of widespread unemployment, destruction of homes and agricultural land, and incessant army forays into neighborhoods reconfig-ures gender relations and relations between the generations. One of these changes pertains to women's strategies for accommodating, resisting, and ne-gotiating patriarchy. We are only beginning to understand these dynamics after nearly four decades of life under occupation.

Much work needs to be done before we can grasp the dynamics of coping, resilience, and survival by household and families. We also need to know much more about the way in which they interact with other community and national institutions, especially in the face of the collapse of quasi-state insti-tutions since the beginning of the second intifada. Current research by some of the contributors into the fate of families and households in the post-2000 era of cantonization, fragmentation of social networks, and separation of com-

2. Joseph (2004) has highlighted the highly contentious nature of family discourses in post-war Lebanon, where war opened up possibilities for challenging gender and age hierarchies within the family.

munities as a result of Israeli policies should help illuminate some of these questions.[3]

Everyday Resistance

Resistance expressed in organized parties and movements has left a deep imprint on the household and family. Very few Palestinian families have escaped the experience of imprisonment of at least one of their members at some point in the long history of struggle against the Israeli colonial system. As an everyday reality, the political activities of members have kept families on constant alert in anticipation of nighttime raids, beatings, arrests, interrogations, imprisonment, and house demolitions, which are only some of the punitive measures devised by the Israeli occupiers. The immense amounts of time and energy that household members, and especially mothers and wives, invest in visiting lawyers and the Red Cross, attending trials, and keeping in regular contact with sons and husbands in prison and catering to their needs for basic supplies and food are other ways in which resistance activities have left their mark on family dynamics such as the division of labor within the household. Family practices such as selection of marriage partners; decisions concerning emigration, employment, and education; and residential choices are also at times strategies to accommodate the social and economic consequences of resistance. For example, the uprooting of wives and children of prisoners who are often forced to live in other households for the duration of the imprisonment of the husband and father is one aspect of the dynamics behind the constitution and reconstitution of the household in Palestine and is directly a consequence of resistance activities. The creation of "female-headed households" as a result of the imprisonment of male members is another obvious example.

But the domestic group is not only acted upon; it is often an active agent in reproducing the ethos of national resistance. Some works emerging from ethnographic fieldwork during the first intifada of the late 1980s and early 1990s have explored how families have been implicated in the construction of a nationalist ethos and the nationalist subject through the transformation or

---

3. The research, conducted at the Institute of Women's Studies at Birzeit University, centers on three communities in the twin cities of Ramallah and al-Bira.

valorization of gendered family relations such as those between mothers and sons and brothers and sisters (Peteet 1994, 1997; Jean-Klein 2000). In her chapter in this volume, Johnson frames everyday practices of kin marriage and kin solidarity as acts through which Israeli colonialism is contested and Palestinian identity is constituted. If we go beyond marriage practices and other "kin work," we find that other, more mundane, everyday practices can also be viewed as acts of resistance, a fact that increases our appreciation of the family as an agent of resistance and as an incubator of national identity, not only the passive "shock absorber" in bad times. One can, of course, view assistance to or solidarity with neighbors and relatives affected by the occupation (in instances of imprisonment, exile, martyrdom, and the like) as expressions of kin or neighborly charity or solidarity, but they can also be seen as acts of resistance. The discourses that accompany and indeed justify these acts are themselves acts of resistance and are often framed as part of the national narrative of resistance and steadfastness.

This ethos is also elaborated through many other everyday practices that are conventionally subsumed under "survival" or "coping" strategies. It may be appropriate to point out here that the meaning of steadfastness and resilience, the twin slogans of the 1970s and 1980s, has undergone a significant transformation in recent years. Hammami (2004a) has noted that under the crushing regime of Israeli sanctions and collective punishment in the form of "internal closures" since 2000, steadfastness (sumud) is now conceived in a more proactive fashion, as a rejection of immobility and a refusal to let the army's roadblocks and closures disrupt life. She notes the collectively understood, but individually achieved, resistance of "simply getting there."

While Hammami is mainly interested in exploring the resistance enacted at and around what she calls the new "public spaces" of the intifada, the checkpoints, she has alerted us to an important shift in the national consciousness. Israel's harsh response to the second intifada, the building of the Wall in the West Bank, and the elaborate system of checkpoints in the Occupied Territories all underline the immensity of the long road to be traversed to liberation. This realization—or reaffirmation—of the enormity of the obstacles facing Palestinians generates a discourse that seeks to find virtue in adversity. To be bearable and tolerable, the drudgery of "simply getting there" must be endowed with political meaning; steadfastness and resilience in the face of physical obstacles thus become resistance to the occupation and its regime of confinement and control. This consciousness is reflected in everyday discourse at checkpoints, in public transportation, and in institutions such as schools and universities, as well as in the media.

It is clear that the household is an important site for the articulation and elaboration of discourses of resistance. As individuals devise solutions for overcoming obstacles and engage in daily recitals of the minute details of their encounters with the Israeli system of control, they increasingly do so with the self-consciousness that they represent something larger than themselves. Thus every person becomes an embodiment of The Palestinian who keeps the struggle going through acts of overt resistance as well as simple steadfastness, stubbornness, and resilience. The household is an important agent in the elaboration of this national ethos, both through its often ritualized practices of solidarity and assistance and in articulating the narrative of resistance through its collectively recollected and reflected-upon rationalizations and meanings. Concerning more ritualized practices, research carried out during the first intifada of the late 1980s and early 1990s by Jean-Klein (2001) offers a window into this ethos by examining widespread and routine practices of "the suspension of everyday life" during the intifada (basically austere self-restraint imposed on public and private conduct and the shunning of leisure and entertainment). She approaches them as both "nationalist" and "resistant" and identifies the domestic space and the neighborhood as important sites for the production of the ethos of nationalism and resistance.

Understanding the Palestinian predicament may necessitate a reassessment of some common terms and assumptions. The warlike conditions since the eruption of the second intifada in September 2000 prompt us to ask whether the term "prolonged occupation" should not be replaced by "protracted war," or more to the point, recognized as another face of the longer-term colonial project for the whole of Palestine, for it has become increasingly clear in recent years that the events of 1948 did not close a chapter in the history of the Palestinians. The military occupation of the West Bank and Gaza, represented not only by the colonies planted there but by the entire system of control put in place since 1967, is part of one and the same process, the steady colonization of Palestine. The Oslo accords of 1993—concluded despite grave reservations by many sectors of society—represented a historic compromise by the Palestinians, the establishment of the first Palestinian authority, and the inauguration of an era that was supposed to result in sovereign statehood and self-determination. That forward-looking scenario was aborted, thereby forcing Palestinians to reexamine their assumptions about the Zionist project in Palestine and to recognize the tenuousness of their claims in the face of the massive forces arrayed against them. The collapse of the "peace process" has dealt Palestinian national aspirations a severe blow and plunged Palestinians into greater uncertainty and vulnerability. While it is possible that a new set of temporary arrangements may be reached, one of the lessons of the post-Oslo period is that it is unwise to view such arrangements in a "post-conflict" framework without examining the overall thrust of the Zionist project.

Similarly, it may be time that we reexamine some of the prevailing depictions of the Palestinian economy. As Kuttab argues in her chapter, the classical "dependency model" derived from an understanding of the relations of colonial dependency between the Palestinian and Israeli economies may no longer capture the full reality of the devastation wrought by a condition of protracted crisis. Describing the Palestinian economy as a "resistance economy," she explores how the understanding of labor force changes and in particular women's economic activity may benefit from an appreciation of people's and families' daily struggles in responding to colonial aggression with "economic resistance" strategies necessitated by highly volatile political conditions. Given these considerations, this volume can be viewed as a modest contribution to efforts to understand the dynamics of families, communities, and societies under prolonged and extreme situations of threat and stress. Social scientists, writers, and artists have tried to understand how civil wars, military occupations, and other forms of strife and conflict affect individuals, families, communities, classes, and nations, and how in turn these various social groups shape conflicts. We hope that this volume can shed some additional light on these issues.

Social Reproduction: The Local and the Global

All the chapters in this volume attempt to come to terms, in different ways perhaps, with the question of social reproduction, the job of ensuring the continuation and renewal of social existence. The practices of everyday existence, as well as the strategic decisions made by individuals and families, are part of this task. Indeed, simple decisions concerning migration, marriage, or education are part of the strategies of social reproduction. Such decisions are rarely made by lone individuals; rather, they are taken collectively by families as they consider their present and contemplate their future. Thus, decisions concerning migration (who migrates, with whom, and to where and for how long), marriage (who marries, to whom, and when) and education (for whom, what level, and where) are usually household or family affairs and are conceived and perceived as decisions bearing upon the continuation of the family and the enhancement of its material, social, and symbolic capital. The levels of risk and uncertainty faced by Palestinians are relevant here and thus constitute the larger backdrop to the decisions.

On another level, social reproduction is also about the task of fashioning identities; forging conceptions of personhood, family life, and family futures; setting horizons; and defining what kinds of sociality are desirable. While the family is not the sole and privileged site of identity-formation or the elaboration of social imaginaries, it is where many of the practices crucial to the outcome of this process are executed, as discussed earlier.

It is inconceivable, once again, that nearly a century's worth of Palestinian encounters with the colonial system would not be relevant to the task of social reproduction or the elaboration of the social imagination. Nor is it possible to ignore the inexorable force of the global circulation of symbols and goods, in whose interstices many of the ideas of personhood, family life, and family futures are made and remade. Appadurai has argued that today's world is characterized by an entirely new role for the imagination in social life; what is new about global cultural processes is the imagination as a social practice, as an organized field of social practices, a "form of work," and a form of negotiation between sites of agency (individuals) and globally defined fields of possibility (1997, 31). He notes that electronic mediation and mass migration have been of signal importance in the work of the imagination as a constitutive feature of the modern subjectivity of ordinary people; the media offer new resources and new disciplines for the construction of imagined selves and imagined worlds, and migration means that "more people than ever before seem to imagine routinely the possibility that they or their children will live and work in places other than where they were born" (7).

It is indeed important to keep in mind that subjectivities and the imagination are today, more than ever before, influenced by global forces, as Appadurai has noted. But it is equally important to recognize that global currents are experienced by ordinary people in specific contexts, and the family is the first-order group where the imagination is elaborated, sensibilities sharpened, dispositions acquired, and horizons established. The family is also bounded by its location, whether the location is the nation, social class, or spatial location.

If we take social class as an example, we find that the family plays a signal role in class production and reproduction, not only through its strategies in education, migration, or marriage, but also in nurturing subjectivities and dispositions directly implicated in the reproduction of prevailing hierarchies of class and prestige. Global currents, of course, do not have the same resonance or indeed value for all classes. A family of machine operators in Hebron, for example, may be impervious to Appadurai's "imagined selves" and "imagined worlds," but an aspiring middle-class family in Ramallah may spare nothing in the pursuit of globally circulated and valued symbolic and material capital necessary for realizing the imagined. Horizons for the self and for the family are bound by class, although the matter of spatial location also appears to be critical here. Cities and locations in themselves can be either enabling or discouraging milieus for the elaboration of sensibilities and dispositions of a global character. In this sense, the more enabling ambience of cities like Jerusalem, Ramallah, or Bethlehem can be contrasted with the more parochial cultural currents prevailing in Nablus, Hebron, or Jenin.

The challenge for us, as we ponder the scene from the bottom up, from the site of the household and family, is to see where the global intersects with the national and the local (neighborhood, camp, city) and finally with the household and family as it lies embedded in hierarchies of class and status. Lisa Taraki and Rita Giacaman's chapter in this volume represents an initial attempt to unravel the different layers of social reality, by contrasting three different social universes in the cities of Hebron, Nablus, and Ramallah.

There cannot be a more global reality than that of transnational migration. Palestinian history itself can be read as a history of this form of migration, as steady waves of migrants have departed the shores and hills of Palestine over the decades, beginning with the eighteenth century, when the first large-scale migrations of Palestinians took place. Migration, like the global mass media, is generally conceived in social science writing in positive terms in the sense that it "expands the horizons" of migrants as well as their old communities; it is believed to accelerate the process of "acculturation" and "cultural change." More recently, postcolonial theory's celebration of hybridity has also privileged migration and dislocation as the sources of innovation and the transcendence of local parochialisms. But there is another face to migration. The migratory experience may reproduce parochialisms and lead to the entrenchment—and indeed discovery—of conservatisms of different kinds. The migrant is not necessarily in search of new and liberatory experiences; he or she may be driven by a desire for better circumstances and above all, for stability. As Aijaz Ahmad has noted, third-world "migrants tend to be poor and to experience displacement not as cultural plentitude but as torment; what they seek is not displacement but, precisely, a *place* from where they begin anew, with some sense of a stable future" (1995, 16).

The Palestinian migratory experience has had contradictory consequences both for migrants and for the society they left behind. Hilal in this volume explores the darker side of migration, specifically the role it plays, together with the renewal and reconstruction of extended family relations, in the reproduction of social conservatism. He elaborates the unintended consequences of migration where the migrants' motives have "not been to change their lifestyle, customs, or identity, but rather to improve their life chances," in the context of statelessness and precarious socioeconomic and political conditions, facilitated by the destruction of the cosmopolitan Palestinian coastal cities after 1948.

This may be an occasion to reflect on the old and problematic dualism of tradition-modernity: is the reproduction of social conservatism by migrants, for example, a sign of the "continuity of traditions?" Is the persistence of kin marriage an instance of the immutability of marriage traditions in a traditional culture? Posing the question in such a way presumes that "cultural traditions" are impervious to or resilient in the face of the dynamics of migration, colonial rule, and all manner of uprooting experienced by Palestinians. It is more productive to conceive of the reproduction of social conservatism by migrants, for instance, as a product of the modern migratory experience that transports people to new national spaces (especially in the case of the Gulf states), spaces where new social groups found there, such as the urban middle classes, are fashioning their own notions of morality and selfhood in a reconstituted public sphere. Likewise, our view of the persistence of kin marriage must take into account the very contemporary transformations against the backdrop of which this time-honored practice continues. The issue is not that kin marriage is an instance of a naturalized adherence to "tradition" on the part of "traditional" subjects; as Johnson explains in her chapter, it is a practice that is part of kinship worlds reconstituted in response to and against the colonial regime, including forms of modernity and in the absence of national security and statehood. As another writer in another context has explained, the "old" practice of kin marriage is not an old choice but a new one; it takes place against the background of the precarious nature of womanhood as it is socially constructed in modern Egypt (Sholkamy 2003).

The Power of Place

One of the surprising results of the household survey was the remarkable significance of region (north, south, and center in the West Bank) as a basis of variation in demographic profiles and social practices and preferences. The social geography of Palestine has conventionally been perceived through the triple lenses of city, village, and camp, assuming some sort of homogeneity within each of these locations. However, it may be that this categorization is not useful for some analytical purposes. In the absence of large-scale rural-urban migration owing to the close proximity of villages, towns, and cities, and because of the marginalization of agriculture, it is becoming less tenable to speak of prototypical villages, cities, and camps. Sharp differences between town and countryside, where they did exist, are being eroded, and the distinction between refugee camp and town or village is not tenable as a social—as opposed to a political—reality. Many of the urban refugee camps are part and parcel of the social fabric of the towns, even though they bear the markings of exclusion and separation as do so many other poor urban communities and neighborhoods the world over.

A more expected finding from the survey, as well as from the 1997 census data, is the existence of important differences among the major Palestinian cities. These differences pertain to basic demographic characteristics, labor force patterns, and lifestyle indicators; together, they suggest that explanations for differences among the cities may be sought not only in the political economy of each city, but also in the nature of the social and moral order, in the particular ethos that characterizes each city.

Two chapters in this volume take up the significance of place in shaping the lifeworlds and practices of individuals and families. Johnson tackles the issue of regional difference, examining it, insofar as marriage practices and familial preferences are concerned, in the context of "economies of symbolic goods" where different forms of symbolic capital have different values. The value of symbolic capital through kin work, she argues, may be higher in some regions than others and may help to explain differences in certain kinds of kin practices and ideologies among regions.

Taraki and Giacaman's chapter also attempts to tackle the thorny issue of regional difference, as well as that of variation among urban centers in terms of their demographic profiles and other attributes, particularly those relating to lifestyles, life pursuits, and the construction of lifeworlds. The differences among the cities are also reflected in representations of these cities in the local imagination as distinct characters, flavors, and ambiences. The historical approach adopted in the chapter aims at explaining the uniqueness of three cities (Nablus, Hebron, and Ramallah) in terms of their pasts and presents and their place within their larger regional contexts. Ruptures and continuities in the relationship of each city with its region, the character of its hegemonic groups, and the diversity of the population seemed particularly relevant to understanding the uniqueness of the three cities. This chapter, together with those of Johnson, Kuttab, and Hilal, can be read as exercises in breathing meaning into statistical "facts." The main difficulty we encountered is the paucity of social and historical evidence at our disposal, because vast areas of Palestinian social history remain unexcavated. A preoccupation with Palestinian political economy and political institutions has precluded a serious study of social and cultural issues. We hope that this volume will be a step in the direction of tipping the balance in recent scholarly work on Palestinian society toward a study of other aspects of Palestinian life, particularly those that pertain to everyday practice and discourse.

Dispossession, Occupation, and Resistance

It is hardly necessary to show that wars, dispossession, exile, military occupation, repression, and resistance are highly salient to the understanding of Palestinian society in all its complexities and contradictions. The contributions to this volume assume this saliency, and each seeks to draw out the consequences and relevance of this turbulent legacy for the issue at hand.

It may be useful to highlight some of the more significant features of the occupied Palestinian territories, particularly in the period since the early

1990s, when a new political regime was ushered in. This new regime was embodied in the establishment of the first Palestinian self-governing authority following the signing of the first Oslo Agreement between the Palestine Liberation Organization and Israel in 1993. Conceived as an interim administration until the conclusion of a final status agreement, the Palestinian Authority was granted some jurisdiction in the administration of civilian affairs in the West Bank and Gaza. However, it was unable to consolidate itself as a central Palestinian authority because of economic dependence on Israel, the division of the West Bank and Gaza into noncontiguous enclaves, and the continued separation of the West Bank and Gaza.[4]

Ironically, at the very time that Palestinians were ostensibly being granted quasi-autonomy in a quasi-state, movement between the West Bank and Gaza and between the latter and Israel was being seriously impeded and the fate of Jerusalem ever more cemented. The emblematic city of Jerusalem, whose eastern part is claimed by Palestinians as the capital of the future state, was in fact being made more securely out of bounds to Palestinians in the rest of the West Bank and Gaza and its inhabitants threatened with further dispossession, containment, and encirclement. The second uprising that erupted in 2000 with the shattering of the Oslo bubble was met with draconian Israeli measures the features of which continue to unfold with the erection of the Wall, the entrenchment of an elaborate system of checkpoints, closures, and siege, and the expansion of Jewish colonies on Palestinian land. The disempowerment of the Palestinian Authority triggered by Israeli assaults on its leadership, institutions, and basic infrastructure in the wake of the uprising continues apace, and is embodied in the dissolution of central authority and the inability to meet the needs of an increasingly pauperized population.

A vast literature documents the major features of the land that has come to be called the Occupied Palestinian Territories; most of the works analyze the economic, political, legal, administrative, demographic, and social consequences of a military occupation that is nearing the close of its fourth decade. Land confiscation, the steady building of colonies on lands captured in 1967, and control over almost every aspect of the lives and livelihoods of the Palestinians living in the West Bank and Gaza have been amply documented.

---

4. For a summary of the accords governing the administration of the West Bank and Gaza, see Roy 2002.

Briefly, the main features of Palestinian society and economy in the years since 1967 have included the marginalization of agriculture, labor migration to neighboring countries and the employment of a significant part of the labor force in Israel (both patterns affected by the highly volatile political climate), arrested urbanization, and significant transformations in the class structure. Another important dimension of social existence for the people of the Occupied Palestinian Territories has been the ubiquitous dynamic of repression and resistance, a constant element in the relation between occupier and occupied. Imprisonment, exile, house demolitions, curfews, house arrests, and myriad other measures (including bombings of civilian areas from war planes) devised by the Israeli army have affected practically every household in Palestine. These measures are very sensitive to fluctuations in local and regional politics; they were significantly stepped up during the massive assault on Palestinian towns and villages after 2000 and particularly during the reinvasion of the major towns in 2002.

Viewed in historical perspective, the Israeli regime of control installed in the West Bank and Gaza in 1967 is in fact an extension of the Zionist project in Palestine. In *Occupier's Law*, published in 1985, legal scholar Raja Shehadeh (1985, 4) maintained that Israeli policy in the West Bank was "intended to drive out the Palestinians, to take over their land, and eventually to annex the occupied territories." Two decades later, Elia Zureik noted that Israelis, both at the level of the public and the leadership, remain committed to the principle of "demographic politics" (2003, 620); the perpetual quest for land and displacement of the Palestinians are still the main items on the Zionist national agenda.

None of this has been lost on the Palestinians of the Occupied Territories whose lives and livelihoods have been profoundly affected by Israeli appropriation of land and water resources; dominance over the economy, including labor policy; and an elaborate system of surveillance and control aimed at containing them in whatever they do, whether it is to register the birth of a child or to drill a well. While many Palestinians continue to use the language of human rights to convey their cause to the world, many others believe that, notwithstanding the Israeli redeployment from the Gaza Strip, the very idea of Palestine is a threatened concept and cannot be captured in the discourse of human rights.

How is the reality of occupation experienced by Palestinians? It was noted earlier that the Palestinians in the Occupied Territories have actually been living in a state of protracted war for many decades; the ubiquitous state of being on an emergency footing may wax or wane, but it is always there, and the awareness that Palestinian existence and identity in the land are under threat is very much a part of the dominant Palestinian ethos. In this sense, the life projects, aspirations, choices, and strategies of individuals, households, and families are very much affected by this state of constant threat generated in turn by the state of protracted war and struggle. People strategize under the shadow of the permit system, the Wall, army forays into neighborhoods, and tens of other ritualized practices of the occupation regime. It is hoped that this volume, conceived with an acute awareness of the heaviness of the baggage Palestinians carry around with them, nevertheless opens new avenues for the investigation of how lives and futures are constituted, reconstituted, and conceived, and how subjectivities, sensibilities, preferences, and practices crystallize in the flow of everyday life.

Living Palestine

1

MODERNITY ABORTED AND REBORN

Ways of Being Urban in Palestine

Lisa Taraki and Rita Giacaman

One of the major consequences of the fateful events of 1948 was the abrupt abortion of Palestine's urban modernity as embodied in the major coastal cities of Jaffa and Haifa and the inland city of Jerusalem. The residents of these cities and their hinterlands were flung into near and distant places of exile, never to form a coherent urban society again. Those parts of historic Palestine that escaped capture by Zionist forces were administered by Jordan (in the case of the West Bank) and Egypt (the Gaza Strip). The Israeli military occupation of the West Bank and Gaza Strip in 1967 marked the drawing of the boundaries of a truncated Palestinian entity in these areas, a place that came to be designated "the Occupied Palestinian Territories." The occupation forced a state of economic dependency and arrested urbanization in these "territories," a process that had set in during Jordanian rule when priority was given to the East Bank. In general, after 1948 and as a result of war, displacement, and forced and "voluntary" migrations, the West Bank and Gaza Strip entered into what we may call a dark period of closure and insularity and were cut off from the dynamic social and cultural currents of the region and the world. While the Arab world's cities were expanding and indeed exploding at the seams, the cities of the West Bank did not exhibit any significant expansion. What was left of Palestinian society in historic Palestine was characterized by many scholars and observers by the persistence—indeed, revival—of a peasant ethos, even though the majority of Palestinians did not live in a peasant economy or have a peasant lifestyle (Tamari 1995; Hilal 1998; Bishara 1998; Barghuthi 1998; Graham-Brown 1989; Muhammad 2002).

Depictions of a peasantized, de-urbanized Palestinian landscape in recent years that lament the loss of Palestine's cosmopolitan urbanity of the

1

Mandate era may be valid as cultural critique on the part of a modernist intelligentsia, but they do not illuminate our understanding of the lived realities of urban life in the country. Such totalizing characterizations gloss over the variety and diversity of urban life in Palestine, especially in the present. While it is true that Palestine's historic encounter with urban modernity was most clearly embodied in the coastal cities and Jerusalem, there were other modes of urban life in Palestine, some of which have persisted into the present. An examination of Palestinian cities and towns reveals palpable differences among them in terms of material and symbolic features, lifestyles, political significance, and economic pursuits. We may add that representations of these cities are also diverse, the inevitable outcome of the process whereby city images are constructed and cities are endowed with particular identities. We maintain that these other modes of urban life are of interest to social historians and sociologists, even if they are found lacking by the yardstick of the urban modernity that set in at the turn of the twentieth century and continued to flourish until 1948.

This chapter is an exploratory investigation of the diversity of urban formations in the West Bank. We attempt to interpret the sometimes striking differences in a range of socioeconomic characteristics and social practices among three cities (Nablus in the north, Ramallah in the center, and Hebron in the south) as reflected in census and other selected data from the Palestinian Central Bureau of Statistics (PCBS) and from the household survey conducted in 1999 by the Birzeit University Institute of Women's Studies in the three cities. Our interpretation has to remain tentative, largely because of the uneven quality and quantity of historical and contemporary evidence. We hope that the questions we raise encourage others to investigate the specificities of time and place, with the aim of understanding better the diversity and variety of urban life in Palestine.

The first step in our approach is to discuss the relevance of the notions of historical continuity and rupture to understanding the variety of contemporary urban formations in Palestine. We argue that the observed (and imagined) differences between our three cities cannot be understood apart from their unique histories. Indeed, the cities can be viewed as embodying different historical experiences, with particular reference to the nature of their relationship to their hinterlands; the character of their ruling groups and the extent and kind of the political power they wielded; the quality of their encounter with modernity, both of the Ottoman and later globalized varieties; and the diversity of their populations. In the case of the older and larger cities of Hebron and Nablus, we argue that while we do not have all the evidence to determine the full extent to which their historical legacies affect their present, some important features of the more distant past persist into the present and thus are probably quite relevant to understanding it. The extent of historical continuity is likely a product of the uneven way in which the dispossession of 1948 and the military occupation of 1967 affected Palestinian communities in the West Bank and Gaza Strip as a whole, not just the two cities. Hebron and Nablus have enjoyed more continuity and stability compared to other cities such as Gaza City and Ramallah. Of particular importance in this regard are the social composition of the population and the origins and dispositions of hegemonic groups. Comparing Hebron and Nablus with the much smaller but of late politically more significant town of Ramallah, we note that the historical ruptures wrought by the dramatic events of 1948, 1967, and 1994 (the last date denoting the establishment of the Palestinian Authority) have more relevance and resonance for the understanding of Ramallah's unique brand of urban modernity than its pre-1948 history. It is important to note, however, that some features of the social history of Ramallah in the first half of the twentieth century are quite relevant to its later elevation as a "capital city" during the rule of the Palestinian Authority.[1]

A closely related notion, but a much more slippery one, is that of region. Data from the census of 1997 and from the household survey have revealed an unexpected pattern of difference within the West Bank. Region, more than the commonsense and dichotomous categories of urban and rural, has emerged as a key basis of variations in some basic demographic and lifestyle indicators, education, employment, and household practices and preferences. It is not surprising that this suggested significance of region in the explanation of difference resonates clearly with historical scholarship on Palestine. There is some evidence, though not yet comprehensive by any

1. Jerusalem, while occupying the place of honor in the Palestinian national narrative as the capital of Palestine, has been in effect peripheralized and cut off from its natural Palestinian extension in the West Bank as a result of Israeli policies of encirclement and siege since the early 1990s. See Tamari 2001 for a history of Jerusalem's recent decline as a Palestinian metropolitan center.

means, that not only cities, but the larger regions within which they were located, have had distinctive identities and social characteristics. That is not to say that cities were not differentiated from villages, but to stress the point that some cities in some regions set the tone for life within the region, or as it were, stamped the villages in their hinterlands with their unique signatures. On the other hand, we also have the case of cities or towns that were not significantly differentiated from their rural hinterlands, producing a situation where a whole region was characterized by the lack of a stark contrast between urban and rural economies and social practices. Given the evidence to be discussed in this chapter, we can make only tentative suggestions about the significance of regionality, leaving the more definitive statement to further exploration (see Johnson's chapter in this volume).

Our main thesis is that Nablus, Hebron, and Ramallah represent three distinct modes of urban life in Palestine. In the case of Hebron and Nablus, the distinctiveness of each city is not only a product of more recent transformations in society and economy, but also an expression of continuity with the more distant past. This continuity with the past is expressed in the composition of the population; the nature and character of dominant groups; the extent of disruption wrought by the *Nakba* of 1948 and the occupation of 1967; the nature of the encounter with modernity, Zionist colonization, and globalization; and their relation to their rural hinterlands. But despite the shared legacy of the weight of past history, each city represents a different paradigm of Palestinian urban life not only in the present but also in the past; it is possible to say that the more "urban" Nablus can be contrasted with the more "rural" Hebron. Ramallah, on the other hand, is a new city, a product of the turbulent developments ushered in by the dispossession of 1948 and its aftermath. In many ways, Ramallah is reproducing, at the dawn of the twenty-first century, some of the same processes that led to the dynamic, hybrid modernity of Jerusalem and some of the coastal cities at the beginning of the twentieth century. It is doing so under vastly changed circumstances, but some of the same processes are at work in the making of the first Palestinian metropolis after the loss of a good part of "modern" Jerusalem and the coastal cities in 1948.

Our discussion of history and regionality begins with the eighteenth and nineteenth centuries. In this first part of the chapter, we discuss the significance of historical continuity and rupture for the understanding of the present lives and identities of our three cities. In the second part, we consider some contemporary features of these cities, including population composition; migration; the types of "publics" or people coexisting in each city; employment patterns and opportunities; and patterns in education, marriage, and standard of living expressed in the ownership of selected consumer durables and goods.

It is important to note here that issues such as migration and patterns of education, employment, marriage, and standard of living cannot be discussed in the abstract, as if "populations" live in a generalized social space. In fact, individuals are very firmly anchored in the concrete world of the family and the household. As such, families and households, especially in the absence of intrusive public sites and institutions in many communities, have a critical role in the production of versions of urban life. Notions of social mobility and conceptions of individual futures and presents, for example, are expressed within and mediated by the family and household. The household and family constitute the nexus within which individual and familial choices are made and the limits of the social horizon set. Nevertheless, whether families tend to reproduce themselves in their own images or to seek different horizons for their members is to be explained not only by reference to the circumstances of the families themselves, but also by reference to their location in a larger social universe, which includes the extent of the public sphere, the structure of the economy, and the availability of opportunities in education, employment, and migration, among other factors.

We will attempt in our analysis to show how these factors impinge on the development of cities and their regions, and by implication, the variety of urban forms in Palestine.

Continuity and Rupture: A Typology of Palestinian Cities

By the turn of the twentieth century, as Palestine was being increasingly brought into the orbit of the world economy, urban life had become differentiated. Ranging from what some have called the "Ottoman modernity" of Jerusalem and Jaffa to the small-town provincial insularity of inland towns such as Hebron and Safad, these cites and towns displayed a diversity that was the expression of the particular trajectories they took in their different encounters with the Ottoman state, the world economy, and of the way they made their living and related to their hinterlands.

We have seen in recent years a heightened interest in the sites of "high modernity" in pre-1948 Palestine, in the cities of Jerusalem, Jaffa, and Haifa. The Institute of Jerusalem Studies has been particularly instrumental in bringing to life the lost cosmopolitanism of late Ottoman and Mandate Jerusalem, through its ambitious program of publishing and scholarship.[2] Interest has also been heightened by scholarly works, memoirs, and autobiographies published or brought to light in recent years chronicling life in pre-1948 Palestine, all pointing to the existence of a vibrant and modern urbanity among the middle and upper middle classes in these cities (see, for example, Seikaly 1995; Said 1999; Karmi 2002; Musallam 2003; Sakakini 1987).

Palestine's other cities, those falling outside the ambit of the "modern" cities of Jerusalem, Jaffa, and Haifa, have received hardly any attention by social historians or sociologists. Disparate studies on the social and economic history of Palestine offer partial glimpses of the quality of life in the less "modern" urban centers such as Nablus, Hebron, al-Lidd, Ramla, Tiberias, and Safad. One notable exception is Beshara Doumani's (1995) social history of the city of Nablus and its hinterland in the eighteenth and nineteenth centuries, a work that has raised many important issues in the historiography of Palestine in general and of urban formations in particular. We will return to this work at length later.

It is possible to piece together from different sources a "stratified" profile of Palestinian cities during the late nineteenth and early twentieth centuries reflecting the ranking of different cities on a continuum ranging from central "modernizing" cities to peripheral "traditional/conservative" cities and towns. Population and economic statistics, as well as records of developments in transportation and communication infrastructures such as railways and roads provide some indication of the position of different cities along this continuum. The rapid population growth of Jerusalem, Jaffa, and Haifa at the turn of the twentieth century can be contrasted with the steady but much slower growth of Nablus and Hebron (Ben-Arieh 1975). In terms of economic activity, there are also many indications of the rising prominence of the coastal cities, especially during the Mandate period and as Palestine became increasingly brought into the orbit of the European and global economies.

2. Some examples are Tamari 2002a, Tamari and Nassar 2003, and Musallam 2003, as well as the Institute's quarterly publication, *Jerusalem Quarterly File* in English and *Hawliyat al-Quds* in Arabic.

Jerusalem, while not a primary center of economic wealth or trade, had a politically hegemonic position because of its status as a religious and administrative center. The rapid development of communication between Jerusalem, Jaffa, and Haifa, especially the improvement of roads, the laying of railroads, and the introduction of telegraph services, has been noted to have been in place toward the end of Ottoman rule in Palestine (Davis 2002). In fact, Ottoman modernization projects dated earlier than that, as in the paving of the first carriage road in Palestine (between Jaffa and Jerusalem) in 1868 (Kark 1989, 58). Diaries and memoirs, exceptionally rich sources of information on the social and economic transformations underway in Palestine, have documented the rise of an urbane way of life as reflected in the spread of places of public entertainment such as restaurants and cafes and the rapid expansion of newspapers and magazines by the early twentieth century.

Alexander Scholch's typology of Palestinian cities in the late nineteenth century is very relevant to our discussion here, based as it is on the criterion of the consequences of European penetration into Palestine. First come Jerusalem, Bethlehem, and Nazareth (these being the abodes of Christian holy sites), followed by Jaffa and Haifa. The second category includes the more peripheral cities of 'Akka (Acre), Safad, and Tiberias, followed by the third category embracing the local economic and trade centers of Nablus, Hebron, and Gaza, which were "indeed washed by the European flood, but were not as swamped by it" (1993, 119) as the first group of cities. It indeed becomes clear from surveying the available historical record that the presence or absence of European institutions, whether of a religious, commercial, cultural, or educational nature, has been of signal importance for setting the tone of social and cultural life in Palestine's cities. This is a point to which we will turn later.

The less quantifiable indicators are possibly of more significance for a typology of cities. These have to do with relations of the city to the hinterland, the nature of dominant groups and classes, architectural styles, and even the "ethos" or predispositions of inhabitants as recorded by travelers, chroniclers, and historians. It is here that we introduce the concept of region into our search for the uniqueness of Palestinian cities. As mentioned earlier, we have been alerted to the significance of region by the striking regional differences observed in our household survey and the 1997 census. Although these regional variations are a contemporary phenomenon, we raised the question earlier whether we can be justified in viewing them as reflections of or a continuation of historical trends. We are encouraged in pursuing this line of inquiry by the work of several scholars whose works, taken together, point to the importance of placing individual cities within the context of the regions of which they were a part. The most comprehensive work in this regard is Beshara Doumani's 1995 work on Jabal Nablus. He was the first social historian of Palestine to draw explicit attention to region as a social and economic organizing principle in eighteenth and nineteenth century Palestine, suggesting that it continues to the present day, at least in regards to some aspects of the social life of Jabal Nablus.

David Harvey (2001, 224–25), while warning against essentialist tendencies in geography that reify the concept of "region," notes that region is an important attribute of social organization in space: "regions are made or constructed both in material form and in imagination, and crystallize out as a distinctive form from some mix of material, social and mental processes. . . . Regionality becomes central to consciousness and identity formation and to political subjectivity." More generally, it has become widely recognized by critical geographers and anthropologists that regions are not "objective" categories but rather constructs, the outcome of processes that are performed, limited, symbolized, and institutionalized through diverse practices and discourses (Paasi 2002, 805).

There could hardly be a better fit between Harvey's conceptualization of region and Doumani's concept of "social space" in reference to Palestine in the eighteenth and nineteenth centuries. It is worth reproducing at length a most significant observation with which Doumani opens his social history of Ottoman Jabal Nablus:

> Ever since its origins as a Canaanite settlement, the city of Nablus has been locked into a permanent embrace with its hinterland. Over the centuries the multilayered and complex interactions between these two organically linked but distinct parts generated a cohesive and dynamic social space: Jabal Nablus. The material foundations of the autonomy of Jabal Nablus were the deeply rooted economic networks between the city and its surrounding villages; and the cultural foundations of its identity were the social and political dynamics of urban-rural relations, especially between merchants and peas-

ants. . . . In this general sense, Jabal Nablus was similar to many others that existed under the umbrella of Ottoman rule, and the centuries-long exis-tence of these social spaces explains the strong regional identifications that are still an important part of popular culture in Greater Syria. . . . [T]he urban centers of Jabal Nablus, Jabal al-Quds, and Jabal al-Khalil occupied different points along the spectrum of possibilities during the Ottoman pe-riod. Hebron was largely an extension of its hinterland, its economic life for the most part focused on agricultural pursuits and on providing essential services to the surrounding villages. . . . Nablus lay somewhere between [Jerusalem and Hebron]: its connections to the hinterland were absolutely vital, but it also contained a large manufacturing base and was a nexus for substantial networks of regional trade. . . . The city of Nablus did not possess the glamour or drama of Jerusalem; nor did it suffer from the relative sleepi-ness and obscurity of Hebron. (1995, 21–22)

Histories and Identities: Nablus and Hebron

Doumani has presented in a nutshell the more conventional typology of Palestinian cities (the glamour of Jerusalem versus the dullness of Hebron), and he may also have provided what may be one of the keys to understanding the uniqueness of the two cities that concern us here. He documents with great detail how both Nabulsi merchants and peasants from the hinterland re-produced the economic networks that bound them together, networks that went beyond purely economic relations of exchange. Whereas Nabulsi mer-chants were the prime agents of rural-urban integration through their invest-ment in the production, trade, and processing of agricultural commodities, middle peasants also played a key role in reproducing urban business and so-cial practices on the village level; eventually, they acquired land, built their own trade and money-lending networks, and set up shops and residences in Nablus (Doumani 1995, 244).

Although much of the evidence is still elusive, it appears that in the earlier part of the twentieth century, a period that lies outside the scope of Doumani's book, the "integration" of urban and rural life continued, albeit in changed circumstances. Graham-Brown, who has noted that Jabal Nablus has the strongest case for constituting a distinct historical entity (1982, 106), notes that by the 1920s landowning families who had stood in near-feudal relations with the peasants working on their land during the Ottoman period expanded their holdings, joined the ranks of merchants and moneylenders, and moved to live in the cities (142). One can only speculate about the cross-fertilization between city and village that the movement of people between these two social sites must have produced. The presence of strong links between merchant-landowners in Nablus and the peasants on the one hand, and the move of former village-based landlords into the city on the other, must have entailed a great degree of ongoing social ties between the city and country, enhancing the continued reproduction of a wider social entity with a distinct identity.

Memoirs recording life in the early part of the twentieth century provide glimpses of this intimacy between city and country. A memoir by Malik Masri, son of a merchant-landowning family in Nablus in the 1920s, documents the continuing involvement of Nabulsi merchant families in village life as overseers of agricultural activity and marketers of agricultural produce, and the ease with which sons of one of these families moved between city and village in the course of family business (Masri 1997). Another Nabulsi, born in 1923, daughter of a family of learned men, notes that her maternal grandfather moved to Tulkarm to be able to supervise his landholdings there, in the process marrying a woman from Tulkarm; her father's family had vast landholdings in the Qalqilya area and in Jaffa, lived from income from the land, and were active in the supervision of production (Salah n.d.). Likewise, the renowned Palestinian writer Fadwa Tuqan notes the frequent visits of villagers to her family's home in Nablus during the 1920s (Tuqan n.d.). One can only imagine the ties of patronage, influence, and deference that these relationships between urban-based landowners and peasants entailed. It is important not to romanticize these relationships; the peasants were most likely locked in relationships entailing a considerable degree of exploitation, conflict, and resistance. But until such time that a subaltern history of Jabal Nablus is written, we can suggest that even exploitative relationships are intimate ones, and that the landlord/merchant-peasant relationship was one factor in the construction of the social universe of Jabal Nablus, as perhaps in other areas.

While Doumani's work is of special interest to us because of its singular focus on the Jabal Nablus area, other works have suggested the existence of similar "social spaces," to borrow Doumani's term. Tamari (1982, 192), although not explicitly concerned with regionalism, nevertheless gives us an insight into this when he notes, in the context of his discussion of factional politics, that the usual urban-rural dichotomy does not have great explanatory value; faction leaders were urban-based "representatives" of a hierarchical system of rural clients and kinsmen. It has also been noted that leading urban families who had dominated their regions since the early nineteenth century contributed to molding disparate villages into a distinct region in their capacity as tax farmers (Kimmerling and Migdal 2003, 42). The part that elites have played in the fashioning of local identities is a subject that has been hardly touched upon in the social history of Palestine. Further work can benefit from Stacul's (2003, 4) observation that the articulation between the constructions of elites and individual social actors' readings of them can be a fruitful avenue for inquiry. The clearest evidence of "regionality" and "regional characters" is presented in Amiry's 2003 study of throne village architecture, a work that we will discuss shortly.

But not all cities, even if they did serve as centers for the regions in which they were located, exercised political and social hegemony in the region. In his work on Hebron in the eighteenth and nineteenth centuries, Karmon observes that the city was an important center of routes of local significance, serving as a meeting place for bedouins from the south and east and peasants from the north and west, as a trading post, center of production, and religious center (1975, 74–78). It did not, however, exercise any political leadership in its surrounding area. This is attributed to what he assumes is the lack of regional interdependence between town and village in a subsistence economy; the absence of a proper regional administration under the Ottomans and thus the predominance of local tax farmers; and the constant danger of attacks by bedouins, which created coalitions of villages whose combined population was much greater than that of Hebron (79).

Karmon's observations about the nonhegemonic position of Hebron in its immediate region give us pause to consider the special circumstances that militated against the assumption by Hebron of a leadership position within its hinterland. In her remarkable book on "throne" village architecture in Palestine during the eighteenth and nineteenth centuries, Amiry has observed that while the Jabal Nablus rural "district lords" (*shuyukh al-nawahi*) were powerful, the ones in Jabal al-Khalil were the least influential. She attributes this marginality primarily to the absence of an economic base for these lords similar to the one that existed in other areas where the *shuyukh* emerged as tax farmers. Because much of the land in Jabal al-Khalil was *waqf* land and thus not subject to taxation, a "feudal" landlord class was not allowed to develop in this area (2003, 216). Furthermore, the dearth of fertile land in the region also meant that agriculture was not the primary activity in this area; animal husbandry, herding, and production were also important. Another unique feature of Hebron noted by Amiry was related to its economic activity and is of signal importance. Whereas in Jabal Nablus and Jabal al-Quds there was a more or less complete separation between agriculture in the villages and trade in the cities, in Hebron this did not hold true. The most fertile lands of the whole region, in fact, were located within the city. Thus Hebron was the only city in Palestine that combined agriculture, trade, herding, and the administration of holy places (216). Scholch confirms this character when he notes that Hebron was a town where different economic pursuits coexisted side by side: agriculture, livestock herding, trade, and the processing of hides and the manufacture of glassware (1993, 162).

A Jerusalem-based Hebronite's recollection of his childhood in the early 1960s is instructive; he recalls that his family in Jerusalem would spend the entire summer out in the vineyards and fig groves in Hebron and its environs, staying there until late fall when the harvesting and processing of grapes had been completed. Families would resist sending their children back to school in the fall, especially if this entailed the long trip to Jerusalem from the fields. Even landless families in Hebron would rent a piece of land for the season, move the entire family there, and return the land to its owner at the end of the season. These "semi-peasant" practices continued until the mid-1960s but have almost completely disappeared today, the result of the loss of agricultural land in the city environs to building expansion and the availability of good roads obviating the need to spend weeks away from home in the city (Ju'beh 2003).

The picture that emerges from these shards of evidence suggests that the "regionness" of Jabal al-Khalil was more a result of the sameness between Hebron and its hinterland than it was a result of the presence of a hegemonic urban center serving as the trading center for the countryside and with an elite ruling (and perhaps serving as a "unifying force" for) the countryside through relations of economic domination and patronage. Amiry's observations about the architecture of Hebron are very significant here: while the palaces of wealthy merchants constituted the basic element in the architecture of

Nablus, the semiurban, semipeasant architecture of Hebron was its main characteristic (216). The abodes of the *shuyukh al-nawahi* in the nineteenth century suggest the less "urban" character of the region as a whole: the architectural remains in the Jabal al-Khalil area are much more modest compared to the palaces and forts left behind by the *shuyukh* of Jabal Nablus and Jabal al-Quds (212–13). It is also quite relevant to note that the *shuyukh* of Jabal al-Khalil, such as the Amrs of Dura, did not move to the city and thus become urban-based, as happened widely in the Jabal Nablus area, where the Abdul-Hadis, Jarrars, and Jayyusis took up residence in Nablus and became its notables and leaders. In fact, it has been observed that in Jabal al-Kahlil, it was the countryside that dominated the city; the Amr clan was the master of the mountain (Ju'beh 2003).

The historical record for Hebron and Jabal al-Khalil[3] from the nineteenth and twentieth centuries, the period of concern to us in this chapter, is extremely poor. Nor do we have the sort of documents, both public and personal, that could shed light on the social history of this peripheral city in Palestine's hill country. This lack may be a reflection of the disposition of the Jabal al-Khalil elite who may not have had the urge to represent their region to the nation and record its accomplishments for posterity in the manner of their more nationally conscious, more intellectually inclined counterparts in the Jerusalem and Nablus areas. An academic from Hebron attributes the "stagnation" of cultural life in Hebron in late Ottoman and Mandate Hebron to the "darkness" that befell Palestine as a whole during this period (Amr 1985, 54). But that was hardly the case, as attested to by the rich cultural production in Palestine's other cities during that period. It may also be a reflection of the historical material poverty of the region, rendering it of little importance to historians and documentarists. One historian has noted that throughout the eighteenth and nineteenth centuries and well into the twentieth, Hebron was a peripheral, "borderline" community, attracting poor and itinerant peasants and those with Sufi inclinations from its environs. The tradition of *shorabat Sayyidna Ibrahim*, a soup kitchen surviving into the present day and supervised by the *awqaf*, and that of the Sufi *zawaya* gave the city a reputation for

---

3. Even today, people from the Hebron region still refer to their different places of residence as al-Khalil (technically the name of the city alone); this may be a reflection of the sameness between the city and its hinterland as inscribed in the language of everyday discourse.

being an asylum for the poor and the spiritual, cementing the poor cast of a town supporting the unproductive and the needy (Ju'beh 2003). This reputation was bound to shed a conservative, dull cast on the city, a place not known for high living, dynamism, or innovativeness.

The character of the ruling groups in the regions and the cities appears to be of significance in "setting the tone" for the cities and perhaps for the regions as a whole. Several scholars have documented the leading role played by Nabulsi notables and merchants in the political life of Palestine, a role extending beyond their regions as well. Doumani (1995, 240–42) documents the emergence of a new ruling elite and notable group in Jabal Nablus in the course of the eighteenth and nineteenth centuries. The Nablus Advisory Council became the forum for this urban elite and played an important role in negotiations with the Ottoman government. Later, in the early part of the twentieth century, the Nabulsi elite formed a central core of the growing nationalist movement (Manna' 1999; Seikaly 1995). Al-Hut's (1984, 656, 658–59) statistics on the composition of the national political leadership during the Mandate is particularly revealing of the significance of Nablus and the peripherality of Hebron: 22 percent of this elite were born in Jerusalem, 16 percent in Nablus, and 1 percent in Hebron. In terms of their place of residence, 35 percent lived in Jerusalem, 15 percent in Jaffa, 13 percent in Nablus, 14 percent in Haifa, and only 1 percent in Hebron. Thirty-six percent of these personalities were teachers, journalists, and other members of the intelligentsia; 34 percent were wealthy merchants and landowners; and 24 percent were government employees. Sixty-five percent had completed some level of higher education.

Doumani (1995, 245) has observed that a preponderant number of leaders of the national movement and Palestinian members of Jordanian cabinets over the past two generations belong to families that constituted the core of nineteenth-century elites: "their political discourse . . . has been encoded by the experiences they and their ancestors had under Ottoman rule." If this is indeed true of the national elite as a whole, can it also be true of the Nablus elite? "Nablus loomed large in the eyes of its inhabitants, implanting in them a strong sense of regional identification and perhaps an exaggerated pride in those social practices they believed unique to their city" (56). Doumani and others have noted the historic continuity of Nablus's elites; merchants in particular continue to play a leading role in economic and political life.

Whether the "essential character of Nablus remains defined by its role as the commercial, manufacturing, administrative, and cultural capital of the surrounding villages" (Doumani 1995, 26) is what concerns us here. This assumption of a historic continuity in the "character" of the city and its regional primacy resonates with contemporary commonsense representations of the city as hegemonic in its social universe. This hegemony, as in the nineteenth century, continues to be crafted and maintained by the dominant social group in the city, merchants and manufacturers. While the links with the hinterland have become very tenuous as a result of the marginalization of agriculture and the spread of wage labor, the elite's cultural and political hegemony has not suffered a corresponding erosion, despite some setbacks in the 1970s and 1980s when the rising leadership of the national movement (many of peasant and refugee origins) entered into a political contest with the landed and commercial elite of the area. Nablus is still the financial and commercial center for the northern West Bank, and Nabulsi families continue to dominate politics in the city of Nablus. In this sense, Nablus continues to be viewed as a unique city, with an *esprit de corps* for which the local elite has set the tone. It is unfortunate that we do not have any comprehensive histories of the leading families of Nablus. An investigation would likely reveal a great continuity over the generations of leadership roles at the local, national, and even regional levels. The Shak'a family is an example. Bassam al-Shak'a was elected mayor of Nablus in 1981 on the nationalist slate; his nephew Ghassan, a Fatah stalwart, was appointed mayor by Yasir Arafat, and other members of the family have considerable commercial interests in the city.

These conclusions must remain tentative for the moment. Detailed research into the composition, function, and regional spread of the Nabulsi elite is necessary to buttress our initial formulation of the issue. For example, we need to know much more about the relationship between the traditional political leadership of Nablus and the new protostate institutions established there after 1994; to what extent do members of the influential Nabulsi families dominate Palestinian Authority institutions such as the governorate, the municipality, the security services and other key institutions? The comparison with Ramallah can be instructive. There, where there is no entrenched local elite (because of the emigration of many of its members in the course of the twentieth century and also because it is designated as a Christian city and thus by definition having a more restricted role in national-level politics), Palestinian Authority institutions are headed by "outsiders," mostly returnees or members of the new elite that does not have historic roots in the city. In Nablus, on the other hand, the Nabulsi elite have managed to integrate themselves into the PA hierarchy; the governorate and the municipality are in the hands of prominent Nablus families.[4]

Gender is a significant marker of the character of places, whether they are cities, regions, or indeed nations. In Palestine, the deportment, dress, and pursuits of women in particular are highly significant markers of regional identities. One of the more enduring features of Nablus's social and cultural life has been the lifestyles and political and cultural activities of its elite women. While the history of middle-class and elite women in Nablus in the twentieth century awaits an author, there is enough evidence to support the argument that the dispositions and practices of this class of women are important markers of the ethos of the city's ruling groups. In the twentieth century, we have ample evidence of Nabulsi middle- and upper-middle-class women's activism within the nationalist movement and later in charitable work. Many scholars and diarists have recorded the lives and accomplishments of Nablus's middle-class and elite women (Fleischmann 2003; Moors 1995; Mogannam 1937; Sayigh 1989; Salah n.d.). These women ranged from the "Florence Nightingale of Nablus," 'Andalib al-'Amad, the founder of the Arab Women's Union in 1921 (Tawil 1979), to businesswomen of acumen (Moors 1995). The late Fadwa Tuqan (d. 2003) was a writer of renown throughout the Arab world, and it is in Nablus that she grew up in the family's home (Tuqan n.d.). In her book on the Palestinian women's movement during the Mandate period, Fleischmann notes that while all the cities and towns had fairly active chapters of the Arab Women's Association/Arab Women's Union, the chapters that received the most publicity were those in Jerusalem, Haifa, Jaffa, 'Akka, and Nablus. She notes the paucity of information about the branch in Hebron, which apparently participated infrequently in nationalist activities such as demonstrations and relief work (2003, 151). The weak evidence for women's activism in Hebron is in itself a good indicator of the likely dearth of such ac-

4. An incident that occurred in Nablus in the early months of the second intifada is very instructive: demonstrations in the city against policemen brought in from Gaza (viewed as "outsiders," even if they were part of the national police) succeeded in driving out the police force.

tivities, compared to the voluminous sources documenting women's activism in Jerusalem (the center of women's activism), the coastal cities, and Nablus.

One of the more striking features of Nablus's middle-class and elite women professionals and activists is the preponderance of single women among them.[5] Anecdotal evidence certainly supports this. Moors (1995, 238–39) notes that since the early part of the twentieth century, single women have played a crucial role as teachers, directors of schools, and board members of charitable institutions, universities, and other public bodies. It is interesting to note that many of these women are involved in national-level institutions, thus emerging as public figures beyond the confines of their city. Hebron, on the other hand, has not produced any women public figures of note, particularly on the national level. Even after 1948, when the Palestinian women's movement lost its dynamic and radical coastal elements from Jaffa and Haifa, Hebron did not emerge as a significant center of women's activism in the manner of Nablus and Ramallah. Jerusalem women maintained their historical hegemony until the 1980s, when mass organizations mobilized by younger women of more modest backgrounds and linked with the various PLO factions took over women's organizing throughout the West Bank and Gaza Strip.

One of the more persistent characterizations of the Nablus elite is its purported "conservative" nature. Graham-Brown (1989, 384) notes that Nablus is still dominated socially by a group of "well-established landowning and merchant families who set a generally conservative social tone. Despite the wealth of individuals and families, it is not a prosperous or outward looking town." Others have also noted this conservative character (Tawil 1979; Tuqan n.d.). Naturally a sense of perspective is required here, as the "conservatism" of Nablus should be placed alongside the "traditionalism" and "conservatism" for which Hebron is notorious. What concerns us here, however, is how to understand these characterizations. We would argue that the encounter with modernity in Palestine was variable and different, producing different expressions in different areas. Thus the encounter with the Ottoman state's efforts at

5. Singlehood for women is not a remarkable feature of Palestinian society as a whole. This phenomenon (which also exists in Jerusalem, Bethlehem, and Ramallah) is likely the product of the dearth of eligible men for accomplished women.

centralization and "modernization," the response to changes in the regional and world economy, and the encounter with the British Mandate and the Zionist movement were different in the different cities. We have already noted the different modes of urban life in Palestine at the turn of the twentieth century, ranging from the cosmopolitanism of Jerusalem, Jaffa, and Haifa to the more "backwater" versions of urban life in the inland towns. This was very much the outcome of the way in which the ruling groups articulated their encounters with the tumultuous changes affecting Palestine.

Representations of Hebron and Nablus going back decades have some resonance for our problematic in this chapter. In an article entitled "Zealous Towns in Nineteenth-Century Palestine," Kushner (1997, 2) notes that Western travelers to Palestine in the nineteenth century singled out Hebron and Nablus as "hostile" and even "violent" toward foreigners, compared to other towns that were more "hospitable" or at least "indifferent." He attributes this to the two towns' relative autonomy from Ottoman rule; later resentment and hostility toward the new and rising class of businessmen in coastal cities and Jerusalem as a result of the "European assault which left these towns in a peripheral position;" and the negligible encounter with Europeans, especially the dearth of resident Europeans, pilgrims, and other foreign or Christian institutions in these towns (4–10). Kushner's observations concerning the homogeneity of Nablus and Hebron compared to Jerusalem and the coastal cities are noteworthy. The encounter with modernity in nineteenth- and early-twentieth-century Palestine involved, among other things, contact with foreigners, missionaries, pilgrims, modern educational institutions, and later the British Mandate authorities. The degree of insularity of the cities' elites, the extent of their integration into the world economy and contact with its foreign representatives, all must have left their imprint on the consciousness and dispositions of the inhabitants.

One of the keys to understanding the different forms of urban life and the urban ethos is an appreciation of the role of education in the creation of elites. The kind and venue of the educational experience appear to be of signal importance. We have enough evidence from memoirs and other similar documents to conclude, for instance, that in the early part of the twentieth century a new educational experience became available for the children of the Nablus elite, while it was lacking for those of Hebron. By the 1920s, several "modern" schools were established in Nablus. It is important to note that even girls were enrolled in these schools and that at least one of these was a church-sponsored institution (run by nuns of the Order of St. Joseph), catering, as in other cities such as Jerusalem, to the children of the Muslim majority. Yusra Salah (n.d), member of a family of Muslim scholars and jurists, notes that she and her sister studied at the St. Joseph Sisters' School in the early 1920s, moving to the Fatimiyya School in 1929, then to the 'Aishiyya School. Her sister went on to study at the teachers' training center in Jerusalem, while she was sent to the Quaker-run Friends School in Ramallah. Many girls of her class went to the Schmidt College in Jerusalem, which was believed by families to be more conservative than the more liberal and "modern" Friends in Ramallah.[6] She then went on to the Beirut College for Women, moving, after a struggle with her family, to the American University of Beirut (graduating in 1946), where her brother also studied.

The experience of study outside Palestine (most notably at the American University of Beirut) brought together members of the Palestinian urban middle class and elite from different cities. Salah notes her friendships with the Sakakini sisters of Jerusalem (daughters of the renowned educator Khalil Sakakini) and associations with men and women from Jerusalem, Ramallah, Nablus, and Jaffa (Salah n.d.). Similarly, education at Palestinian schools and colleges such as the Arab College and Schmidt College in Jerusalem and the Friends School in Ramallah played an important role in the production of a "national" Palestinian urban class uniting Muslims, Christians, and individuals from different cities.[7]

Hebron's educational system remained traditional throughout the 1920s and 1930s, and it has been noted that no foreign educational institutions (which in Palestine were mostly church-sponsored or run by missionaries, as in Jerusalem, Nablus, Jerusalem, Jaffa, and Haifa) were established there. Even in the 1950s, most of the school teachers in Hebron were from outside the region (Ju'beh 2003).

It is very significant for our argument that no written document of note

6. Among the girls from Nablus who studied at Schmidt College were Saba 'Arafat (who later became a member of the Board of Trustees of Birzeit University), Rashda al-Masri, Naziha Abdul-Majid, and Nabiha Tuqan (Salah n.d.).

7. This is amply documented in Palestinian memoirs from the pre-1948 period (for example, Sharabi n.d.; Tuqan n.d.; Masri 1997).

has been left behind by Hebron notables or public personalities in the course of the nineteenth or twentieth centuries. Compared with the wealth of memoirs, diaries, and chronicles bequeathed to the social historian by public figures and intellectuals in Nablus, Jerusalem, Haifa, and Jaffa, the offerings of Hebron have been indeed meager. This can be taken as a reflection of Hebron's peripherality in national life on the one hand, and the lack of interest or desire on the part of its elite to memorialize in writing their accomplishments and contributions on the other.

To recapitulate, it may be appropriate to return to the two interrelated questions we raised at the start of this chapter. First, how much of the past is embodied in the present, and to what extent are the "characters" of the two cities, Nablus and Hebron, a reflection of their social identities and histories in past decades? How much continuity has there been, and what significance have the ruptures of the past four decades had? The second broad problem continues to confound: is there still such a place as a "social space" as conceived by Doumani for eighteenth and twentieth centuries Jabal Nablus and Jabal al-Khalil? For instance, Johnson (in this volume) argues that the southern area of the West Bank (primarily the region around Hebron) may have denser webs of kin and community relations. The question remains, however, as to what accounts for this persistent difference, as reflected in census and survey data.

Historical Rupture and the New City: Ramallah

The history of Ramallah as recorded by historians and its own "native sons" (and some daughters) in the early twentieth century is not the history of a cosmopolitan city such as Jerusalem, Haifa, or Jaffa. Nor is it the history of an established inland city such as Nablus or Hebron. Until the end of the nineteenth century, Ramallah was a village like many others in its environs. An architectural history of Ramallah has shown that its architecture was not distinguishable from that of other villages in the hilly district, and the building styles reflected the lifestyle and needs of peasants (Ju'beh and Bishara 2002, 22). Its population was small, and agriculture was the main economic pursuit. Families spent much of the summer months tending their orchards and vineyards (Shaheen 1982, 46), much in the manner of Hebronites noted earlier. The winds of change, however, began to prevail by the mid-nineteenth century, when a number of public buildings were erected, reflecting the increasing presence of foreign churches and religious missions in what was a town of Greek Orthodox Christians. The proximity to Jerusalem and the fact that the village had a majority of Christians were obviously factors in the attractiveness of Ramallah to foreign missionaries and churches. By the beginning of the twentieth century, the Catholics, Greek Catholics, Protestants, and Quakers had established their presence in the town and had built churches and schools. The first modern school in Ramallah was established by the Germans. The local Greek Orthodox Church was the last to do so, no doubt feeling the competition from the other institutions. Its slowness may be a reflection of the fact that the Greek Orthodox Church had taken its constituency for granted, only to discover that it was losing members to the newer churches. Financial incentives and the promise of education abroad were probably factors in the attractiveness of the new churches to the local Christian population.[8]

The first expansion of Ramallah into a town occurred in the early part of the twentieth century, with the dramatic increase in emigration to the Americas. Gradually, remittances from abroad began to change the face of the town, as émigrés began to invest in building residences and establishing community institutions, businesses, and services. Ramallah became a service and commercial center for the region (Ju'beh and Bishara 2002, 38). The period of the British Mandate was another turning point in the history of this village's transformation into an important regional town. Ramallah began to attract migrants from other regions, particularly Jabal al-Khalil, because of employment opportunities created by the emigration of its natives and the abandonment of agricultural pursuits by the younger generation. The expansion of building outside the confines of the old town nucleus (modern-day Lower Ramallah) also attracted many builders and craftsmen from surrounding villages and the Hebron region (Ju'beh and Bishara 2002, 42). During this same period, villagers from Jabal al-Khalil were also moving into Jerusalem in search of livelihoods, a feature that is mainly characteristic of the Hebron region and not generalizable to other areas in Palestine (except for the migrations to the

8. Muslims were not targets of the foreign churches' missionary efforts; missionaries concentrated on the already sizeable Christian population in Ramallah (as well as in Bethlehem, Jerusalem, Nazareth, and other Christian towns and villages in Palestine).

coastal cities from Jabal Nablus during the Mandate period). Extreme poverty and scarcity of tillable land were all factors contributing to this pattern of internal migration. In that sense, Palestine's first labor migrants during the early part of the twentieth century were the Khalilis; the history of this migration (and its considerable impact, especially on Jerusalem), spurred by poverty and possible land alienation, has yet to be told.

The slow crystallization of a middle class during the Mandate was important in the history of Ramallah's gradual transformation into a regional center. Emigration was one important source for this development, as investments by émigrés in construction, institution-building, and commercial activities began to change the face of daily life in the growing town. Periodic visits by emigrants to seek wives and husbands, to oversee the progress on their investments, or to collect rents were all important factors in the development of a new middle-class ethos, increasing the "openness" of Ramallah to the outside world, in this case the diasporas in the Americas, particularly in the United States.[9] Several nonchurch and secular institutions of note were established during this period, notably the Scouts in 1928, and the First Sariyya Group in 1930. Four important women's associations were formed between 1925 and 1941 (Shaheen 1982, 71–72), giving an opportunity for the small group of educated and community-minded women to develop and legitimize roles in the public sphere.

The real turning point in Ramallah's trajectory of transformation into a town with a distinct middle class came with the dispossession of 1948. We have noted earlier that Ramallah and Gaza City are the two Palestinian towns most affected by the war and dispossession of 1948. While Nablus and Hebron, the two largest cities in the West Bank, did receive some refugees (Nablus many more than Hebron), Ramallah in the West Bank became a city of refugees and internal migrants after 1948. But what distinguished Ramallah (and to some extent Bethlehem and Jerusalem) from other towns receiving refugees was the fact that many of these new exiles were middle-class Christian refugees from the coastal towns of Jaffa, al-Lidd, and Ramla. Mostly engaged in commerce, this group of urban refugees augmented the already dwindling original Chris-

9. Much the same process was occurring in Bethlehem, also a Christian town. The majority of Bethlehem's emigrants were in Central and South America. Their emigration had begun in the eighteenth century.

tian population of Ramallah and formed the nucleus of its new middle class of shopkeepers, petty traders, government employees, teachers, and later, professionals. It is important to note that these middle-class refugees became part of the fabric of the town itself, not isolated in refugee camps on the periphery, both physically and socially. Peasant refugees, on the other hand, were set apart in several refugee camps within and outside Ramallah. With time, they formed a significant component of the working and underclass of the town, along with migrants from the Hebron region.[10]

By the 1950s, Ramallah had become a hybrid town of natives and refugees, people with city ways and new arrivals from villages. Even though it had lost its former Christian majority (despite the influx of Christian refugees from the coastal cities and their environs), it kept its unique Christian cast and consequently more "open" way of life; its Christian schools, especially the Quaker-run Friends Schools, continued to attract students from other Palestinian cities and even from surrounding Arab countries. Despite some reservations by conservative Nabulsis and others concerning the open atmosphere at these schools, enough of them seem to have admired these Christian institutions for the kind of education and values being offered to send their children there.

The role of emigration in the development of Ramallah into a town of some diversity cannot be neglected. Emigrés' periodic visits to Ramallah to maintain ties with the "old country" *(il-iblad)* normalized strange ways of dress and deportment, especially by Americanized youth from urban communities such as San Francisco and Chicago. Overall, Ramallah's diversity and reputation for openness and tolerance became a factor for further heterogeneity, and the town became a magnet for those wishing to escape the oppression of villages and other towns. Small numbers of intellectuals, professionals, and political activists from other areas settled in Ramallah.[11]

10. This does not mean, however, that middle-class refugees (whether Christian or Muslim) or migrants from other areas were given "citizenship" in Ramallah by the dwindling community of "original" Ramallawis. The fact is not only reflected in the discourse and practice of everyday life but also in municipal regulations. Living one's entire life in Ramallah does not confer a Ramallah identity upon a person.

11. Histories of Ramallah and other literary and historical documents bear this out (e.g. Abu-Rayya n.d.; Qaddura 1999; Shaheen 1982; Shaheen 1992; Dajani 1993; Barghuthi 1998).

One of the keys to understanding the transformation of Ramallah from a sleepy village to a vibrant small town and later a city on its way to becoming the primary urban center in the West Bank has to do with its Christian identity. It has been decades since Ramallah lost its Christian majority,[12] yet the original Christian identity continues to figure in representations of the city, both in terms of its self-image and its place in the national imagination. We would argue that over the years, different social groups—professional and other white collar migrants from other towns, students coming to study at nearby Birzeit University, political activists, Christian refugees, and the dwindling population of natives—had a common interest in furthering the notion of Ramallah as a Christian town, and by association and extension, as a town tolerant of openness, difference, and diversity. Today, under the rule of the Palestinian Authority, whose major seat Ramallah has become, the Christian identity of Ramallah endures and is embodied in its relatively lax and free social atmosphere enabling the mixing of men and women, leisure activities, and a restaurant and café culture where men and women can feel comfortable in public and where alcohol can be served.[13]

Ramallah is unique among our three cities in that it does not have a hegemonic social group with historic roots in the city. This, we believe, is one of the keys to understanding its urban modernity, in sharp contrast with the more conservative cast of Nablus and the entrenched conservatism of Hebron. A good part of Ramallah's "original" families emigrated throughout the twentieth century, making Ramallah a town that belonged to no one and thus to everyone. Because there was no hegemonic, entrenched group of town "elders" or notables in place, "strangers" and "outsiders" came to assume positions of influence in the town, especially after the 1970s and with the growing power of the hegemonic national movement. A good number of political activists of rural origins or from other towns took up residence in Ramallah and began to wield effective political power through the growing network of national institutions such as universities, political parties, mass organizations,

12. Figures from the 1997 census indicate that 32 percent of the city's population are Christian (PCBS 2000a).

13. Jerusalem, Ramallah, and Bethlehem are the only cities in the West Bank where alcohol is served in restaurants and sold in shops. Even in Ramallah's twin city of al-Bira, a stone's throw away, municipal regulations prohibit the sale of alcohol.

women's associations, and student federations. The arrival of the Palestinian Authority in 1994 further intensified this trend. Marginalizing the town's mayor (who according to custom has to be a Christian "native" of the town), the president's office, the governorate, and the various security services took over the leadership of the town. This situation must be contrasted with Nablus and Hebron, where, owing to the relative stability of the population and the negligible migrations into the cities, the local power structures have been largely local and more stable over time.

Ramallah captured the imagination of the many students, intellectuals, and political activists who spent time in the town or who eventually settled there; it was also the site of many awakenings. This vitality is vividly captured in a book of testimonials to Ramallah published recently by the Ramallah Public Library. It is actually a celebration of the vitality, hybridity, and diversity of the city and contains many essays documenting the coming of age of students fresh from the village, and the making of intellectuals and nonconformists (Qura 2002). It is hard to imagine such a volume being published to celebrate Nablus or Hebron, cities that have not been as deeply touched by war, dispossession, migration, and upheaval. Nablus belongs to the Nabulsis and Hebron to the Khalilis. It is only Ramallah that has become the city of all.

By the 1960s, and despite the relatively small size of its population, both native and migrant, Ramallah had become a town of some significance in its region, primarily as a market and administrative center and as the site of a number of educational institutions. In the period stretching from the Israeli occupation in 1967 to the arrival of the Palestinian Authority in 1995, Ramallah's status as a district center was further cemented by the annexation of East Jerusalem and the presence of the military administration for all of the West Bank, courts, main hospital, public libraries, banks, and other public services. Ramallah's central location in the West Bank and proximity to Jerusalem were no doubt important factors here. Birzeit College in the nearby village of Birzeit, which was until then a two-year institution, became the first Palestinian university in 1976 and expanded in the 1980s to encompass an increasingly diverse student population and faculty drawn from all parts of the West Bank and Gaza. By the 1980s, Ramallah had become more diverse, a major market center during the day for villagers from the area, and a site of investment for village entrepreneurs (Yunis et al. 1991), but also, more importantly, a place drawing youth from outlying villages to demonstrations, political rallies, book fairs, voluntary work camps, and the ubiquitous annual "Palestine Week" held in local colleges and at Birzeit University. In short, and despite the fact that many of the visitors to the city and investors were from villages and thus did lend a ruralized cast to the town (Tamari 1995), the town had accumulated enough cultural capital as a site of modernity and diversity to later become the seat of Palestinian politics and an important node in the national economy.

The coming of the Palestinian Authority enhanced Ramallah's status as a central Palestinian city. The optimistic political atmosphere surrounding the Oslo agreements and the establishment of the Palestinian National Authority (PNA) encouraged local and expatriate entrepreneurs to invest in construction and to launch businesses. The years after 1994 saw the initiation of several relatively large-scale private-sector investment projects in upscale and middle-class housing estates, hotels, a shopping mall, supermarkets, a medical center and hospital, and several private radio and television stations. Ramallah's image and reality as an "open" city and the availability of private education were also factors encouraging the resettlement of a small but culturally significant group of Palestinians returning from exile. While the men may have stayed in Gaza City to work in PNA institutions, their families established themselves in Ramallah. Commuting to Ramallah from Gaza became impossible after 2000, prompting many such families to establish residences in Ramallah rather than stay in Gaza City.

Over the course of the last few decades, the popular imagination has endowed Ramallah with a unique character. It is important to note, however, that representations of Ramallah as a relatively prosperous, open, and "free" city are bounded by the contexts in which those doing the imagining live their lives. Recent research on youth (Giacaman et al. 2004a) and life quality (Giacaman et al. 2006) in the West Bank and Gaza has revealed that a good life was generally defined by youth as the ability to move freely, the availability of educational choices, and possibilities for leisure activities. Yet this definition seems to also represent a gauge for lives worse than one's own; imaginations of Palestinian locales were as much a function of a person's freedom of access as of the perception of relative deprivation. For instance, youth in Gaza thought that life on the West Bank as a whole, and not only in Ramallah, was good. For teenagers in Qalandia refugee camp, close to Ramallah, a miserable life was not part of their perception of their own lives but pertained to the lives of Gazans. Thus, the youth of Qalandia assessed their life quality in terms of more miserable conditions in Gaza, the epitome of misery in the national imagination. In contrast, youth at Am'ari refugee camp, located within Ramallah city boundaries and in fact part and parcel of the city fabric, described their lives in the camp as a "prison within a prison" compared to the high life in "Ramallah." In other words, youths' perceptions of their life quality are partially a function of their concrete experiences in place. However, these perceptions also articulate with representations derived from national imaginings of Palestinian locations; in these imaginings, Ramallah comes highest in terms of life quality, and Gaza lowest.

A further factor in the assumption of prominence by Ramallah was the intensification of Israeli policies of siege and encirclement, especially those targeting Jerusalem. By the late 1990s, movement within the West Bank and between the West Bank and the Gaza Strip had become increasingly difficult. Many Palestinian Authority institutions, including the president's office, diplomatic missions, and Palestinian NGOs, relocated their headquarters to Ramallah. Ramallah's central location within the West Bank and the existence of an infrastructure of services and a small but essential pool of professionals and service workers were no doubt important factors in this process. By the year 2000, most if not all the major Jerusalem-based NGOs had established permanent offices in Ramallah. Further restrictions on movement during the second intifada since late 2000 have resulted in an influx of employees of Palestinian Authority, NGO, and private sector institutions who used to live outside Ramallah. The social heterogeneity of Ramallah continued to expand.

A unique feature of Ramallah after the establishment of the Palestinian Authority, and the most relevant for our purposes here, is the way in which Ramallah has inserted itself—primarily through its new middle class—into the evolving and dynamic hybrid trans-Arab urban culture, epitomized in the major cities of the Arab world such as Cairo, Beirut, and more proximately, Amman. This globalized and modernist urban middle-class ethos has captured the imagination of the city's new middle class and is reflected in the sensibilities, dispositions, life projects, and practices of wide sections of the urban middle strata. Consumption, predictably, is the field par excellence for the elaboration of this ethos and way of life. We show in the next section how this ethos finds expression and is reflected in lifestyle indicators related to consumption but also to education, employment, and women's visibility and participation in the public sphere.

The Production of Difference

We now examine some of the contemporary features of our three cities as reflected in data from the census, our survey of households, and some recent studies. We attempt to draw out the uniqueness of each city from these seemingly dry statistics; we suggest that the sharp contrasts in terms of demographic, socioeconomic, and lifestyle indicators reflect differences in the ambience and ethos of these cities. We came to realize these important differences among cities as we were analyzing our household survey data, focusing specifically on Nablus and Hebron.[14] Hebron consistently appeared to be more caught up in an insular and conservative way of life compared to Nablus as evidenced by the early marriage of its women, the high proportion of children within the household, large family sizes, lesser educational levels for both men and women, the type of work people do to earn a living, housing arrangements, and the lower level of modern amenities in homes. Utilizing the PCBS 1997 census and the labor force survey 1999 data sets,[15] as well as selected indicators derived from the household survey, the comparison expanded to include Ramallah city. Our aim has been to establish the coexistence of different modes of urban life in one national space, from the unabashed globalizing urbanity of Ramallah to the intermediate "traditional-urban" of Nablus and the generally "traditional-peasant" way of life in Hebron.

This typology not only has local historical resonance, as we have seen in our examination of the forces of continuity and rupture in Palestine, but also reflects the reality of contemporary urban formations in the Arab world as a whole. Arab cities today can be placed along a continuum ranging from the

14. The household sample survey size was too small to yield comprehensive meaningful analyses for Ramallah City.

15. The 1997 census data set (PCBS 2000a) for districts as well as the 1999 Labor Force survey data set (PCBS 2000c) are sample data sets representing different districts and locales (urban, rural, and camp) but not individual cities. City-specific census data were also kindly released by PCBS for use by the Institute of Women's Studies in this analysis.

large globalizing metropolises to the relatively insular peripheral cities at the margins of the national and global economies and cultural hegemonies. It would appear that the pace of integration into the world economy and the place of the city in the international division of labor, the nature of the hegemonic groups, and the size and nature of the middle class are among the principal factors that set Arab cities apart. Cities are different not only in terms of the size of their populations or their economic growth indicators, but also in terms of the kinds of cultures they nurture and the images they project. The globalized "modern face" of Cairo, Beirut, Amman, Tunis, and other capital cities can be contrasted with the more traditional urban ambiences of Aleppo, San'a', or Baghdad (at least before the occupation). These are yet differentiated from peripheral cities that are no more than large villages. The coexistence of the city and the village in the same urban space is of course another matter altogether and has been widely noted by urban sociologists. What we are referring to here is the public face of the city, its "official" representation, as defined by hegemonic groups (and often governments, as in the case of those intent on attracting tourism and international business links by presenting their cities as oases of modernity in the Arab desert landscape).

The Demography of Difference

Table 1.1 demonstrates the sharp demographic contrasts among the cities, differences that we propose reflect differing conceptualizations of family life, family futures, sociality, and sociability, and even the self. The family and household constitute the sites where such conceptualizations are elaborated and take shape.

Beginning with basic demographic indicators, we find that Ramallah has the lowest rate of children under fifteen years of age, compared to Nablus and Hebron (the latter denoting high fertility levels there). Ramallah also has the highest percentage of persons over sixty-five years old, compared to Nablus and Hebron, a reflection, once again of high fertility levels in Hebron. Thirty-nine percent of Ramallah women over fifteen years of age are single, compared to 29 percent for Nablus and 24 percent for Hebron. Finally, the age at first marriage seems to confirm a pattern of early marriage for Hebron's women that is consistent with the other findings, with over half of Hebron

Table 1.1
Selected Demographic Indicators by City, 1997 Census (%)

Indicator	Nablus	Ramallah	Hebron
Children under 15 years	39.0	34.0	48.0
Persons 65 years or older	3.8	4.7	2.6
Average household size	6.9	6.4	8.0
Single women over 15 years	29.0	39.0	24.0
AGE AT FIRST MARRIAGE: WOMEN			
11–14	6.6	3.9	8.9
15–17	30.0	22.0	42.0
18–24	49.0	56.0	43.0
25–34	13.0	15.0	5.0
Over 34	3.4	3.1	1.1

Source: PCBS 1999a

women having been married before they reached the age of eighteen years, compared to 37 percent for Nablus and 26 percent for Ramallah women.

Interesting patterns emerge when we compare cities with the villages of their district. While on the whole children under fifteen years of age constitute 46 percent of the population in West Bank villages and 44 percent in cities, the figures for specific locales reveal features unique to those areas. If we examine rural-urban gaps within districts, we find that the largest gap between the city and its hinterland is recorded for Ramallah, followed by Nablus and Hebron. Hebron and Hebron district rates are the highest overall. In contrast, we find that the proportion of children in Nablus villages is 46 percent, compared to 39 percent in the city, indicating a more significant gap between city and countryside compared to Hebron. In the Ramallah district, the gap between city and village is even greater. We are thus presented with two unique cases, Hebron and Ramallah, two cities on opposite ends of the urban continuum, each with a population profile reflecting its unique history, both distant and more recent.

A similar pattern is noted when examining the proportions of single women in these cities compared to their rural areas. With Nablus's proportion of single women over fifteen years of age found to be 29 percent, its rural areas have a lower proportion at 26 percent. Ramallah again stands out in the level of contrast with its rural areas. Hebron is the most similar to its rural area, with only 24 percent of its women fifteen years or over single, compared to 26 percent in its hinterland. A comparison between cities and their rural extensions in terms of the proportions of women who marry under eighteen years of age is even more remarkable: while Nablus city's rate is 37 percent of all its married women having married below the age of eighteen years, the rate of its rural areas is 36 percent, that is, almost the same; Ramallah city marriages under eighteen years of age stand at 26 percent, compared to 37 percent in its rural areas; finally, Hebron city seems to even surpass its rural areas with 51 percent of its marriages having occurred when the women were under the age of eighteen compared to 42 percent in its rural areas.

Demographically then, Hebron resembles its hinterland rather than other Palestinian cities as indicated by its large household sizes, large proportion of children under fifteen in households, and low levels of singlehood among women over the age of fifteen years. Moreover, Hebron women tend to marry at significantly lower ages than women in the Jabal al-Khalil rural areas, pointing to a peculiarity of its inhabitants' practices and dispositions. Nablus on the other hand displays important contrasts with its countryside, but not as dramatic as in the case of Ramallah. Ramallah stands out in terms of urban-rural demographic comparisons by not only having the lowest levels of children, early marriage, and family sizes and the highest levels of singlehood, but also in terms of the sharp differences in these indicators between Ramallah city and its rural areas.

How do we read these statistics? On one level, it would appear that these three cities represent different "moments" in the process of urbanization in Palestine. One would be tempted to view these cases as representing three stages in the process of modern urbanization. Yet it is important to keep in mind that these three cases may also represent three different paradigms of contemporary urban formations, paradigms that are not necessarily best understood in an evolutionary framework or in terms of traditionalism and modernity. From the perspective of regional (Arab) urban patterns, one could say that it is likely that our three cities represent three different types of social universes according to their degree of integration into global systems of economic exchange, culture, and consumption; the nature of their hegemonic social groups; and the size and importance of their new middle classes.

Having said this, it is important to underline the uniqueness of place and location in Palestine. Under the stifling regime of closure, separation, and fragmentation (especially in the West Bank), Palestinians have lost their mobility, the one dynamic factor in urban transformation in the Arab region. If these Israeli policies continue, Palestinian society will be locked into localisms of a kind not observed anywhere else in the region today; we will find ourselves with the curious case of a "cosmopolitan" localism in Ramallah, as insulated from the rest of Palestine as the "localized" localisms of insular Hebron or Nablus. Palestinians' social worlds are contracting, ironically at a time when the internet and satellite television have accelerated access to the globe (Giacaman et al. 2004a).

Education: How Much, and For What Purpose?

Educational levels of the three cities' inhabitants conform to the patterns noted earlier. With the highest percentages of lower levels of education scored by Hebron city (26 percent having had no more than six years of schooling), we find that Nablus city is in between and Ramallah has the lowest levels (table 1.2). In comparison, Ramallah residents have higher postsecondary educational levels, compared to Nablus and Hebron. Consistent with our main arguments, the demographic characteristics and educational levels of these city's inhabitants are understandably interlinked, with higher levels of education corresponding to lower household sizes, smaller percentages of children in the community, higher levels of singlehood among women, and lower rates of early marriage.

Table 1.2
Educational Attainment by City
and District Rural Area (DRA), 1997 Census (%)

Educational level	Nablus		Ramallah		Hebron	
Population over 15	City	DRA	City	DRA	City	DRA
Up to 6 years	21	39	13	33	26	50
7–9 years	25	27	17	25	33	29
10–12 years	29	16	33	21	28	12
Postsecondary	25	18	37	21	13	9
Total	100	100	100	100	100	100

Source: PCBS 1999a

The contrasts among the cities and the district rural areas where the cities are located also support our hypothesis. With the gap between city and countryside largest for Hebron in the lower educational levels, the gap diminishes substantially for the seven to nine years of education group. The rates almost even out for Nablus, with 25 percent of the city's inhabitants having had seven to nine years of schooling compared to 27 percent for its rural area. Ramallah has the largest gap between the city and the countryside. The data seem to suggest that Hebronites believe that seven to nine years of education are sufficient for the children to manage their future lives, perhaps for the same reasons that Hebron district's rural dwellers reach a similar conclusion. Postsecondary educational levels reveal a similar trend, where the gap between city and village dwellers in Hebron is 4 percent in favor of the city, widens to 7 percent for Nablus, and widens even more for Ramallah, to 16 percent.

We can only speculate here on the meanings of these patterns. One conclusion could be that formal education is not perceived to be as relevant to the lives and futures of Hebron's residents as it is for those of Nablus or Ramallah. This finding seems to be consistent with economies where formal education and training are not prerequisites for employment; furthermore, it reflects an ethos where prospects for social mobility are not linked with higher educational levels and the acquisition of skills that are marketable in a modern, globally oriented economy. The contrast between Ramallah and Hebron then can be expressed as one between two social, economic, and cultural universes with different horizons: one valorizing social mobility through the acquisition of higher levels of education, and the other with a more restricted and provincial horizon where social mobility in the sense of a change in lives has less resonance. This issue is not necessarily one of individual choice; in the social universe of Hebron, people are not presented with visions of alternative lives and livelihoods—the horizons are more restricted, and those desiring more dynamic and different futures have to pursue these elsewhere. Ramallah is one of those places where such futures can be contemplated, and the city does have its share of Hebronites, Nabulsis, and others in search of a middle-class and different life. Sites of migration farther away and outside Palestine are also contemplated by individuals desiring a transformation in their lives, although the chances of realizing the migration dreams of the previous generation seem to have evaporated with restrictions on the movement of Palestinian labor in the Gulf and beyond.

It is interesting to note that the differences in educational levels between the sexes in these cities are not very substantial. This attests to the overall rapid increase in women's education in Palestine, with 25 percent of Nabulsi men and women each with post-high school education, 36 percent of Ramallah men and 37 percent of Ramallah women with post-high school education, and 14 percent of Hebron men and 12 percent of Hebron women with post-high school education. In Ramallah, then, there seems to be a very high proportion of women with postsecondary education compared to the other cities. This statistic cannot be explained solely by the higher levels of education of the population, as post-high school education among women in Ramallah is one and one half times that of women in Nablus and three times that of women in Hebron, strengthening the argument that the real and perceived work opportunities and openness of milieu encourage educated women to move there. The situation in Hebron appears to be exactly the reverse, with Nablus situated between the two.

We can argue then that our three cities represent three different modes of urban life, where one of the defining marks of difference resides in openness and diversity, the opposite of which are insularity and sameness. Education appears to be highly relevant here, because its level (and type, as we demonstrate below) seems to be strongly linked with ways of living, working, and being. We have some support for this conclusion in the finding related to the countries where the highest educational levels were received. Ninety-one percent of Hebronites reported that their highest degrees were obtained in Palestine; 83 percent of Nabulsis and 77 percent of Ramallah residents reported receiving their education in Palestine. The highest levels of degrees obtained in the Arab world came from Nablus at 11 percent, compared to 10 percent for Ramallah and 6 percent for Hebron. That is, 97 percent of Hebronites who responded to the question about where they had received their highest degrees reported completing their education either locally or in the Arab world, followed by 94 percent for Nablusis and 87 percent for Ramallawis. Finally, and most interestingly, 13 percent of Ramallah residents reported having received their degrees from other world universities, compared to 5 percent for Nablus, and 3 percent for Hebron. These results can only reinforce the view that experiences outside Palestine, including the encounter with higher education in non-Arab milieus, contribute to differences in lifestyles. Ramallah thus stands out as a place that attracts individuals in search of a space tolerant of differing ways of life. This conclusion may be appear to be dampened some-what by the recognition that the availability of work opportunities in more modern types of occupations in Ramallah may be the magnet that attracts graduates of world universities and thus explains the attraction of the city. But it is equally plausible to suggest that once there, the diverse mix of people cre-ates qualitatively new realities that become part of the lived experiences of in-dividuals and families as they try to negotiate their way in their new worlds.

Work as a Vocation

The survey data regarding work show that 43 percent of our cities' men and women fifteen years or over are reported as working, both part-time and full-time; 5.3 percent are reported as unemployed; 14 percent are full-time stu-dents; and the rest are either housewives, unable to work, disabled, or not working for other reasons.[16] Important differences among the cities emerge when we examine gender gaps (table 1.3). Twenty-one percent of Ramallah women work for pay outside their homes, while 3 percent are seeking work. This brings the total to 24 percent who are part of the labor force. For Nablus, the rates are lower: 13 percent of women are reported as working and 4 per-cent are reported as seeking work, bringing the total to 17 percent. Only 7 per-cent of Hebron women work, and 1 percent are seeking work, that is, 8 percent consider themselves in the labor force, an understandable situation given the large family sizes there and the relatively low level of education. These results match the results on education and demographic characteristics observed previously: Ramallah women marry later, are more educated, work, and have smaller family sizes. Hebron women work mostly at home, marry early, have large families, and are not highly educated. Nabulsi women fall somewhere in between.

Almost one-quarter of women fifteen year old or older in Ramallah report that they are students; the rates are 15 percent for Nablus and 14 percent for Hebron (table 1.3). Male students are found at higher levels in Ramallah as well. In contrast three quarters of Hebron males and the same percentage of Nablus males are working, compared to 69 percent for Ramallah males.

---

16. These statistics pertain to 1997, that is, before the widespread unemployment caused by economic distress and the severe restrictions on movement during the second intifada.

Table 1.3
Employment by City and Sex, 1997 Census (%)

Employment status[a]	Nablus		Ramallah		Hebron	
	M	F	M	F	M	F
Working	74	13	69	21	74	7
Unemployed, seeking work	8	4	9	3	8	1
Students	13	15	17	24	12	14
Other	5	68	5	52	6	78
Total	100	100	100	100	100	100

Source: PCBS 1999a
[a]For persons fifteen years old or older

These differences can be explained by the higher proportion of students living in Ramallah. That is, Ramallah is unusual in that it has significantly more working and educated women and significantly more male and female students as well. Given that both Nablus and Hebron house universities within the city, these results suggest that Ramallawis tend to pursue educating their children to a larger extent than either Nablusis or Khalilis. Once again, we speculate that these data not only reflect the different economies and employment opportunities of the three cities, but also different notions of social mobility and the avenues available for pursuing it.

Indeed, support for this argument is further found when examining data on children six to seventeen years old. Table 1.4 reveals that about 6.5 percent of children who should be attending school in both Nablus and Hebron work, mostly fifteen hours or more, compared to 3.3 percent for children in Ramal-

Table 1.4
Child Labor and Schooling by City, 1997 Census (%)

Status[a]	Nablus			Ramallah			Hebron		
	T	M	F	T	M	F	T	M	F
Works 1–14 hours	0.5	1.0	0.0	0.3	0.7	0.0	0.4	0.8	0.0
Works 15 hours or more	6.0	12.0	0.1	3.0	6.0	0.1	6.2	12.0	0.2
Student full time	87.0	83.0	91.0	92.0	89.0	95.0	85.0	81.0	89.0
Other	6.0	4.0	9.0	5.0	4.0	5.0	8.0	6.0	11.0

Source: PCBS 1999a
[a]For children six through seventeen years of age

lah city. The percentages of children who are full-time students in the three localities suggest that children's education is perceived as less relevant to life and work in Hebron and more relevant in Ramallah. As for the rest of these children who are not in school and not working, either they were registered as unemployed persons seeking work, they were working at home with the family, or they were unable to work. We may also note that child laborers are predominantly boys, with 13 percent of boys working in both Hebron and Nablus compared to 7 percent for Ramallah. Ramallawis appear to value children's education and discourage child labor and attrition from schools, while in both Hebron and Nablus some sectors within the population appear to believe that their children can manage their lives without much education. This difference must be related to the types of economies, both material and social-symbolic, that valorize one conception of individual and family presents and futures over others.

Data on employment status in the PCBS labor force survey of 1999 are helpful here.[17] Table 1.5 indicates that the highest level of self-employed men fifteen years old or older and reporting themselves as working are found in the Hebron-area urban areas, suggesting the presence of a domestically based, perhaps informal type of economy and relative lack of absorption into the broader framework of employment in formal institutions. That is followed by the Nablus urban areas, with the lowest levels of self-employment found in the more developed economy of Ramallah, which has the highest levels of the employer category, implying the development of structures that allow inhabitants to set up and operate their own private enterprises.

The sector where people are employed is revealing as well. Although the "private national" sector is dominant in all cities, census results reveal that 63 percent of Ramallah employment is held in the private national sector compared to 66 percent for Nablus and 68 percent for Hebron (table 1.6). National government employment is 18 percent in Nablus and 17 percent in Ramallah but only 12 percent in Hebron, affirming both Ramallah's and Nablus's relative importance as seats of government compared to Hebron. If we consider employment with international organizations and local non-governmental organizations, we find that overall, 9 percent of Nablusis are

17. The 1999 PCBS Labor Force survey data set does not allow for specific city comparisons, but rather urban-rural and district comparisons.

Table 1.5
Employment Status by District Urban Area, 1999 (%)

Employment status[a]	Nablus	Ramallah/al Bira	Hebron
Employer	13	16	10
Self-employed	20	18	22
Wage worker	60	60	61
Unpaid family work	7	6	7
Total	100	100	100

Source: PCBS 1999e
[a]Of men fifteen years old or older reported as working

Table 1.6
Employment Sector by City, 1997 Census (%)

Employment sector[a]	Nablus	Ramallah	Hebron
Private national	66	63	68
Private international	6	6	3
National government	18	17	12
Outside establishment	7	6	15
Other[b]	3	8	2
Total	100	100	100

Source: PCBS 1999a
[a]For those reported as working and ten years old or older
[b]NGO, UNRWA, international bodies, etc.

employed by such organizations, compared to 14 percent for Ramallah and 5 percent for Hebron. This finding is a reflection of the relative preponderance of local nongovernmental and international organizations in Ramallah, facilitated by proximity to Jerusalem, the availability of modern services, and better communication and other links to global institutions and networks, and perhaps an openness of milieu as well. Such employment also requires good educational levels and a range of skills, such as English language and computer and Internet skills that are only acquired through higher levels of education. These observations suggest the emergence of a professional class in Ramallah personified by the prototype consultant dubbed by one analyst (referring to Jordanian technocrats) as "English-speaking people with Power-Point presentations" (Ryan 2005).

The data presented above once again point to the different types of economies and ways of life in these cities. What is interesting about table 1.6 is also the category "outside establishment," explained by PCBS as institutions that are not counted as official establishments. The highest levels of employment in such establishments are recorded for Hebron, followed by Nablus and then Ramallah. While these results must be interpreted with caution, as this definition does not constitute an adequate definition of the informal sector, it is nevertheless interesting to point out that Hebron has substantially larger employment in these establishments located in this seeming twilight zone than either Nablus or Ramallah, and perhaps testifying to the presence of a less modern economy, based on small-scale and possibly home-based production.

The occupational status of these cities' inhabitants is also quite revealing and testifies to the presence of work opportunities for more highly educated people in Ramallah in modern occupations, compared to Hebron with the majority of its workers absorbed in seemingly smaller-scale, possibly home-based, productive settings (table 1.7, 1997 census). For all those reported as working, Ramallah boasts the highest levels of legislators, managers, and professionals, compared to Nablus and Hebron. Likewise, Ramallah has the highest percentage of technicians, clerks, service sellers, and sales workers, compared to Nablus and Hebron. In Hebron city, 66 percent of the working population can be categorized as workers (semiskilled and unskilled workers,

Table 1.7
Occupation by City, 1997 Census (%)

Occupation[a]	Nablus	Ramallah	Hebron
Legislators, managers, professionals	16	27	8
Technicians, clerks, service sellers, and sales workers	34	41	26
Craft and related workers	32	18	32
Machine operators	7	7	18
Elementary occupations	11	7	15
Other	0	0	1
Total	100	100	100

Source: PCBS 1999a
[a]For those reported as working and ten years old or older

artisans, plant and machine operators, and those in "elementary occupations" i.e., manual workers), compared to 50 percent for Nablus and 32 percent for Ramallah. In Hebron and Nablus, 32 percent of workers are crafts and related workers, compared to 18 percent in Ramallah. Fifteen percent of the working population in Hebron are machine operators, compared to 11 percent for Nablus and 7 percent for Ramallah. This is likely a reflection of the many shoe manufacturing establishments in Hebron. Finally, Hebron also boasts the highest level of elementary occupations at 15 percent, compared to 11 percent for Nablus and 7 percent for Ramallah. Clearly, the occupational picture supports our thesis that Ramallah's inhabitants are employed in a more modern economy requiring special skills and an approach to work and life that can only be attained through education, while Hebron's inhabitants are still absorbed in an economy that relies on other types of skills, such as those related to crafts and to operating machines, skills that can be acquired without formal education, and where manual rather than mental labor is determinant. The demographic, employment, and education data reviewed thus far are consistent with our idea of the existence of different urban paradigms in Palestine. As noted earlier, these data reflect sometimes striking differences in the way people conceptualize their individual and family lives and futures.

Standard of Living and Lifestyles

The availability of home amenities (such as ownership of computers, video cassette recorders, cars, libraries, and central heating) may be viewed as a reflection of households' and families' ability to purchase various household items, their perceived need for these items in relation to the family's expenditure priorities, and their actual need to purchase them because of their importance for work, study, and similar purposes. On a more general level, however, the issue of amenities must be viewed within the context of lifestyles, life agendas, and life projects as elaborated by individuals and families. We believe that the notable differences in the ownership of amenities observed among our three cities are a reflection of the divergent lifestyles nurtured by the various social groups in these cities. In turn, differences in lifestyles can be viewed as differences in the kinds of social imaginaries or imaginations hegemonic at any given moment. Charles Taylor defines social imaginaries as "what enables, through making sense of, the practices of a society" (2002, 91) and considers them "ways in which people imagine their social existence," the "common understanding which enables us to carry out the collective practices that make up our social life" (106). Appadurai's "imagination" is a closely related construct that also captures the essence of this social and cultural force. The imagination is "an organized field of practices, a form of work . . . and a form of negotiation between sites of agency (individuals) and globally defined fields of possibility" (1997, 31). In his view, ethnography in this age of globalization should illuminate the power of large-scale, imagined life possibilities over specific life trajectories and display "a new alertness to the fact that ordinary lives today are more often powered not by the givenness of things but by the possibilities that the media . . . suggest are available" (55).

We believe that the differences displayed by our three cities in the possession of home amenities can thus be viewed also as a reflection of differences in social imaginaries and imaginations, each with its own conceptions of self, family life, and family futures. We can only speculate about the range of possibilities available to families in Hebron compared to Ramallah: how much is life fueled by the givenness of things compared to the possibilities that are perceived to be available? Consumption is the medium par excellence for the elaboration of social imaginaries, especially of the "modern" social imaginary. It can take material form in the shape of home amenities and comforts, but it also has powerful symbolic expressions in the consumption of other commodities such as particular types of education (here conceived in the wider sense of the term to denote the acquisition of tastes, dispositions, and life skills of various sorts).

Ramallah, as by now one would expect, comes out first and Hebron last in terms of our "lifestyle indicators," with Nablus again somewhere in the middle (table 1.8). Ramallah families boast higher levels of private car ownership, compared to Nablus and then Hebron. The same pattern is noted for the other amenities, such VCR machines, computers, home libraries, and central heating, all signifying a more comfortable and "modern" way of life. House ownership takes the opposite pattern, with the highest levels of home ownership found in Hebron, then Nablus, and finally Ramallah. Notice that the gap in home ownership in favor of villages is highest for Ramallah city at 40 percent difference, followed by Nablus, with a gap of 25 percent, and Hebron, with a gap of 18 percent in favor of its villages. This pattern of home ownership is once again suggestive of a rural way of life in Hebron more so than Nablus

Table 1.8
Ownership of Selected Items by City
and District Rural Area (DRA), 1997 Census (%)

Ownership	Nablus		Ramallah		Hebron	
	City	DRA	City	DRA	City	DRA
AMENITIES						
Private car	36	19	54	25	30	21
Central heating	3	0.2	18	1.5	3	0.2
Home library	26	13	31	15	14	9
VCR	22	9	49	18	12	7
Computer	10	3	21	3	5	2
HOUSE						
Own	56	81	48	88	75	93
Rent	33	5	46	4	12	2
Other	11	14	6	8	13	5

Source: PCBS 1999a

and much more so than Ramallah. It also suggests a more stable community, one in which home ownership has probably continued for some generations in the same family. Ramallah, on the other hand, is a city of migrants and transients, and thus its home ownership patterns are consistent with a more dynamic population composition. We may also note that the table consistently demonstrates a minimal gap between Hebron city and its rural area in terms of amenities, while the gap for Ramallah and its rural areas is considerable.

The People Living in These Cities

Who are the people who live in these cities, and where do they originally come from? Our hypothesis would be further supported if Ramallah is found to have the largest number of migrants (refugees and other migrants), with Nablus falling in the middle, and Hebron with the lowest levels. Census data reveal that only 39 percent of Ramallah residents are nonrefugees, compared to 76 percent in Nablus and 82 percent in Hebron. A very high level of refugee residents is found in Ramallah, at 61 percent of its total inhabitants of all ages, and compared to only 10 percent for its district villages. In Nablus, 24 percent of its inhabitants are of refugee origins, compared to 11 percent for Nablus district villages. In Hebron, only 18 percent of the population is of refugee origin, and that is also the case for the population of the villages in the Hebron district. Thus the level of refugee absorption has been highest in Ramallah, with very low levels in its district villages, and very low in Hebron, with rates exactly the same as its villages, again denoting the stability of the Hebron population in ways that are comparable to its own district villages.

Also of note is that 32 percent of Ramallah residents are Christians, compared to 0.8 percent for Nablus and 0.1 percent for Hebron. A large proportion of Christians living in Ramallah are urban Christian refugees from the coastal cities of the pre-1948 period. They are not peasant refugees pulled to the city in search of livelihoods, but rather urban dwellers who became refugees because of war.

Mothers' places of residence at the time of birth (thus, residents' places of birth) is another indicator pertaining to the diversity and homogeneity of the population of our three cities. We find that 86 percent of Nablus residents were born inside their district, with 7 percent abroad, 3 percent in northern districts other than the Nablus district, and 3 percent inside the 1948 line, with the rest in other districts. For Ramallah, 61 percent were born in the district, 10 percent were born abroad, 7 percent were born inside the green line, and the rest were born in other districts. As for Hebron city residents, 93 percent were born in their district, 4 percent abroad, 0.5 percent inside the green line, and the rest in other districts.

Taking each city separately, we note important differences. Analysis by age shows that in Ramallah the proportion of the population resident in the city since birth decreases for each ascending age group, with the highest proportion (73 percent) in the 0–14 age group and the lowest (16 percent) in the population over fifty. The age profiles for Nablus and Hebron are very different, indicating stable populations over time. There, we see a significantly smaller gap among the age groups (the percentages for the 0–14 age group are 90 percent and 95 percent for Nablus and Hebron respectively, while the percentages for the over fifty group are 52 percent for Nablus and 71 percent for Hebron).

Data on change of residence by city are also indicative of the population profiles of our three cities (table 1.9). We note that 50 percent of Ramallah residents at the time of the census reported that they had moved from another place to Ramallah city, compared to 27 percent for Nablus and only 13 per-

Table 1.9
Change in Place of Residence by City, 1997 Census (%)

Event	Nablus	Ramallah	Hebron
Changed residence	27	50	13
REASON FOR CHANGE			
Work	13	13	11
Study	6	11	6
Marriage	15	14	19
Companion	39	41	43
Expulsion	7	10	7
Other	20	11	14
Total	100	100	100

Source: PCBS 1999a

cent for Hebron, confirming that Ramallah has the highest level of recent in-migration and not only the highest proportion of refugees of the 1948 and perhaps even the 1967 wars. The reasons provided for why the move to these cities was made are also interesting: Ramallah has higher levels of in-migrants who moved to the city for the purpose of study (11%) and because of expulsion (10%), compared to 6 percent reporting migration for study purposes for Nablus and Hebron and 7 percent for expulsion for each of the other cities as well. Nineteen percent of residents who moved to Hebron did so because of marriage, compared to 15 percent for Nablus and 14 percent for Ramallah. For work, the differences are small, with 13 percent of incoming residents of both Nablus and Ramallah reporting work as a reason for moving to the city, compared to 11 percent for Hebron. This signifies a higher level of possibilities for finding work in Ramallah and Nablus compared to Hebron.

Disaggregating the census data further by sex (table 1.10), we find a higher proportion of women who reported having moved to Ramallah compared to 50 percent for both sexes (table 1.9). The level of migration of women compared to men is about the same for both Nablus and Hebron. In other words, Ramallah seems to attract more women residents than men, in addition to attracting the largest proportion of in-migrants overall. Moreover, Ramallah seems to attract the highest levels of in-migrants for work and study, compared to Hebron, with Nablus once again being in between. In contrast, a

Table 1.10
**Change in Place of Residence by City,
Women Only, 1997 Census (%)**

Event	Nablus	Ramallah	Hebron
Changed residence	27	54	14
REASON FOR CHANGE			
Work	2	4	2
Study	4	14	2
Marriage	29	24	36
Companion	46	43	49
Expulsion	7	9	5
Other	12	6	6
Total	100	100	100

Source: PCBS 1999a

higher proportion of Hebron women moved there for marriage purposes, the ultimate traditional reason for women's movement out of their communities, compared to Nablus and then Ramallah. Again, moving for the purpose of accompanying others—probably men—is highest in Hebron compared to Nablus, then Ramallah. In all, and given that women's movement into cities can be regarded as a good measure of the openness of milieu, Ramallah stands out in that it pulls women for work and study rather more than the other cities and less for the more conventional patterns of women's movement to accompany men.

More recent population movement data are also important to consider. Of all those reporting ever having changed their place of residence among a representative sample of people of all ages in the West Bank and Gaza, the highest proportion of residential change was for the Ramallah District, followed by the Hebron and Nablus Districts. Likewise, the highest proportion of respondents who reported having changed their place of residence had bachelor's degrees or more (8.3 percent of respondents), compared to 4.6 percent with secondary schooling, 3.2 percent with preparatory, and 2.3 percent with elementary schooling or below.[18]

18. These figures were obtained from the PCBS Demographic and Health Survey (2004) data set. The data set was made available to the authors by the PCBS.

These data suggest that we may be witnessing a specific rather than general type of population movement involving educated professionals to a larger extent than other migrants, and to Ramallah more than to the other two cities. With the intensification of closures and siege since September 2000, this population movement suggests the emergence of pockets of economic growth and prosperity (centered in Ramallah), but also the rise of pockets of destitution in other areas where the less educated are trapped and unable to move out. In this regard, it is important to consider the differential impact of Israeli military policies on the three cities. It is reasonable to expect that the particularly harsh Israeli army onslaught on Hebron, for example, is highly relevant to understanding the kinds of people who live in the city. The implantation of Israeli settlers in the heart of Hebron has led to widespread flight of merchants and families from the old city area, and the constant frictions arising from the presence of armed settlers and soldiers at religious sites and settlements in and around the city have taken their toll on the city. According to the Palestine Red Crescent (2005), Hebron city spent a quarter of its time under curfew in a three-year period from 2002 to 2005, compared to 20 percent in Nablus and a mere 11 percent in Ramallah. Hebron is thus hardly the most welcoming environment for migrants; if anything, it may be proving to be unlivable to those with the material and symbolic capital necessary for mobility, capital that they can more profitably invest in a place like Ramallah.

We conclude that in Hebron and Nablus, the majority of families have lived there for generations, thus with fewer refugees and outsiders, with less than a quarter of their populations each in-migrating to the city for work, study, in marriage, or otherwise, and with the original inhabitants continuing to form a solid majority population. In contrast, the original Ramallawis are clearly a minority, composing certainly less than half of the population, and constituting thus a weaker social force than in the other two cities. In essence, the majority in Ramallah are outsiders in more than one sense. First, they are outsiders in that they originally belonged somewhere else, because in the Palestinian consciousness one's family's place of origin determines one's identity. Second, they are also outsiders in that they are able to pursue their own way of life in the absence of an established and hegemonic local social group. Finally, they are outsiders in the sense that they have few or weak links with local (native) social networks, making it more possible for them to pursue the lives they choose.

Our household survey data on migrants abroad may also be of importance for our analysis. In this volume, Jamil Hilal utilizes household migration data to demonstrate that migration is implicated in the production of conservatism, which may help us better understand and partially explain the lifestyle differences among our cities. While the sample size here is small (708 migrants in total), the survey data reveal a significant difference among the cities in terms of where migrants from the city reside, and relevant to our general argument concerning the factors important in the production of difference. Table 1.11 shows that 78 percent of Hebron migrants reside in Jordan, compared to 59 percent for Nablus and 35 percent for Ramallah. The Gulf and Arab countries seem to attract Nabulsis to a higher extent than Ramallawis and Hebronites, perhaps explaining the intermediate situation of Nablus in terms of the exposure of its inhabitants to the ways of life of their kin abroad extending beyond those available in Jordan, but not as wide as ways of life available in non-Arab countries. Finally, 50 percent of Ramallah city migrants reside in the United States and Canada, compared to only 9 percent for Nablus and a mere 3 percent for Hebron. In view of the return visits of migrants to the home country on a periodic basis for holidays, marriage, and other purposes, the influence of migrants on the cities themselves cannot be underestimated and may well partially explain differences in lifestyles and life pursuits.

There are other lifestyle indicators that the household survey also reveals as important in understanding the differing types of urban life in each of our cities. Although the small sample size of the household survey warrants caution in interpreting some of the results, the patterns are clear. One example is

Table 1.11
Migrant Residence by City, 1999 (%)

Migrant residence	Nablus	Ramallah	Hebron
Jordan	59	35	78
Gulf and Arab world	25	14	10
U.S. and Canada	9	50	3
Other	7	1	9
Total	100	100	100

Source: IWS household survey, 1999
$p < 0.000$

the schooling of children. In Ramallah, 41 percent of girls and boys attend private schools, compared to 13 percent for girls and 17 percent for boys in Nablus, and 9 percent for girls and 10 percent for boys in Hebron. While private schools do exist in Hebron and Nablus, their nature, philosophy, and the type of schooling they offer can be very different from those found in Ramallah. Many, if not most, of the charitable institutions and groups operating schools in Hebron (and to some extent in Nablus) are Islamic organizations, and their schools are strictly segregated by sex and offer a curriculum strongly colored by Islamist conceptions of morality, selfhood, and good conduct. Many of Ramallah's private schools, in contrast, are sponsored by Christian churches but also have strong international links and nurture school cultures reflecting the social agendas and modernist dispositions of the globalized Arab middle classes. Despite its small size, and as noted earlier, Ramallah's new middle class is located firmly within the universe of the trans-Arab urban middle and upper-middle classes, and looks to them for guidance in matters of cultural competencies, tastes, skills, education, and other cultural standards. The history of emigration to the United States is also relevant here for a segment of the middle class in Ramallah; contact with emigrant relatives on a regular basis has been another channel for the elaboration of new lifestyles and dispositions. On the other hand, and despite the links that we can assume exist between Hebronites and Nabulsis with their kin in Jordan or the Arab world, it is likely that these links are with social groups not on the "cutting edge" of global consumer cultures in their countries of emigration. It may be paradoxical that while Ramallah's new middle class has the Arab new middle class as a point of reference, its knowledge of this class is not necessarily based on kinship ties and networks. It is rather a product of less personal means, the most significant of which are trans-Arab satellite television (a recent influence but extremely powerful), the educational system in private schools (many of which have similar counterparts in Jordan, Egypt, and other countries), the electronic media, trans-Arab tourism, and advertising.

In our search for the uniqueness of the three cities, we may also examine how families conceive the futures of their daughters and sons. The household survey reveals that, in terms of education, 39 percent of Hebron respondents reported an intention to educate their girls up to only high school, compared to 16 percent for Nablus and 7 percent for Ramallah. For boys, the overall intended level of education is higher, but nevertheless, also with significant differences among the cities; 82 percent of Ramallah and Nablus respondents report intending to educate their boys up until the bachelor's level, compared to 70 percent for Hebronites. Hebron parents also reveal that they prefer their daughters to have the same number of children as they had themselves (43 percent of respondents), compared to 31 percent for Nablus and 15 percent for Ramallah. This preference indicates a stronger desire on the part of Ramallah residents for a change in their daughters' lives. In Hebron, 39 percent of respondents thought that their daughters should not work outside the home, compared to 30 percent for Nablus and 18 percent for Ramallah. In contrast, 54 percent of Ramallah residents reported that they would like their daughters-in-law to work outside the home, compared to 39 percent for Nablus and 21 percent for Hebron.[19]

In other words, in terms of expectations and aspirations, Hebron residents reveal the most conservative attitudes toward women and their place in society. Nablus comes second, and Ramallah reveals the most openness regarding the newly generated roles for women within society and the economy, all consistent with our main argument regarding the differing types of urbanities emerging in the West Bank today.

Conclusion

This chapter has explored the diversity of modes of urban life in Palestine in the twentieth century and the first years of the twenty-first. Using historical material as well as statistical data from the first Palestinian census, other studies, and a subsequent household survey, we have attempted to explain the uniqueness of each of the three cities in terms of their place within their regions and their more immediate and distant pasts and their present realities. The story of this chapter began when the research group of which we were a part set out to examine household data to answer questions about how individuals in households (and families), in the words of the initial report produced for the research, "negotiate roles and responsibilities, and strategize for more secure and prosperous futures" (Giacaman and Johnson 2002b, ix). But the survey had not been designed with a view to studying the modalities of urban life, even though it was conceived as a community-based study and thus

---

19. All the household survey results comparing cities were statistically significant.

specifically targeted certain cities as sites for the survey. Also, and in keeping with current research orthodoxies, the survey design was undertaken with the familiar triple categories of urban, rural, and refugee camp, although region was also identified as a meaningful category for exploring difference. Recognition of the signal importance of region was forced upon us as we began to examine the data. However, it also became apparent that the uniqueness of some regions could not be understood without reference to the cities encompassed therein. We thus set out to explore this uncharted terrain in the sociology of Palestinian society.

While Ramallah has captured the world's attention as the site of Yasir Arafat's bombed-out headquarters and final resting place, it has fueled the local imagination as a site of modernity, dynamism, and diversity. It is indeed remarkable that despite the devastation wrought by repeated Israeli assaults upon the city, it has managed to remain true to the prevailing representations of the city in the local imagination. Even though by day the city appears to be taken over by rural bodies and rural inflections, by night, and after the last Ford *service* has dispatched its passengers at their rural destinations, Ramallah wakes up to another life and to other pursuits. To understand how this has become possible after the abortion of Palestine's urbanizing trajectory at the turn of the twentieth century has been one of our aims.

Hebron and Nablus represent very different social universes. We may venture to state that Ramallah's gaze is set on the future and at the world outside, while that of Hebron and Nablus is turned inward, to the mundane, the familiar, the same. It appeared to us that understanding the ethos of these two older cities required examining their relationship to their immediate surroundings, Jabal al-Khalil and Jabal Nablus, and looking for continuities and ruptures in the history of this relationship. But this exploration must remain tentative, as noted at the outset, largely because of the lacunae in our knowledge about aspects of the social history of Palestine in the late nineteenth and early twentieth centuries, particularly in regard to the city of Hebron.

2

LIVING TOGETHER IN A NATION IN FRAGMENTS

Dynamics of Kin, Place, and Nation

Penny Johnson

> The cousin [*ibn il-'amm*] — my darling!
> How sweet it is on his breast to rest!
> The stranger — the clumsy one!
> May he be wrapped in his grave clothes!
>> — Women's song praising marrying relatives,
>> southern West Bank village of Artas, 1920s

> Buy not the ass whose mother is in the same street.
>> — Proverb warning men against marrying relatives,
>> southern West Bank village of Artas, 1920s

In her foundational study of marriage practices in the southern West Bank village of Artas in the 1920s, Finnish folklorist Hilma Granqvist took an acid view of earlier writers who "quite inconsistently with the great differences in country and people" conflated nineteenth- and twentieth-century Palestinian peasant life with its biblical equivalent. The same writers also inflated their own local observations into generalizations, which were "quite unconcernedly given out as Palestinian in general" (Granqvist 1931, 10). Although the biblical approach to Palestinian society has been abandoned by scholars, if not by all politicians, the tendency to generalize about Palestinian families, marriage practices, and domestic life is still prevalent. Since Granqvist penned her warning, Palestinian families have passed through major social and economic transformations and turbulent histories, including an unfulfilled, highly contested, and ongoing national project against Israeli colonialism. Do these "great differences" in local marriage practices, family and kin dynamics, and domestic life still exist and if so, what do they mean? If specific marriage practices and family and kin dynamics—such as marriage to relatives, or kin marriage,[1] a main focus of this chapter—persist over time, how do we explain such persistence in a society whose economic, social, and political changes have been so heavily marked by dispossession, dispersal, military occupation, colonial modernities, and national resistance? In the context of the profound transformation of Palestine, persistence in practices is remarkable; indeed, stability may require more explanation than change.[2]

In the Institute of Women's Studies (IWS) 1999 community-based survey of 2,254 households in nineteen communities in the West Bank and Gaza, region—defined as Northern, Central, and Southern West Bank, Gaza, and East Jerusalem—emerged as an important determinant of difference in a range of family and household practices and preferences. These included patterns of kin relations, marriage to relatives, and parents' preferences in marriage, education, and work for sons and daughters, among other things. Regional variations were also found in demographic features such as fertility, occupational and educational status of household members, migration patterns, and family composition. Variations in most of these preferences and practices were stronger among households living in different regions of the West Bank and Gaza than among households living in rural, urban, or camp localities, or households with varying degrees of wealth.

Regional demographic differences in the Palestinian territory are also found in analysis of the rich data of the first Palestinian national census, conducted in 1997 by the new Palestinian Central Bureau of Statistics (PCBS), as well as in other PCBS reports. Although these differences might be expected between the West Bank and Gaza, with their territorial separation and different political and economic histories in the 1948–67 period,[3] distinct regional differences within the West Bank are less expected and thus require analysis.[4]

---

1. I am using the term *kin marriage*, rather than the more precise category of endogamy, partly to escape from kinship terminology, but also to indicate that both definitions and practices of kin-based marriages are not fixed.

2. Thanks to an anonymous reviewer for a clear formulation of this point.

3. The Gaza Strip was under Egyptian administration from 1948 to 1967, and the West Bank was annexed to Jordan.

4. In the analysis of data from the 1999 IWS household survey, the West Bank was divided into the southern, central, and northern regions; the samples in Jerusalem and Gaza were ana-

Kin marriage in particular seems persistent in Palestinian society; the IWS survey found that about a quarter of women were married to first cousins and over half to relatives of any sort, similar to findings in PCBS surveys, as discussed below. There were also marked regional differences, particularly in the marrying of relatives other than first cousins. The contrast between parental preference for their children's marriages expressed in the IWS survey—where an overwhelming majority of parents do not favor first-cousin marriage and express their reasons largely in terms of a modernist discourse of genetics—and the persistence of kin marriages in actual practice, will be explored, with attention both to persistence and its regional variation. Patterns of postmarital residential living and preferences for marriage choice for sons and daughters and employment and education for daughters and daughters-in-law will shed additional light on family and kin dynamics.

One may posit with some confidence that daily life and practices in the Palestinian context—who men and women marry; how parents exercise their responsibilities and care for children; how adolescent girls and boys dream, plan, and work for the future—are deeply marked by the struggles between a colonial regime of control and dispossession and an unfulfilled national project of independence and sovereignty. This chapter argues that these everyday practices of marriage and "kin work"[5] are sites where Israeli colonialism is contested and Palestinian identity is constituted. These practices respond not only to a hostile Israeli rule that threatens Palestinian identity and existence, but also to the shadow of an absent Palestinian state until 1994, and to the contradictions of limited Palestinian rule since that time. Whereas kinship solidarities have often been counterposed to national/state loyalties and public citizenship, the Palestinian case offers a more complicated model. For example, "the logic for marrying close," to use Sholkamy's apt phrase (Sholkamy

---

lyzed separately. In PCBS data, differences between the West Bank and Gaza are routinely analyzed; some of the PCBS studies considered here also give data by the nine administrative districts in the West Bank and the three in Gaza, or combinations thereof. Bornstein (2002, 42–43) makes the interesting point that the Israeli military government in 1967 decided to administer the West Bank through these nine independent districts; under Jordanian rule, the three administrative centers were Hebron, Jerusalem, and Nablus, Israeli rule ab initio thus further fragmented the West Bank.

5. See Stack 2003.

2003, 65), may be at the same time an implicit response to public insecurity and the risk of family and social disintegration and an assertion of an oppositional Palestinian identity, as well as the outcome of particular family dynamics and marriage choices. The separation and fragmentation of Palestinian communities, not only in the years since the outbreak of the second Palestinian intifada (October 2000) but also in the interim period of Palestinian self-government (1994-) as a whole, make the question of local practice and localism, including emerging new forms, particularly germane.

How does the production or reconstitution of local (and different) practices function in this context? Households and families "as the first level of economic and political institution," as Mundy (1995, 3) has suggested in her study of kinship, community, and polity in Yemen, are one critical site where the relationship of local practices and national dynamics is articulated. In turn, viewing Palestinian households in "place," in their specific locations within a dense web of kin relations and practices, opens up an understanding of how these local practices produce sociopolitical identities in a context of national oppression and prolonged military occupation. Rather than viewing local differences and practices as vestigial, I argue in this chapter that regional difference in marriage patterns and preferences are shaped by specific place-centered symbolic economies of kinship, or "economies of symbolic goods," to use Bourdieu's framework for understanding marriage and marriage exchanges (Bourdieu 2001, 96). I use Bourdieu's related concepts of habitus and capital to explain how marriage and kinship practices can be understood not as rule-bound or archaic vestiges of tradition, but more as makers of forms of sociality that are living features of Palestinian identities and producers of local and national meanings.

My argument is not that kin marriage is pursued for nationalist reasons, but that the kin marriages are practical and expressive acts that consolidate related local and Palestinian identities and are shaped by Palestinian histories, as well as family and individual interests, including those of women. Kinship economies, or kinship worlds, to use a broader term, persist and are reconstituted in response to and against the colonial regime, its political economy, and forms of modernity and in the absence of national security and statehood.

Bourdieu's notion of nonmaterial forms of capital is particularly useful in the Palestinian context: the repeated assertion by Palestinians that education is a form of portable capital (cultural capital) for a dispossessed and stateless people is both a discursive and empirical example. In this example, the value of education as capital lies also in its ability to be translated into economic gains, reminding us that nonmaterial forms of capital are inherently convertible, with varying levels of difficulty (Calhoun 1995, 140), although not always or in all contexts. In my analysis the more elusive notion of symbolic capital is used first to explain how "kin work," and in particular kin marriage, conserves and produces certain forms of symbolic capital or symbolic goods, or "the economic gathering, exchange and circulation of nonmaterial forms, qualities and values" (Connor 1996, 370). One such key value in the Palestinian context of insecurity and risk is clearly kinship solidarity and its contribution to individual, family, and national survival. Symbolic capital also denotes social identity and its recognition[6] and even more broadly, "social importance and reasons for living" (Bourdieu 1998, 241). The notion of symbolic capital is closely related to the more widely used notion of social capital, where individuals invest in social relationships, networks, or membership in groups, which provide support, information, and access to power and opportunity. However, symbolic capital in this analysis provides the social recognition of these relationships, although I stress that such recognition is always differentially distributed and relations of dominance and coercion are present, as well as solidarities. Nonetheless, to use a monetary metaphor, the overall persistence of kin marriage in Palestinian society in the West Bank and Gaza and the significance of sharp regional differences in its practice suggest that symbolic capital is a shared national currency but with varying values in local symbolic economies.

Local Identities, Habitus, and the Rural-Urban Divide

Regional differences in kin marriage and marriage and kin practices and preferences raise the question of place. Borrowing another notion from Bourdieu, that of habitus or systems "of durable and transposable dispositions" (1990, 54), allows us to explore the relationship of place, kinship practices, and iden-

---

6. In his editor's introduction to Bourdieu's *Field of Cultural Production,* Johnson defines symbolic capital as "degree of accumulated prestige, celebrity, consecration of honour and is founded on a dialectic of knowledge (connaissance) and recognition (reconnaisance)" (Bourdieu 1993, 7).

tities. Generally, habitus is a structured domain of learnable social practices, relations, dispositions, and perceptions that is etymologically and, here argued, conceptually rooted not only in habit, but in the physicality (and sociality) of habitat, or place,[7] much in the same way that Raymond Williams's "structure of feeling" has a physical and social embodiment in place (Harvey 2001, 177). In my reading, habitus has both a temporal and spatial dimension, grounded both in place and local histories as expressed in family and kin practices and relations, and in the larger national history of dispossession and disruption. Bowman posits a relevant distinction (and relation) between habitus and identity, noting that identity abstracts and reduces elements from the "wider range of sociality" that is habitus—and crucially when those elements are under threat of negation (1999, 53). Indeed, a "sense of place" implies an attachment, which is actively constructed; Tuan contrasts a self-conscious "sense of place" with an incurious and un-self-conscious "rootedness" (Parmenter 1994, 4). In the post-1948 Palestinian context, a sense of place is almost invariably self-conscious because it is informed by loss or threat of loss and conquest. For these reasons rather than in spite of them, place is an important site of identity and meaning. Scholars have pointed out that Palestinian family and kin identities, at least after 1948, are imbued with a sense of place. As Ghabra has noted in his study of Palestinian families in Kuwait and the role of expanded and reconstituted kin networks in family and national survival and identity, "it is meaningless . . . to identify a Palestinian family in isolation from its village or city of origin" (1988, 79–80). In the IWS survey, regional differentiations among households were in general sharper than those among types of localities, in particular the categories of city, refugee, camp, and village that are often used to analyze Palestinian society. Although these categories remain useful, the rural-urban divide should be interrogated in the Palestinian context of the loss of the major Palestinian coastal cities (Jaffa,

7. De Certeau (1988, 59) objects to Bourdieu's connection of habitus and place, whereby "habitus becomes a dogmatic place" and the problematics of place "win out" over the problematics of practice. However, De Certeau raises this criticism in examining "technocratic societies" where practices and practical logic "work independently of the place that controls its functioning in traditional societies" (55). In the Palestinian context and in examining the question of how practices such as kin marriage persist, the relation of habitus to place—both existing, imagined, and lost places—is important.

Haifa, Acre) and their urban populations in 1948, which effectively halted dynamic processes of urbanization after 1948. Most West Bank towns are perhaps better defined as "ruralized townships" (Tamari 1983) rather than centers of urban life, with the recent exception of Ramallah, as pointed out in Taraki and Giacaman's contribution to this volume. The "de-peasantization" of Palestinian villages in the West Bank since 1967 as subsistence and other agriculture gave way to unskilled and semiskilled work in Israel also raises questions about the nature of "villages." An enduring third category since 1948 is the supposedly transient term "refugee camp"; whereas camps continue to display distinct administrative, social, demographic, political, and economic features, camp boundaries are increasingly blurred as camps are transformed into urban slums, particularly in the post-Oslo period. How do these three abstract spatial categories (city, camp, village) relate to the specifics of place?

Tamari's observation on peasant identities in an earlier period is useful: he notes the importance of the "city-village dichotomy" in the consciousness of Palestinians in the early twentieth century but adds that it was mediated through "regional loyalties, religious affiliations and clan affiliations" (1983, 28). In contemporary Palestinian society, these affiliations may also mediate, rather than conflict with, national identities from the standpoint of family, kin, and place affiliations.

Historically, regionalism, particularly in the central highlands of Palestine[8] (the West Bank), is linked to specific patterns of economic and social relations between towns and their surrounding villages: "Each market town and its hinterland had its own deeply rooted and locally specific social formation and cultural identity," notes a historian of the late Ottoman period (Doumani 1995, 4). In the West Bank, Jerusalem's urban history has distinct features related to its administrative and religious roles, but the Jabal Nablus region, centered on the city of Nablus, and the Jabal Hebron region, centered on the city of Hebron, conform to the market town/hinterland paradigm. Today Hebron

8. In contrast to the Mediterranean coastal areas in the Ottoman era, where the principal plains were subject to Bedouin raids and "virtually void" of a settled population until the mid-nineteenth century, the central highlands were continuously settled throughout the Ottoman period: the "lion's share" of Palestine's rural population lived in this hilly region (Gerber 1987, 75–76).

is the largest West Bank city (population 119,401 in 1997), slightly larger than Nablus (100,231), and more than six times as large as the town of Ramallah (18,017 in 1997).[9]

Identities of Place, Kin, and Nation

Local and regional affiliations are important components of Palestinian identity as it emerged in the twentieth century. Khalidi sees the "powerful local attachment to place" as a critical element in the formation of Palestinian identity and modern national consciousness (1997, 153). When confronted with a "national" crisis, in particular the challenge of the Zionist movement and the profound crisis of the 1948 war or *Nakba*, identities of place mobilized resistance but had serious limitations.[10] In the wake of the expulsion and dispersal of over 750,000 Palestinians, a majority of whom were peasants, from their "place," family, kin, and clan in 1948, both place and kinship took on new meanings in unstable and threatening circumstances.

In the West Bank and Gaza, a quarter of a century of direct Israeli military occupation (1967–93) blocked the development of any form of Palestinian national sovereignty or national political institutions. At the same time, Israel's political and civil repression and colonial economic policies unleashed both political and economic commonalities. Palestinian national resistance spurred oppositional national political identities, while Israel's economic policies created both a dependent economy and its most distinct feature: wage labor in Israel that was common to the occupied territories, although more prominent in some regions (Gaza) and settings (refugee camps and villages, rather than towns) than others. In the interim period of limited Palestinian rule (1995 to the present) in which the survey was conducted, a first national authority (and emerging nation-state) ruled over an increasingly

9. This number does not include the population of al-Bira, Ramallah's twin city.

10. Examining narratives of the 1948 *Nakba* by those who lived through it, Tamari remarks: "Above all, however, there is an overriding sense of localism. What happened then is seen as having happened to this town or village in a context isolated from an onslaught that affected Palestine as a whole" (2002b, 2). Interestingly, the narratives Tamari examined were told fifty years later during commemorations of the *Nakba* held in the Palestinian territory in 1998, thus the raconteurs project a localism of the past—but also of the present.

physically fragmented society. Using a definition of place as possessing three necessary and sufficient characteristics—geographic location, material form, and investment in meaning and value (Gieryn 2000, 464–65)—we can say that places shape kin relations and marriage practices, but also that the social logic of kin relations contributes to the constitution of the meaning and value of place.

At the same time as local or regional differences are evident in the 1999 IWS household survey, there are characteristics and attitudes (the value of education, for example, in the household survey and a range of political and social attitudes and practices in other literature) that seem to be "national" and tied to the Palestinian national and social field as a whole. It can only suggest how this social geography is both crucial and unsettled during the profound national crisis generated by the present emergency conditions of intifada, where Palestinian communities are separated by physical barriers and spatial regimes.

Domestic Economies and Economies of Occupation

A main line of inquiry in this chapter is how marriage, kinship, and parents' expectations and hopes for male and female children locate the household in particular systems of reproduction and economies of "symbolic goods," and how the persistence of practices such as kin marriage, and the regional differences therein, might be explained in terms of these economies. In examining the persistence of masculine domination and gender differences, Bourdieu argues that a decisive factor in the perpetuation of differences is "the permanence that the economy of symbolic goods, of which marriage is a central component, owes to its relative autonomy, which allows masculine domination to perpetuate itself unaffected by the transformations of the economic modes of production" (Bourdieu 2001, 96). This evocative statement contains an internal contradiction: if the domestic economy and family relations are only relatively autonomous (see also Bourdieu 1990, 54), surely they interact in some way with economic and social transformations, even if they are not determined by these processes, or by a reigning mode of production. Bourdieu himself presents a method of understanding this interaction through his notion of habitus as "embodied history" or "the active presence of the whole past of which it is a product" (1990, 56). This notion suggests that kin and family relations and the economy of symbolic goods that sustain them are not solely products of the present moment and contemporary economic and social realities. Instead, they contain the "active presence" of the past, enacted (or embodied) by the practices and dispositions of men, women, and children in families as they act to meet their present needs, interests, and yearnings.

Did the massive and systemic economic changes that Palestinian families have experienced over the last half-century, and particularly since 1967, change "traditional" marriage practices? The overarching economic transformation of the West Bank and Gaza since 1967 has been the decline of agriculture, including the subsistence agriculture of many West Bank villages where the majority of the West Bank population lived,[11] and the massive entry of West Bank former peasants and Gaza refugees, overwhelmingly male, into the Israeli labor force, as well as the accompanying dependent and colonial relation of the Palestinian economy to Israel. This transformation is inseparable from the political conditions of military occupation and its accompanying widespread land confiscation for Israeli settlement, restrictions on water and land use, personal insecurity, dispersion of families, and lack of rights. Work in Israel and labor migration to the Gulf, particularly in the 1970s, contributed at times to greater economic prosperity for individuals and families, but it was prosperity without economic development (Roy 1987, 35). While the interim period brought a Palestinian Authority with limited powers and less territorial sovereignty, many of the political conditions of occupation did not wither away—and some intensified with increased closure of the Palestinian territories. It would be hard to argue that the dynamics of one of the most prolonged occupations in modern history have not affected most Palestinian households and families, including their internal dynamics, processes, and economies. But households and families are not simply acted on: they utilize their resources, whether material or symbolic—including their "embodied history," or the active presence of the past—to respond to changing and often threatening circumstances. These responses may well help to explain the persistence

11. The 1997 national census found 47 percent of the population in the West Bank living in villages, with an equal 47 percent living in cities and 6 percent in refugee camps (PCBS 1999f, 161). In the Palestinian territory as a whole, 53 percent of the population is urban, 31 percent rural, and 16 percent camp residents.

in kin marriage, examined below, as well as other persistent features of Palestinian family life, such as high fertility and preferences for large families.

Thus, the regions of the West Bank may have lost distinct systems of production and exchange in the course of the twentieth century, but they have retained more distinct symbolic economies where the production of symbolic capital through kin work has considerable currency. These symbolic economies interact with, but are not solely determined by, material economies—and they also respond to systems of domination, as well as systems of production and consumption. Indeed, seeing Palestinian local symbolic economies and kin worlds as responding to systems of domination, lack of legitimate authority, and profound insecurity helps explain how local kin solidarities and identities may not necessarily detract from Palestinian national identity but may constitute an important component of national identity, as is suggested in the conclusion of this chapter.

Survey data, whether from the IWS household survey, the national census, or other sources, are inadequate for fully addressing the theoretical and empirical problems in understanding these complex relations, but they are helpful in an initial formulation of questions, areas of inquiry, and conceptual problems for further investigation. For example, the IWS survey finding that southern West Bank (Hebron) region parents supported more freedom of choice for daughters and sons in marriage will be scrutinized, as will regional differences in preferences for cousin and other kin marriages for sons and daughters and attitudes toward daughters versus daughters-in-law, and preferences for education and work for children and their spouses. National census data will also be utilized, as well as studies of consanguinity.

In sum, this chapter proposes a very initial reading of the nation—and to some extent of Palestinian society—from the practices and preferences of households/families and their members as they are located in specific communities from which they experience national dynamics of economic dependence and uncertainty, colonialism, and resistance.

Kin Marriage: Problems and Paradigms

An investigation of the persistence, as well as the diverse practice, of kinship-based marriage among Palestinians in the West Bank and Gaza logically turns for conceptual and empirical assistance to previous scholarship on consanguine marriage, whether in Palestine, the Arab region, or elsewhere. This scholarship, however, has several problems that need to be addressed. The modern history of Palestine has great relevance in explaining the hiatus in Palestinian scholarship on the issues identified by Granqvist working in Artas in the 1920s, such as patterns of marriage, divorce, and dower. Introducing his study of family patterns in the West Bank in the 1980s, Ata (1986, 3) noted that there were areas in family studies "where no research has been done since Granqvist's work." While Ata's observation is too sweeping and work of great interest has been published since Ata's survey-based study,[12] it is fair to say that research on marriage practices and family and kin relations in Palestinian society has been uneven and interrupted.

Turning to regional research, a first problem is simply that the ideal of first-cousin marriages, or more specifically of marriages with patrilineal parallel cousins, and their preferential practice is such a stock feature of ethnographic descriptions of Arab and Mediterranean societies that it may seem drained of interest as a subject of inquiry. New and productive directions in scholarship on the Arab world and the Middle East in gender studies or household and family studies have largely been conceptually separate from kinship studies.[13]

This unfortunate division reflects the two "zones of theory" Abu Lughod (1989) finds in the anthropology of the Arab world, between the *harem* (women's lives) and the *hamula* (men's domain), a division Rothenberg (1999, 24) also identifies in anthropological literature on Palestine. Because the *hamula*, defined as a patronymic group often made up of several patrilineal lineages, is usually envisioned as a "group of men" (Cohen 1965, 110), gender dynamics receive little attention in its analysis. This division artificially constructs a public/private divide that the social practice of kinship continu-

12. Since Ata's investigation, several rich veins of inquiry have been opened, in anthropological studies (e.g., Moors 1995); legal studies (e.g., Welchman 1992); ethnographic work (e.g., Malki and Shalabi 1993); and surveys of living conditions, marriage, inheritance, labor, and demography, in particular the publications of the PCBS and of the Norwegian Fafo Institute for Applied International Studies.

13. This is true of scholarship beyond the Arab region. Although feminist scholarship has brought new interest to the study of gender and families, the anthropological study of kinship, one recent undergraduate textbook ruefully admits, is "noted more for its difficult jargon and tortuous diagrams than for the light it sheds on gender." (Stone 1997, 10).

ally crosses. On the other side of the divide, an interest on the part of women's studies scholars in changing, rather than seemingly stable, practices, such as kin marriage, may also contribute to a division between gender and kinship studies. Here, Kandiyoti's insight that crisis in patriarchal (or other) systems does not seamlessly lead to change is helpful in turning attention to these seemingly stable practices. She argues, for example, that women may resist, rather than accept, changes in the prevailing, male-dominated order if "other avenues to security and well-being" are not available (1988, 278).

A second problem is that scholars interested in kin relations and endogamous marriage patterns in the Arab world have tended to study such marriages primarily in tribal or rural settings, and often see such marriage practices as premodern, placing them in a tradition/modernization binary. In the Arab and Islamic region in general, the logic of consanguine marriages is ascribed to family/kin defense against land partition where primogeniture is not practiced and sons inherit equally and daughters partially: a strategy thus of prevention of "the alienation of property from the lineage" (Holy 1989, 112), or, in other words, a strategy to keep sons and daughters in the family. This practice should thus fade away when its rationale is eroded by urbanization, modernization, and migration. However, regional and Palestinian data analyzed below challenge a reductionist model of modernization. In an extensive 1998 survey of living conditions in Jordan, researchers pondered the "dense web" of kin relations and kin living patterns and noted cautiously that "it is possible to argue that the tendency to continue basic patterns of localisation and the importance of family relations dominates over modern processes" (Hanssen-Bauer, Pedersen, and Tiltnes, 1998, 263). This observation could perhaps be reformulated to posit that patterns of kinship and localization (identities of place and local practices) offer (modern) strategies to respond to modernity and its challenges to families in maintaining not simply their material capital but their "symbolic capital" (Holy 1989, 113).

While an economic imperative to keep family land intact (and land in the Palestinian context has a symbolic, as well as material value) may well still influence marriage patterns and the devolution of property and the accompanying control of reproduction is integral to the institution of marriage, the frequency and persistence of endogamous marriage, in the Arab region and Palestine as noted below, even when there is "nothing to divide" (Tillon 1966, 38), suggests that this explanation is insufficient.

Tillon's own explanation, in a small 1966 volume that is perhaps sui generis in the boldness of its speculation, and a brief but pungent critique of Tillon by Sayigh (1981), underscore several other problematics. Tillon hypothesizes that the "Mediterranean determination not to exchange women" (38) is a social innovation of great duration.[14] She contrasts the Mediterranean "republic of cousins" with earlier "primitive" exogamous societies and with the modern European "republic of citizens," making the weighty claim that the republic of cousins "lies at the root of a persistent debasement of the female condition" (1966, 13) and paralyzes "social evolution a whole" (18). This essentialist reading at least has the virtue of linking gender, kinship, and marriage practices with social and political life, but its failings are aptly, if sharply, criticized by Sayigh:

> In common with other Orientalists, Tillon makes no attempts to discover history, region or class variations in women's situation. . . . This republic of cousins . . . is presented as unchangeable, tribal, aggressive, expansionist, pronatalist, endogamous and oppressive to women. It is an ideal formation that rests on an idealized view of European social structure and totally ignores the role of the state in structuring social relations. (260)

Sayigh is particularly helpful in foregrounding the notion of diversity[15]—frequently neglected in studies of Arab kinship—and the role of the state. Her short intervention does not pretend to provide a coherent new framework to explore practices of kin-based marriage in different contexts in the Arab world, but she does provide two key elements that dislodge an essentialist and rule-based model of kinship.[16] Bourdieu also moved beyond rule-based models by

14. She locates it in technological and social transformations in the late neolithic world (agriculture, "cities," herds) permeating the ancient world and persisting in the Mediterranean region and beyond for most of human history.

15. Mundy notes that "the exploration of diversity has not been a central concern of Western academic studies on Arab kinship and domestic structures" (Mundy 1995, 90).

16. Tillon's book was written in an earlier wave of anthropological interest (and intellectual confidence perhaps) in establishing the rules and patterns of human kinship and marriage in "traditional" or even "primitive" societies. Even in Levi Strauss's theoretically sophisticated work on kinship and marital systems of exchange (Levi Strauss 1968), endogamy is considered as a kind of violation of the rules of exchange. Rule-based models of kinship often presume rule-based behavior, which is both problematic and limiting in understanding kinship practices.

opposing "genealogical" or official kinship to "practical kinship" where men and (especially) women produce and reproduce kinship as strategies to satisfy material and symbolic interests (Bourdieu 1990, 166–67). These interests and the rationales of men and women, of mothers, fathers, and children, in pursuing marriage arrangements obviously may vary. In the contemporary setting of a village in Upper Egypt, Sholkamy examines the "rationales that make youth in the 1990s seemingly continue to make choices similar to their ancestors" (Sholkamy 2003, 62) and concludes: "This marriage preference is not an old choice; but rather a new one." (66)

Taking this logic to a general level, kin marriages broadly examined can be a response not only to perennial problems of land partition but to new threats of family and community dispersion and disintegration. Analyzing a 1992 survey of Palestinian communities in the West Bank, Gaza, and East Jerusalem, Hammami believes that marriage arrangements based on kinship persist "as a way to preserve the continued identity of dispersed communities" (1993, 286). I would not argue that this is the sole reason for kinship-based marriage, but I do argue that the logic of "marrying close" draws its operative power both from the embodied history of habitus, its salience as a response to threat and insecurity and a source of symbolic capital, and from particular ways it furthers women and men's perceived material and symbolic interests. It is thus a "new choice" that is embedded in history, body, and place.

Regional and Palestinian Persistence in Consanguinity

Reviewing nuptiality patterns in the Arab world, Rashad and Osman (2003, 29) note that consanguinity is "generally high:" seven Arab countries out of thirteen surveyed in the 1990s registered at least 30 percent of all ever-married women aged fifteen through forty-nine married to their first cousin (table 2.1). In Jordan, a country not included in Rashad and Osman's review but of particular interest given its majority Palestinian population, researchers in 1998 found 26 percent of ever-married women married to their first cousins, with about half of these to a father's brother's son (ibn 'amm). Another 21 percent of marriages were contracted with other relatives "within the hamula," making almost half of all marriages kin marriages (Hanssen-Bauer, Pedersen, and Tiltnes, 1998, 274–75). These patterns are strikingly similar to those in the West Bank and Gaza. Also of relevance is that Rashad and Osman's analysis

Table 2.1
Ever-Married Women (15–49) Married to Their First Cousins
in Thirteen Arab Countries

Country	Year	%
Algeria	1992[a]	26
Bahrain	1989[b]	23
	1995[c]	24
Lebanon	1996[a]	18
Libya	1995[a]	43
Egypt	1991[a]	31
	1992[d]	25
	1995[d]	24
Kuwait	1987[b]	30
	1996[c]	26
Oman	1988/89[b]	33
	1995[c]	34
Qatar	1987[b]	35
Saudi Arabia	1987[b]	36
	1996[c]	31
Sudan	1992/93[a]	56
Syria	1993[a]	35
United Arab Emirates	1987[b]	26
	1995[c]	24
Yemen	1991/92[d]	31
	1997[d]	34

Source: Data are from Rashad and Osman 2000, 6
[a]Maternal and child health surveys
[b]Child health surveys in Gulf countries
[c]Family health surveys
[d]Demographic and health surveys

shows that "changes in consanguinity are not very significant" (2003, 30) although an examination of their data shows a slow decline in some countries and other countries where the practice is relatively low. In Lebanon, for example, a lower 18 percent of ever-married women were married to first cousins in 1996.

A relatively high rate of first-cousin marriages is also found in the West Bank and Gaza. In the 1999 IWS household survey, over a quarter (27 percent) of ever-married women aged fifteen through forty-nine were married to first cousins (table 2.2); this is similar to figures found in the 1995 and 2000

Table 2.2
Ever-Married Women (15–49), Degree of Consanguinity by Region, 1999 (%)

	No. West Bank	C. West Bank	So. West Bank	Gaza	Jerusalem	Total
First cousin	21	26	27	30	32	27
Relative of father	8	12	10	17	7	12
Relative of mother	6	7	5	5	4	5
Nonrelative, same community	31	25	40	10	16	27
Nonrelative, other community	34	31	19	28	42	28

Source: IWS household survey, 1999, unpublished data

demographic and health surveys of the PCBS (2002a). In the 2000 survey, 28.4 percent of ever-married women aged fifteen through forty-nine are married to their first cousins (26.8 percent in the West Bank and 31.5 percent in Gaza).[17] In the 1995 survey, 28.8 percent of ever-married women in that same age group were married to their cousins (31.6 percent in Gaza and 27.2 percent in the West Bank; PCBS 2002a, 29; see table 2.3). This rate of first-cousin marriages is slightly lower than the 30–35 percent calculated by Rashad and Osman for Egypt, Saudi Arabia, Syria, Qatar, and Oman (or the very high rates in Libya and Sudan), but slightly higher than Algeria, the UAE, and Kuwait.

What is even more interesting in the Palestinian context is the strong majority practice of kin-based marriage in general. In the 2000 survey, another 20 percent of women married "distant cousins"; thus, about half of women married kin. In the 1995 survey, the percentage marrying "distant cousins" is a much higher 36 percent (see table 2.3). However, this probably does not reflect a great change in the ensuing five years, but simply that PCBS used different categories in the two surveys. In the 1995 survey, women were asked if they were married to first cousins, relatives from the same *hamula*, relatives from a different *hamula*, or nonrelatives. In the 2000 survey, respondents chose among first cousins, relatives from the same *hamula* (termed in the En-

17. The gap between the West Bank and Gaza widened in data from the 2004 health survey, which found 32.2 percent of women aged fifteen to forty-nine married to first cousins in Gaza and 24.6 percent in the West Bank (PCBS 2004b, 13).

Table 2.3
Distribution of Ever-Married Women (15–49) by Relation to Spouse
and Background Characteristics in 2000 and 1995 (%)

Background characteristics	First cousins	Distant cousins[a]	No relation
2000			
REGION			
West Bank	26.8	19.3	53.9
Gaza Strip	31.5	21.0	47.5
AGE			
15–19	29.7	18.4	51.9
20–24	29.0	19.2	51.8
25–29	28.6	19.0	52.4
30–34	27.2	20.8	51.9
35–39	30.2	18.5	51.3
40–44	27.5	22.8	49.7
45–49	26.9	21.2	51.9
TYPE OF LOCALITY			
Urban	28.4	19.5	52.1
Rural	27.8	23.3	48.9
Camp	29.8	15.2	55.0
YEARS OF SCHOOLING			
0–6	29.4	23.1	47.5
7–9	28.1	20.4	51.5
10–12	30.4	19.0	50.6
13 or more	21.5	14.3	64.2
Total	28.4	19.9	51.6

glish translation "distant cousins"), or nonrelatives, and the problematic category of "different *hamula*" was discarded. Thus, in 1995, about half of the
women responded that they were married to first cousins or relatives from the
same *hamula*, similar to the half of women reporting kin marriage in 2000,
but another 19 percent reported marriages with relatives from another
hamula. Here the border between blood kin, affinal kin, and putative kin may
be very blurred, as will be discussed later in this chapter.

At least for the last half of the twentieth century, which witnessed the frag-

Table 2.3 (*cont.*)
Distribution of Ever-Married Women (15–49) by Relation to Spouse
and Background Characteristics in 2000 and 1995 (%)

Background characteristics	First cousins	Distant cousins[a]	No relation
1995			
REGION			
West Bank	27.2	38.8	33.9
Gaza Strip	31.6	31.6	36.7
AGE			
15–19	29.9	36.5	33.3
20–24	28.4	35.9	35.6
25–29	29.9	34.2	35.9
30–34	29.3	34.4	36.3
35–39	27.3	39.4	33.1
40–44	28.4	37.5	33.8
45–49	27.6	38.2	34.1
TYPE OF LOCALITY			
Urban	26.9	33.6	39.4
Rural	30.3	41.7	27.9
Camp	29.1	29.8	41.0
YEARS OF SCHOOLING			
0–6	31.0	39.9	28.9
7–9	28.1	37.5	34.4
10–12	29.4	34.3	36.1
13 or more	20.8	27.1	52.1
Total	28.8	36.3	34.9

Source: PCBS 2002a, table 18, using data from PCBS national demographic and health surveys
conducted in 1995 and 2000
[a] In the 2000 data, the category "distant cousins" in the original Arabic questionnaire reads "from
the same hamula"; in the 1995 data, the category "distant cousins" combines two categories
in the original questionnaire: "from the same hamula" and "from a different hamula"

mentation of historic Palestine and many subsequent wars and upheavals, the
rate of consanguine marriage in the West Bank and Gaza may not have
changed dramatically. Stokke, using data from PCBS's 1995 Demographic
Survey, believes that endogamous marriage practices in Palestinian society in
the West Bank and Gaza have been relatively stable over time; women born in

1940–49 and women born in 1960–69 had roughly the same rate of first-cousin marriage at about 28 percent (Stokke 2002, 81–83). This finding is confirmed by PCBS's data showing kin marriage by age groups, where rates of first-cousin marriage are similar for all age cohorts of women in both 1995 and 2000. Indeed, in both 2000 and 1995, the older age group (45–49) registered a slightly lower rate of first cousin marriage than the youngest (15–19). Type of locality (urban, camp, or city) and refugee status also made little difference. Rather surprisingly, educational level also was not highly significant in either survey: only women with more than thirteen years of schooling registered a lower proportion of first-cousin marriage at 21.5 percent in 2000 (table 2.3).

However, Hammami has argued that "the logic of contemporary marriage arrangements in the West Bank and Gaza are both diverse and different from those in the past" (1993, 286). Her point is valid even if Stokke's contention (that first-cousin marriage is relatively stable) is accepted. First, the evidence suggests that the proportion of first-cousin marriage is more stable than the proportion of kin marriage in general. Second, marriage patterns, whether in Palestine or elsewhere, are reproduced through active practices, family dynamics, and choice both by partners and other family members, as well as shaped by political, social, and economic circumstances. Indeed, it is possible that consanguinity might even have increased since the beginning of the twentieth century. In her detailed and meticulous work in the Bethlehem village of Artas in the 1920s, for example, Granqvist (1931, 81–82) found that the majority of men in fact marry "strangers" (only 13.3 percent of men marry a *bint il-'amm* [female patrilineal first cousin]), and 42.8 percent marry wives from outside the village entirely.

When Endogamy Increases: Contexts of Crisis and Dislocation

National patterns are always abstract and local realities may be very different. For example, in the 1970s Tamari (1983, 327) found a rate of 58 percent of first cousin marriages in the Jordan valley village of Zbeidat (mostly patrilineal), with another 15 percent of marriages within the same subclan. Although Tamari is not explicit, the reason for the high proportion of first-cousin marriages seems to be that residents were resettled from a Bedouin tribe in the Naqab (Negev) and thus have lost their marriage pool of other kin. An even more relevant case is patterns of increased endogamy in Arab villages in the

Galilee in the 1950s, after the founding of the state of Israel, large-scale Palestinian dispossession and the institution of military government for the Palestinian population that remained. Rosenfeld (1976, 115), for example, found that patrilineal endogamous marriage (of men with women from their own *hamula*) had almost doubled among Muslim villagers and more than doubled among Christians. He points to one dynamic that Galilee villagers share with the "resettled" Bedouins of Zbeidat: a shrinking of the marriage community in that seventeen of the villages within a fifteen-mile radius of the village in question "no longer exist" (121); in other words, their residents were expelled or fled in 1948 and the villages razed. A similar dislocation is also identified by Cohen (1965, 11–12) in border villages whose residents experienced a "sudden isolation" after 1948 when the new political border "cut mountain and plain apart" and severed villagers from their kin and from economic and cultural ties to the Jabal Nablus region. Cohen also finds a high rate of kin marriage; more than two-thirds of the marriages in "Bint al Hudud" over two generations involved members of the same *hamula*.[18]

Rosenfeld located an explanation for increased endogamy in social and economic factors, primarily the role of male villagers as an "insecure proletariat outside the village and backward agriculturists inside it," so that wage labor does not offer an alternative to village social structure, and security rests in "the manipulation of women within the marriage system" (1976, 116, 120). Despite some power to his argument, Rosenfeld's economist explanation is too narrow; it neglects the profound political insecurity behind the "insecure proletariat." His attribution of unequivocal power to males in marriage arrangements is also highly questionable, as will be explored below.

Given the persistence of insecurity and domination, amid the many changes that have swept Palestinian society, understanding marriage practices as strategies by both men and women to ensure security, survival, and development in a highly insecure world is a fruitful avenue; a similar framework has been useful in explaining the persistence of Palestinian high fertility (Giacaman 1997).

18. For a critique of Cohen's ideological biases and theoretical weaknesses, see Asad 1975. As Asad points out, Cohen does not problematize the concept of *hamula* but rather considers the *hamula* as a "basic principle of the political economy of the Palestinian peasant" (23), regardless of changing conditions.

Regional Variations

Although first-cousin marriage remains fairly constant across Palestinian localities, the wider practice of kin-based marriage exhibits strong regional [19] differences. It is also noteworthy that the district with the highest percent of kin
marriages in the West Bank, Hebron, also has significantly higher fertility, although Stokke (2002, 80) maintains that overall fertility rates are not influenced by kin relations. PCBS 1995 demographic data show a total fertility rate
for the Hebron district at 6.83 compared to rates of around 5 for Bethlehem,
Jenin, and Nablus (table 2.4). In the 1999 IWS household survey, almost a
quarter (23 percent) of married women aged fifteen through forty-nine from
the city of Hebron had seven children or more, while only 12 percent of
women from the city of Nablus did.

In the 1995 demographic survey (table 2.5), variations in first-cousin mar-

19. When referring to the IWS 1999 survey, the term "region" refers to the southern, northern, and central West Bank, as well as Gaza. More generally, "region" in the West Bank is related
to the historic configurations of the Jabal al-Khalil (south), Jabal al-Quds (central), and Jabal
Nablus (north) regions. PCBS data analyze data by districts, which are administrative units. The
IWS's category of "southern West Bank" roughly corresponds to the Hebron District; only one
small locality in the southern West Bank sample is outside the Hebron District.

Table 2.4
**Total Fertility Rate (TFR) and Median Age at First Marriage
in Nine Districts, 1995 (%)**

District	TFR	Median age at first marriage	
		Female	Male
Hebron	6.83	18	22
Bethlehem	4.97	17	22
Jerusalem	3.95	18	24
Ramallah/al Bira	5.41	18	24
Nablus	5.01	18	24
Tulkarm/Qalqilya	6.63	19	24
Jenin	5.06	19	24
Gaza: north	7.29	18	22
Gaza: south and central	7.56	18	22

Source: PCBS 1997c, table 24

Table 2.5
Ever-Married Women, Degree of Consanguinity by District, 1995 (%)

District	First cousin	Other relative (same hamula)	Other relative (other hamula)	No relation
Hebron	30.6	25.6	30.6	13.2
Bethlehem	27.4	22.2	15.6	34.7
Jerusalem	27.1	16.2	9.8	47.0
Ramallah/al-Bira	24.4	24.7	16.5	34.4
Nablus	24.3	15.8	17.2	42.7
Tulkarm/Qalqilya	26.2	15.0	17.2	42.7
Jenin	29.9	17.2	15.6	37.3
Gaza: north	32.1	16.5	7.7	43.7
Gaza: south and central	31.0	24.2	16.1	28.7

Source: PCBS 1997c, tables 25, 59

riage among the seven administrative districts in the West Bank and two in Gaza were not large, although they were slightly higher in Hebron and Gaza than in other districts. Differences among districts in other forms of kin and stranger marriage were more significant: the survey, using categories of marriage to first cousin, same *hamula*, other *hamula*, and no relation, found only 13.2 percent of ever-married women (aged fifteen through forty-nine) from the Hebron district reporting that they were married to a spouse who was no relation, while over a third of women in other districts (with the exception of south and central Gaza) reported being married to nonrelatives. The differences in Gaza are interesting, with highs in both first-cousin and stranger marriage in northern Gaza. Patterns in the Hebron region (southern West Bank) may help clarify the logic of kin-based marriage arrangements and their relationship to place, local economies, and cultures.

Logics of Land and Dower: Material Explanations

Are the two standard economic reasons given for kin marriage—avoiding land alienation and avoiding dower payment—valid in the Palestinian context? In the IWS survey, 24 percent of heads of households in the southern West Bank owned land in addition to their own dwelling, as opposed to a 15 percent rate of ownership for household heads in the northern and central West Bank (table 2.6). However, while land as a factor in marriage patterns cannot be dis-

Table 2.6
Land Ownership of Heads of Households by Region, 1999 (%)

Ownership	Northern West Bank	Central West Bank	Southern West Bank	Gaza	Jerusalem	Total
Heads of households owning land other than dwelling	15	15	24	8	4	14
Owned land is within city, camp, or village boundaries	65	87	73	69	90	72

Source: IWS household survey, 1999, unpublished data

counted, the material and symbolic significance of land ownership requires explanation. Land ownership clearly does not translate directly into wealth: not only does the Hebron district register significantly higher levels of poverty than every other district in the West Bank (NCPA 1998, 51, table 3) except the Jenin district, but also livelihoods from agriculture play a marginal role in local economies. Indeed, the Hebron district is more distinguished by its greater dependence on wage labor in Israel than other districts in the West Bank: three-quarters of the labor force in the Hebron district, and 72.5 percent in Hebron city, were reported as wage labor in 1999 (table 2.7). The overall dynamic of a decline in agriculture and uneven and insecure proletarianization, with a strong dependence on work in Israel, are shared among regions, whatever the important difference in local economies—from shoe factories in Hebron to sewing workshops in Gaza to stone quarries in Bethlehem.[20] Greater land ownership in Hebron could thus be seen less as a material source of wealth that can be immediately utilized than as a symbolic (as well as material) resource to be preserved through strengthening the symbolic economies of kinship.

Another intriguing difference to consider are patterns of dower. Both

20. In the IWS survey, about 4 percent of the labor force in the southern West Bank were machine operators in shoe factories with none found elsewhere, while about 4 percent of the Gazan work force worked sewing clothes. However the most significant difference was that 11 percent of Gazans worked in the police or security forces, compared to less than 3 percent elsewhere.

Table 2.7
Employment Status in Three West Bank Districts and Cities, 1997 (%)

	Hebron		Nablus		Jenin	
	District	City	District	City	District	City
Employer	5.5	6.5	7.9	12.9	5.6	8.6
Self-employed	16.3	17.3	16.7	17.9	21.8	21.9
Wage	75.0	72.5	71.8	66.7	68.5	65.6
Unpaid family member	2.4	2.4	3.2	2.6	3.8	3.7
Other	0.8	1.3	0.4	0.5	0.3	0.2
Total	100.0	100.0	100.0	100.0	100.0	100.0

Source: Calculated from PCBS 1999c (92, table 14); 1999b; 1999d (100, table 14)

Notes: Employed persons over age fifteen are included. The IWS survey recorded higher levels of self-employment in Hebron as defined by the respondent, while PCBS figures reflect institutional categorization. In fact, "wage" labor can be day labor or other forms of irregular labor where relations with employers are transient, and it is interesting that workers, particularly in Hebron, may perceive themselves as "self-employed."

Moors and Welchman have clearly documented the sharp decline of the prompt dower in favor of the deferred dower since 1967 (Moors 1995; Welchman 1992). The prompt dower is received by the woman upon marriage; the deferred dower is paid in the case of divorce (unless the divorce is by mutual consideration, where women waive their financial rights[21]) or widowhood. The prompt dower served historically as an important source of property for rural women; a pattern of registering only token prompt dowers and deferring the rest of the dower payment began in some urban locales in the 1960s and spread in the years thereafter. Surveying Islamic court *(shari'a)* records in Hebron, Bethelehem, and Ramallah for the years 1965, 1975, and 1985, Welchman finds sharp declines in the registration of prompt dower in all three districts, although there is a lesser drop in Hebron. While 95 percent of Hebron marriage contracts in 1965 showed a greater prompt dower than deferred dower, 25 percent did so in 1985. In Ramallah, 65 percent of marriage contracts registered a greater prompt dower in 1965 and only 3.8 percent in 1985, whereas for Bethlehem the decline in the same twenty years went from 95 per-

21. *Khal'*, or *khul'*, divorce by mutual consideration, is by far the most common form of divorce in the West Bank and Gaza. The husband agrees to divorce his wife in return for her giving up all her financial rights.

cent to 4.2 percent (Welchman 1992, 129). These findings are interesting in light of the greater proportion of kin marriage in the Hebron district: first, the decline in preference for the prompt dower is clearly a national pattern, and second, about a quarter of Hebron marriages in 1985 continue to register a larger prompt dower. While there are other marriage expenses not examined here, the logic of kin marriage as avoiding dower payments does not seem to be operative: the economies that operate in marriage transactions appear to be more complicated.

Kinship as a Social Category: The Dynamics of "Sameness"

Aside from first-cousin marriages, the 1995 PCBS demography survey inquired about marriages in two categories termed "other relative, same *hamula*" and "other relative, different *hamula*." Comparing the results to the 1999 IWS household survey, one can begin to see kinship as a social category rather than simply as a relationship of consanguinity. Overall in the IWS survey, 27 percent of ever-married women aged fifteen through forty-nine were married to first cousins, 12 percent to other relatives on their father's side, 5 percent to other relatives on their mother's side, 27 percent to nonrelatives from the same community, and 28 percent to nonrelatives from other communities (table 2.2). In the southern region (primarily the Hebron district), 27 percent were married to first cousins, with similar proportions for other relatives; however, 40 percent were married to nonrelatives from the same community, and only 19 percent were married to nonrelatives from other communities. It seems likely that marriages to the "same community" (*nafs al-mujtama‘*) would include marriages based on the same social relations that were identified in the PCBS 1995 survey as "relative, other *hamula*." This is confirmed in the 2000 PCBS demographic and health survey where the "other *hamula*" category was not used and the percentage of kin marriage dropped accordingly (PCBS 2002a). Moors points out the complex notion of "sameness" and its "various meanings in different contexts," observing that in the Palestinian context she studied (Jabal Nablus), " 'sameness' is associated with 'closeness' (*qaraba*), a relative rather than an absolute term which also means 'kinship' " (1995, 87). Hildred Geertz makes a similar observation about Moroccan society, where *qaraba* is "sometimes used to include people who have become part of the group in other ways than birth or marriage"

(Geertz 1979, 376). In Moors's view, marriage dynamics are based not simply on sharing blood, but, class, culture, and space (or place). In his ethnographic study of the Ramallah-area village of Baytin in the 1960s, Lutfiyya also notes the idiomatic use of kinship: " 'We are all cousins' is a remark often made to a stranger who may ask a villager if he were related to someone in the village who is not a close relative" (Lutfiyya 1961, 175). More recently, Palestinian migrants to the United States call each other *ya qaraba* (O relatives!), even when they share neither kin relations nor the same specific village or town origin, but simply come from the same region of Palestine.[22] In both the Palestinian territory and the Diaspora, Palestinians employ the vocabulary of kinship to establish social relationships and social worlds, whether an older man is addressed with the respectful term of *'ammo* (paternal uncle), or women evoke shared experiences with the vocabulary of sisterhood. This is particularly striking in shared public spaces, whether public transportation or the endless lines in which women wait for bureaucratic "favors" (e.g., residency permits, prison visits, or food rations).

When villagers become refugees, "sameness" may be affirmed and reconstituted in marriage practices. A particularly telling example of these dynamics is found in a study of marriage patterns since 1948 in Burayj refugee camp in the Dayr al-Balah district of Gaza. After constructing genealogical maps of six "patrilineal lineages,"[23] founded either by individual males or groups of brothers exiled to Gaza in 1948, Tuastad found that two-thirds of 538 married individuals had married a refugee descended from the same village in Palestine; about one-half (of the 538) married from the same lineage as well (Tuastad 1997, 112). He observes that the larger category of *hamula* has been fragmented by refugee life and believes that it is no longer an operative category. After 1948, reorganizing kinship networks was one of the few options for Palestinian refugees for social and political organization: Tuastad notes that kinship organization located "refugees in space and time" and reproduced "home as a social and cultural state" in a new physical environment (1997,

---

22. Information supplied by Rita Giacaman from personal experience.

23. Tuastad (1997, 110) calculated the average lineage size as seven households, although a majority was from lineages of 10 or more households, ranging from 50 to 500 relatives living in the same camp. Nonetheless, there were a substantial number of households (248) were single households without other relatives.

112). The rise of the Palestinian national resistance movement and Palestinian political factions created new forms of political activism and solidarities in Burayj, which were dominant during the first Palestinian intifada; however, factional and family politics in the interim period crisscrossed in multiple ways, with family politics serving as a "second tier" (131) to buttress power and position.

Although Tuastad insists that "patrilineal," rather than matrilineal, lineage is the basis of Palestinian social and political organization based on kinship, he does note that the refugees themselves refer to these lineal descent groups simply as *'a'ila* (families) (1997, 113). Patrilineal descent may be too strict a notion in understanding the dynamics of these refugee marriage patterns. When marriage to relatives is so pervasive, the description of a marriage as matrilineal or patrilineal can be a matter of choice, as spouses may be related through both their mothers and fathers, although the patrilineal link may be more dominant in discourse and practice. Marriages of Burayj camp residents to original Gaza residents were extremely rare, while an overwhelming majority, as noted above, found partners from the same original village in Palestine. Here marriage patterns seem to reproduce a particular form and history of lost village life, where kin "re-places" or embodies place.

Preferences for Change: Do They Signal a Decline in Kin Marriage?

Granqvist used her finding of the prevalence of stranger marriage in Artas to underscore the "dissonance between idea and reality" (1931, 92) in ideologies and practices of family life, given her respondents' strong and consistent valorization of patrilineal first cousin *(ibn il-'amm)* marriage and the fact that most marriages were made with "strangers" from outside the village. In contemporary Palestine, the dissonance partially works the other way: while over a quarter of ever-married Palestinian women are actually married to first cousins and over one-half are married to kin of various degrees, less than 10 percent of parents in the IWS survey prefer first-cousin marriage for a randomly selected male or female child and only 16 percent a relative of any type (including first cousins) for their sons and 19 percent for their daughters (Abu Nahleh 2002a). Almost half (45 percent for sons and 48 percent for daughters)

Table 2.8
Respondents' Preferred Spouse for Son by Region, 1999 (%)

Preferred spouse for sons	No. West Bank	C. West Bank	So. West Bank	Gaza	Jerusalem	Total
Relative	12	27	10	21	5	16
Nonrelative	47	42	35	47	61	45
From same or original town	15	4	7	7	23	10
His decision	22	19	42	21	11	25
Other/not important	4	8	6	4		4
Total	100	100	100	100	100	100
Ns	351	129	337	597	64	1,478

Source: IWS 1999 survey data from Giacaman and Johnson 2002b, table 7.3

Table 2.9
Respondents' Preferred Spouse for Daughter by Region, 1999 (%)

Preferred spouse for daughters	No. West Bank	C. West Bank	So. West Bank	Gaza	Jerusalem	Total
Relative	13	25	16	25	4	19
Nonrelative	50	52	38	50	60	48
From same or original town	18	5	9	12	18	12
Her decision	8	6	22	6	5	10
Other/not important	11	12	15	7	13	11
Total	100	100	99	100	101	100
Ns	331	138	314	581	57	1,421

Source: IWS 1999 survey data taken from Giacaman and Johnson 2002b, table 7.4

explicitly chose nonrelatives, 25 percent left the decision to their sons, and 10 percent left the decision to their daughters (tables 2.8 and 2.9).

Of particular interest is the finding that women aged fifteen through forty-nine who were married to first cousins were less likely to prefer kin marriages for their sons and daughters than women married to other more distant kin. Women married to first cousins exhibited only a slightly greater preference for kin marriage (first cousins or other relatives) than the average. However, women married to relatives other than first cousins had a pronounced higher

Table 2.10
Preference for Daughter's Husband by Mother's Relation
to Husband, 1999 (%)

Preference for daughter's husband	Mother's relation to husband		
	First cousin	Other relative	Nonrelative
Relative	22	33	16
Nonrelative	47	39	55
Same community	11	11	14
Her decision/not important	20	19	15
	100	100	100

Source: IWS household survey, 1999, unpublished data
Note: Sample size: 684 married women aged 15–49; 186 married to first cousins, 134 to other
    relatives, and 364 to nonrelatives

Table 2.11
Preference for Son's Wife by Mother's Relation
to Husband, 1999 (%)

Preference for son's wife	Mother's relation to husband		
	First cousin	Other relative	Nonrelative
Relative	19	30	13
Nonrelative	49	32	51
Same community	8	10	9
His decision/not important	24	27	27
	100	100	100

Source: IWS household survey, 1999, unpublished data
Note: Sample size: 692 married women aged 15–49; 168 married to first cousins, 136 to other
    relatives, and 388 to nonrelatives

preference for kin marriage (see tables 2.10 and 2.11). That suggests that first-cousin marriage may be a more troubled environment than other forms of kin marriage and that women married to first cousins may feel such marriages are too close for comfort.

How do we understand the fact that a majority of women married to relatives seem to prefer nonrelative marriage for their daughters and sons? Overall, the IWS survey data seem to indicate a strong preference for change in principle on the part of both male and female respondents: aside from marriage preferences, parents generally supported much higher levels of education for sons, daughters, and potential spouses than their own educational attainment, and they also supported to a significant extent daughters and daughters-in-law working outside the home, an expectation often quite different from their own lives and the environment around them (Abu Nahleh 2002b). These findings inevitably raise a series of questions about how to interpret the meaning of stated preferences. These preferences may best be taken as normative statements: as Holy notes, preference is a "phenomenon that clearly belongs to the notional, cognitive or cultural level of social reality" (1989, 9). There is also the obvious fact that preferences may be difficult to translate into practice. People marry kin for reasons other than a normative ideology: working in Morocco where marriages with first cousins were relatively common, Hildred Geertz observed that a "normative preference for marriage with the father's brother's daughter . . . was rarely, if ever, expressed to me unsolicited" (1979, 372), adding that reciprocated marriage among kinsmen over generations had produced a "ramifying thicket of ties" that defy simple classification. Inside this "thicket," kinship may be more idiomatic than strictly biological.

These notes of caution, however, do not mean that the survey data are meaningless; it is significant that women and men in the IWS survey expressed marital preferences for their children that were substantially different from their own experience. However, an interpretation of this significance must be situated in the context of married women and men being asked in a formal interview to express a marriage preference for their children: their responses may not only reflect their experience in a particular social world or community of dispositions (habitus) and the constraints and opportunities therein, and their preferences for change, but also how they might wish to project or communicate that world to outsiders.

The Freedom to "Decide": Closeness and Choice

Consider the quarter of respondents in the IWS survey who did not express a preference for either relative or nonrelative marriage for their son, instead affirming that it was up to their son to decide on whether his marriage partner was a relative or not, and the 10 percent who gave the same response for their daughters (table 2.12). Individual choice of marriage partners is often seen as a marker of modernity: how do we explain that an elevated preference for personal decision was found among parents in one of the most "traditional" regions of Palestinian society, the southern West Bank, where kin marriage is also disproportionately present? About twice as many southern West Bank parents chose to let their son decide on his partner than the sample average, and about three times as many chose to let their daughters decide (tables 2.8–2.9). Parents in rural and camp households also chose to let their sons and daughters decide to a greater extent than parents in urban households, also contrary to a logic where urban modernity fosters individualism.

Aside from gaps between stated ideals and actual practice, choice obviously takes on different meanings in varying contexts. Not only are personal preferences in marriage notoriously subjected to familial and communal imperatives, but the conditions of choice may limit options. Palestinian communities in the present warlike conditions provide an obvious example: in communities that are under curfew, surrounded by barriers, or literally walled in, the drastic reduction in the zone of socialization and the inability to activate social networks recall the isolation of Palestinian villages inside the Green Line after 1948. In the case of southern West Bank parents responding in 1999 prior to the intifada, a degree of physical insularity is certainly present—but forms of social insularity are perhaps more pertinent.

A preference for personal decision for their children in marriage choices explains why southern West Bank respondents exhibited the lowest preference both for relative and nonrelative marriage. While there is a considerable gender gap in allowing sons and daughters to decide on marriage partners, the parents in the southern West Bank, at first glance, seem to support individual rather than family decision making in marriage, in seeming contradiction to the conservatism and family-centered economies and social life usually attributed to the region and in particular to its major center of population, Hebron. In contrast, parents in Gaza more rarely express a preference for individual choice. Gaza and the southern West Bank share actual high levels of first-cousin and kin marriage (tables 2.2, 2.5; Stokke 2002, 7), even among younger age cohorts, but express somewhat different preferences for their children's marriages: what difference does this in fact express? It is not necessarily that southern West Bankers have a greater desire for changing patterns of kin

Table 2.12
Preferred Spouse for Daughter or Son by Type of Locality, 1999 (%)

Preferred spouse	City		Camp		Village		All	
	Daughter	Son	Daughter	Son	Daughter	Son	Daughter	Son
Relative	18	14	17	17	22	20	19	16
Nonrelative	52	50	50	38	38	36	50	45
From same or original town	12	11	7	7	15	10	11	10
Her/his decision	7	22	14	33	14	30	10	25
Other/not important	11	3	12	5	11	4	10	4
Total	100	100	100	100	100	100	100	100
Ns	853	916	230	214	338	348	1,421	1,478

Source: IWS 1999 survey data from Giacaman and Johnson 2002b, table 7.6

marriage. Almost half of Gazan relatives explicitly prefer a nonrelative spouse for their sons, for example, as opposed to only a third (35 percent) of southern West Bank parents.

The reasons for the southern West Bank exception are speculative, but, given existing marriage patterns there and strong kin relations in such matters as living arrangements, as noted below, the southern West Bank—dominated by the Hebron city sample—may have denser webs of kin and community relations where trust and restricted exposure to some extent can replace control in marriage preferences. In another context, Barakat notes that parents in Lebanese villages allow their children more independence than city-dwellers because of the familiar surroundings (1993, 106). Using the wider definition of kin as "sameness" noted above, parents in the southern West Bank may also feel more certain that their children's marriage preferences will conform to their own, given their children's experience of social life at least in part as a world of kinship and the values and dispositions embedded therein. Physical and social restrictions on meeting possible marriage partners from outside kin and community also play a part.

The differences between urban, camp, and village respondents also point in this direction. Urban respondents were the most conservative in allowing children freedom of choice in marrying kin or nonkin: twice as many camp and village parents as urban parents preferred choice for their daughters. Urban parents also registered lower preferences for sons' freedom to choose than village or camp parents (table 2.12). However, a majority of urban and camp residents preferred nonrelatives as husbands for daughters, as opposed to only 38 percent of villagers. Parents in the cities of Nablus, Ramallah, Jerusalem (Old City), and Gaza City have a lower preference for choice; the small and ruralized town of Jenin was more like the large but also ruralized city of Hebron in greater preference for personal decision. Here urban environments with greater mobility and access for youth may cause parental distrust of children's freedom to choose, whereas rural and camp parents may believe to a greater extent that their children will "naturally" conform to their wishes. In these locations, as in Hebron, the social organization may also be more constricted; institutions that provide a context for individual choice and offer opportunities for young men and women to intermingle—whether workplaces, educational or leisure institutions, or political parties and movements—are much more prevalent, for example, in Ramallah and Jerusalem than in Hebron, and in cities more than villages.[24]

Genetics versus Choice: Discourses of Modernity

When parents were asked the reasons for their preferences in children's marriages, it is striking that the greatest overall reason cited is "avoiding genetic problems" (table 2.13). While the questionnaire effect may well have prompted this concern for consanguinity by asking marriage preferences in terms of kin or stranger relations, it is nonetheless incongruent in a society in which kin marriage is so prevalent. Direct or family and community experience of birth abnormalities may well play a part: PCBS's 1996 health survey found about 10 percent of disabilities as inherited (14 percent in Gaza and 8 percent in the West Bank), and 39 percent as congenital (PCBS 1997b, 83); families might also perceive congenital disabilities in the framework of genetic disorders. The rationale of avoiding genetic problems may at the same time be seen as a normative discourse of modernity: parents may employ this discourse defensively, of course, as well as presenting it as an expression of intent to change. It is very likely that respondents have also reacted to modernizing discourses of genetics from the media, health providers (both Palestinian and Israeli), health information campaigns, and exposure from visits or relatives abroad, particularly in the United States, where anecdotal evidence suggests that Palestinian and Arab immigrant couples find themselves trying to conceal their kin marriage relations in a society that socially (and in some states, legally) stigmatizes such relations. A genetic discourse may be newly normative, but its translation into practice (and the interpretation of genetic threat in various contexts) remains a question to be explored, given the thinness of the normative when confronted with the thickness of kin relations.

A lesser thirty percent of southern and central West Bank parents ex-

24. Jamil Hilal drew my attention to the important issue of the social organization of choice. Peteet's observation of a new discourse of girls choosing their own marriage partners in the context of the Palestinian Resistance in Lebanon is also pertinent. Young women choose spouses but go through the appropriate steps of family approval: "Marriage remains enmeshed in larger kin structures and strategies" (1991, 180).

Table 2.13
Reasons for Choosing Child's Spouse by Sex of Child, 1999 (%)

Reason for choosing child's spouse	Daughter	Son	Total
AVOIDING PROBLEMS			
Avoiding genetic problems	38	37	37
Avoiding family problems	18	15	17
PROTECTING CHILDREN			
Relatives will take care of her/him	10	2	6
Staying close to family	5	2	3
Knowing about child's future	2	7	4
Sharing customs	2	3	2
FAMILY POWER AND SUPPORT			
Strengthening family ties	3	5	4
Expanding circle of acquaintance	3	3	3
FREEDOM OF CHOICE			
She/he is mature enough to decide	13	18	16
Avoiding his/her blame	0	7	4
Other	4	1	2
Don't know	2	0	2
Total	100	100	100
Ns	1,429	1,480	2,909

Source: IWS 1991 data from Giacaman and Johnson 2002b, table 7.6

pressed a concern with "avoiding genetic problems," whereas a strong majority of Jerusalem parents (57 percent) and 40 percent in the northern West Bank gave this as their rationale for marriage preference. Instead, southern West Bank parents were again concerned with choice in their rationale, citing either the maturity of their sons and daughters, or avoiding blame from sons (but not daughters) as reasons for leaving the decision to their children. Interestingly, women married to first cousins had concerns that were similar to those of the general population: their own marriage circumstances did not lead to an elevated concern with genetic problems.

This bare statistical outline of "preference" leads to several observations and some interesting questions. Discourses of genetics and of personal choice at first glance might seem to be both modernizing discourses, but in our respondents, they are contrasted: southern West Bank parents are less drawn into genetic rationales for marriage partners than other parents, but they are much more likely to opt for personal choice. Similarly, 41 percent of urban residents chose avoiding genetic problems as a main reason for the choice of wives for their daughters, but less than 25 percent chose to let their sons decide on partners; 29 percent of villagers chose personal decision for sons, but only 31 percent chose avoiding genetic problems. Here, modern knowledge about genetic dangers seems to accompany increasing parental direct control of choice.

Only 10 percent of southern West Bank parents were explicitly worried about "avoiding family problems" in their choice of spouse for sons and daughters, as opposed to 28 percent in the Old City of Jerusalem and 18 percent in the northern West Bank. Given that the genetic rationale — also cited to a lesser extent in the southern West Bank and by villagers — is also directed at avoiding problems, we can perhaps posit that parents in the southern West Bank are less likely to see marriage choices as a source of tension and problems, while parents in other urban environments have a greater tendency to view marriage as an institution fraught with problems that must be avoided. Overall, in fact, the rationale of avoiding problems — whether genetic or familial — is prominent. Interestingly, a very small minority of parents anywhere (less than 5 percent) explicitly explained their choices by the rationales that are often given by social scientists for marriage: strengthening family position and ties through marriage alliances, while about three times as many parents cited reasons of protection, closeness, and knowledge of spouses (table 2.13), all presumably reasons for kin marriage.

Given the serial crises that have beset Palestinian families, the protection of family and children is both a central concern for Palestinian parents and a continuing crisis in actual capabilities to protect (Johnson and Kuttab 2001). If we view parental preferences and actual marriage practices in this light, we can see that a dynamic of sameness in marriage partners may help preserve families that are literally embattled. Where environments foster sameness and closeness, parents are more willing to trust their children to choose suitable spouses. Parents are highly sensitive to dangers for their children and grandchildren: a genetic discourse is both a normative statement of modernity and an expression of real fears. As the section below explores, mothers and fathers project hopes and high expectations for a better life for their sons and daughters in terms of education and employment. These are often "unrealistic" in terms of current educational and employment patterns: a gap between ideal and practice is not uncommon, but what seems operative in the Palestinian context is also an imagining of a better, more stable, world.

Daughters and Daughters-in-Law: Marrying Equals

The IWS survey showed an overwhelming and consistent desire of parents for higher education for their sons and daughters, with 87 percent aspiring to a bachelor's degree or higher for their sons, and 72 percent for their daughters. Given that almost half of the heads of households in the IWS survey were educated only to the sixth grade—including a quarter that were illiterate or could barely read—this commitment to higher education, whatever its practical possibilities, is an important part of family dynamics and aspirations and perhaps even a key component of Palestinian national hopes and identities. Within this national consensus for education, there are gaps both between and within genders. Of particular interest is the difference in preferences in education and work for daughters and daughters-in-law.

Normative and actual marriage patterns in the Middle East have been broadly generalized to privilege "marriage between equals (homogomy)" or "marriage of a man of higher rank to a woman of lower rank (hypergamy)" (Holy 1989, 112). Holy notes that hypergamy serves to reproduce agnatic solidarity, as younger generations are more likely to be bound to the husband's family and its greater resources and status. Recognizing that rule-based models of kinship and marriage are highly limiting, can we find preferences for homogomy and hypergamy in the available data, and if so, what do they mean for characterizing particular communities of dispositions, or a specific habitus?

Generally in the IWS survey, parental expectations and preferences in both education and work outside the home differ for daughters and daughters-in-law. Most fathers and mothers prefer higher levels of education for daughters than daughters-in-law, and more parents approve of work outside the home for daughters than daughters-in-law. Position and roles within the family thus complicate gender expectations, and a tendency to hypergamy in the marriage of sons is distinguished. While there is a generally high approval of female work outside the home, mirroring findings in a number of Palestinian public opinion polls, 68 percent of parents approve their daughter's employ-

ment, either unconditionally or in certain circumstances, or give her the freedom of decide, and only 59 percent their daughter-in-law's employment, with
fathers generally more conservative than mothers (Abu Nahleh 2002b; tables
2.14 and 2.15). Parents also prefer lower levels of education for their son's
wives than their own daughters.

However, the differences in preferences and expectations in education
and work for daughters and daughters-in-law were less among southern West
Bank parents. While parents in most regions opted for higher levels of education for their own daughters than for their daughters-in-law, southern West
Bank parents were more egalitarian; they also preferred similar educational
levels for sons and for sons-in-laws. This "all in the family" perspective perhaps
flows from a framework of marriage as bringing kin or "like" together where
the daughter-in-law is not a stranger and thus should be treated as a family
member. Marriages are thus more likely to be between equals (or homoga-
mous): I would argue that a wider preservation of kin solidarity, rather than
simply agnatic solidarity, is the cultural context for such practices.

The contrast with Gazan parents is telling, given that Gaza and the Hebron district share similar dynamics in terms of high first-cousin marriage, unusually low female labor force participation, high fertility rates, and early
marriage. Gazans had the largest gender gap in their preferences for relatively
low levels of education for son's wives and relatively high levels for daughter's
husbands, suggesting a stronger preference for hypergamy. Gazans were also
generally more negative about employment for daughters, perhaps reflecting
the more insecure conditions and low opportunities in Gaza,[25] but they were
even more strongly opposed to the employment of daughters-in-law: 44 percent of Gazan parents opposed paid employment for their daughters-in-law in
contrast to 34 percent of parents in the southern West Bank (Abu Nahleh
2002b, 140). It is tempting to explain the Gaza-Hebron difference by the very
low refugee population in the Hebron region and the very high refugee population in Gaza—a culture of cousins contrasted with a culture of refugees is
clearly an over-generalization, but it may offer a paradigm for consideration.

Interestingly, these preferences for children and their spouses exhibited
no strong pattern based on wealth and standard of living, suggesting that habi-

25. In a survey of public opinion polls, Hammami (2004b) argues that female employment
is viewed more positively in times of relative security and stability.

Table 2.14
Preference for Daughter to Work by Region, 1999

Preference for daughter	Region No. West Bank	C. West Bank	So. West Bank	Gaza	Jerusalem	Total
Should not work	108 (33%)	43 (31%)	82 (26%)	207 (35%)	15 (27%)	455 (32%)
Should work	193 (58%)	86 (62%)	149 (47%)	293 (50%)	37 (66%)	758 (53%)
Should decide	31 (9%)	10 (7%)	89 (28%)	84 (14%)	4 (7%)	218 (15%)
Total	332 (100%)	139 (100%)	320 (100%)	584 (100%)	56 (100%)	1431 (100%)

Source: IWS 1999 survey data from Giacaman and Johnson 2002b, table 9.5a

Table 2.15
Preference for Daughter-in-law to Work by Region, 1999

Preference for daughter-in-law	Region					
	No. West Bank	C. West Bank	So. West Bank	Gaza	Jerusalem	Total
Should not work	158 (45%)	53 (41%)	113 (34%)	262 (44%)	18 (28%)	604 (41%)
Should work	153 (44%)	63 (49%)	107 (32%)	261 (44%)	35 (55%)	619 (42%)
Should decide	38 (11%)	12 (9%)	116 (35%)	73 (12%)	11 (17%)	250 (17%)
Total	349 (100%)	128 (100%)	336 (100%)	596 (100%)	64 (100%)	1473 (100%)

Source: IWS 1999 survey data from Giacaman and Johnson 2002b, table 9.5a

tus, and the symbolic economies of kinship operating therein, may override social stratification in certain contexts. As researchers on Palestinian living conditions have observed, "family bonds may cut across stratification lines, contributing to a complex pattern of socioeconomic interdependence" (Heiberg and Ovensen 1993, 244).

Living with Family and Kin

The prevalence of kin-based marriage is matched by kin-based living arrangements, despite the prevalence of nuclear households. According to both the 1997 national census and the IWS survey, about three-quarters of Palestinian households in the West Bank and Gaza are nuclear, a percentage that does not vary substantially across regions. Yet this widespread nucleation, while obviously having implications for conjugal life and household dynamics, does not necessarily sever nuclear households from family and kin networks, as indicated by the significance of other forms of kin-based living arrangements as described below. Significantly, these arrangements do vary by region.

The IWS survey investigated kin-based living through households that physically share a building or attached dwelling with relatives. Of those households living in apartments or attached dwellings, over 90 percent in the southern West Bank and 80 percent in Gaza share these residences with relatives, compared to about half in the central West Bank and in the Old City of Jerusalem (table 2.16). These figures are similar to those found in 1992 in the living conditions survey conducted by Fafo; more than 75 percent of households in multihousehold buildings shared the dwelling only with kin and 40 percent with brothers, pointing to the key importance of this sibling relationship (Heiberg and Ovensen 1993, 93). In her examination of a neighborhood in the Jordanian city of Irbid, McCann termed the dominant household form "patrilineal co-residential units," consisting of fathers and married sons who own housing and property jointly but live in separate nuclear residential units and sometimes work together on economic and social ventures (1993, 1).

Can we also assume that family and kin cluster in neighborhoods, even if dwellings are separate? Evidence from Jordan suggests that this pattern may also exist in neighboring Palestine: researchers in 1998 (Hanssen-Bauer, Pedersen, and Tiltnes, 1998) found that two-thirds of households had family members or other relatives living in the neighborhood or within walking dis-

Table 2.16
Housing Arrangements by Region, 1999 (%)

Housing	No. West Bank	C. West Bank	So. West Bank	Gaza	Jerusalem
Separate	20	58	51	19	28
OF THOSE IN APARTMENTS OR ATTACHED DWELLINGS					
Share with relatives	68	54	91	81	53
Share with 1st-degree relative	58	50	86	74	39

Source: IWS 199 survey data from Giacaman and Johnson 2002b, table 4.2

tance, with no differences between refugees and nonrefugees, indicating that the majority refugee Palestinian population in Jordan conforms to this pattern. Interestingly, more refugees than nonrefugees live with ten or more relatives within walking distance, although fewer refugees have both lineal and collateral relatives in the neighborhood (262–68). These kin-based living arrangements among refugees living outside Palestine constitute further evidence of how practices of kinship are reconstituted in changing circumstances and places.

Living closely with first-degree relatives points to the embeddedness of households in what might properly be called "family," rather than kin—or in Arabic *ahl*, rather than *qarayib*, *hamula*, or other terms that denote larger kin groups. Other scholars have pointed to the dominance of the extended family rather than the extended household in Arab countries, a family that is nuclear in form and extended in function (Farsoun 1970). We can only speculate on the significance of nuclear households embedded in kin-based social and living arrangements for relations between household and family members. In European family history, some scholars have proposed that the separation of the unit of parents and children (one form of family) from extended kin networks occurred generally since the eighteenth century (Nicholson 1997, 31), leading to increased partnership and conjugality between spouses and a more distinct role for mothers in socializing children. However, more detailed studies in local European contexts have discovered a more complicated picture, asserting a reorganization of kinship ties in the nineteenth century.[26] In Palestine, Moors's examination of patterns of dower, inheritance, and paid labor in the Jabal Nablus region led her to hypothesize an increase in conjugality in the Palestinian context, dating from the 1920s, with kinship "less important as a social principle of organization" (Moors 1995, 125). Moors is careful to limit her observation to the Jabal Nablus region, and her attention to changes in the material economy of kinship is extremely useful. However, an increase in conjugality might not necessarily lessen the importance of kinship as a social principle of organization, particularly when kin marriage continues to be

26. Working with parish records in southern Germany, Sabean found that kinship relations became more important in the nineteenth century, and endogamous marriages, particularly of cross-cousins, increased, and other scholars have found increased co-residence with extended kin in cities undergoing industrialization (Doumani 2003, 5).

widely practiced and when kinship is an important constituent of social and political identities, as this chapter suggests. Working in two Beirut neighborhoods in the late 1960s, Khuri advances the thesis that parallel cousin marriage "nullifies" the effect of marriage on natal family relationships, diminishing not only conjugality but other possible new affinal relations. While his observation suffers from male bias—it is the man who acts to perpetuate the same family relations he had before marriage—and does not address other forms of kin marriage, the general point that marriage to relatives may weaken conjugality is well-taken (1970, 597).

I am not arguing that kinship has remained stable over the course of the twentieth century; this would be a highly untenable proposition, and the changes Moors identifies are important to take into account, as are other trends and transformations that change family relations and create new loyalties and interests, such as increased market relations, new political institutions and practices, and the spread of education, among others. Rather, my emphasis is on the persistence of a "kinship universe" (Holy 1989, 119) or universes reconstituted by kinship practices in varying settings and with varying values. A model of linear decline (which is not, however, what Moors suggests), cannot capture the continuing, and often re-created, significance of kinship and family in various contexts in Palestinian society.

Working with Family and Kin

Moors's assumption that kinship is "less important" as a social principle of organization does at first seem borne out by the very low rate of kin-based economic enterprises found in the IWS survey. Only 3 percent of household heads reported partnership in an economic enterprise with kin, mostly in shops or services. This rate is very low, even if there is underreporting of economic enterprises in general. There was little regional differentiation: a slightly higher rate in the central West Bank is probably attributable to a slightly greater ownership of some types of property. In fact, ownership of property (outside land and dwelling) is only 6 percent, which partially explains the low reporting of kin-based economic partnerships. Of those with property, 9 percent report kin partnerships. One suspects, however, that the sharing of kin in economic activity is largely informal, given occupational patterns where the overwhelming majority are wage workers, such as, for example, a striking three-quarters of employed persons in the Hebron district.[27] Kin relations in work thus might focus on informal cooperation rather than formal economic ties. Investigating work in Israel in a 1980 case study of a village in the Ramallah District, Tamari notes that "in all cases interviewed, work was obtained in construction sites through a brother or cousin who was already employed by a Jewish boss" (Tamari 1983, 228). Experienced workers often established a team: for example, one worker's team might include two cousins, a younger brother, and a distant relative. Family relations are also used in aspects of the management, recruitment, and work environments of the small-scale and sometimes family-run workshops that make up a large portion of Hebron city's manufacturing sector. In one infamous example, poor working conditions in a cigarette lighter factory in Hebron led to a fire that killed fourteen young women workers in 1999; most lived in the same neighborhood of the village of Dura, and five were in the same family grouping.[28]

In an initial review of kinship data in the IWS survey, Taraki made the important observation that eliciting information about the "regular and usual patterns of cooperation" means leaving out the occasional assistance and informal cooperation based on need and reciprocity that perhaps is "what mutual assistance is really all about" (Taraki 1999, 6). While there is no doubt that economic transformations, and in particular the decline of agriculture, including subsistence agriculture, and the rise of waged work, have dramatically altered family economics and social relations—particularly between fathers and sons and husbands and wives—kin dynamics seem to be also at work in new economic contexts. Just as the predominance of kin-based living arrangements discovered in the IWS survey calls for a more contextual analysis of the meaning of nuclear households, assumptions that market relations solely prevail because of the dominance of wage labor also bear evaluation and refinement.

27. In the 1999 IWS survey, labor force participants in the southern West Bank also had a higher rate of working inside Israel (at 23 percent as opposed to 14 percent in the northern West Bank and 13 percent in Gaza), mostly as semiskilled or unskilled labor.

28. For the full story of this tragic incident, the search of families for compensation, and the utilization of customary law, see Labadi 2004.

Kin Marriage: In Whose Interest?

The transition from subsistence agriculture to male wage labor led Moors to posit an accompanying transformation in the roles of women from "productive daughters" to "dependent wives" (1995, 150), a transformation that, if true, not only weakens women's roles and responsibilities in the family setting but would probably weaken the material rationale for kin marriage. The economic transition is indubitably true, but the accompanying social transition may be highly uneven. The persistence of kin marriage is one important example of a countervailing dynamic: there arises not only a question on the nature of the symbolic economies that produce this persistence but also the perennial query: in whose interest? Rosenfeld (1976), in his examination of endogamous marriage patterns in several Arab villages in the Galilee in the 1950s and early 1960s, places power and decision making firmly with males in the context of strengthening their own kin or (in his view) their *hamula*. In an earlier work reviewing marriage patterns and preferences in various villages in Arab countries, based mainly on his fieldwork among the Libyan peasantry, Hilal (1970) argues that first-cousin marriage is driven at least partly by the desire of women to secure family protection and support. In thinking about women's strategies in marriage, the interests of mothers and daughters, of mothers for daughters, and of mothers versus daughters, should be considered, together with the influence of larger circles of female kin. The domain of practical kinship, and thus practical marriage arrangements, is often the province of women (Bourdieu 1990). Studies on Palestinian society have also pointed out the dominant role of mothers in arranging marriage. In Burayj camp, for example, Tuastad observes that the "social contacts and preferences of mothers" dominate marriage arrangements (1997, 107), and that parents, usually mothers, find it more practical and secure to find marriage partners for their children within the lineage—perhaps in contrast to the insecurity and risk of strangers. Hoodfar finds a similar dynamic among poor women in Cairo in the 1990s, where most women said, "it was best for women to marry kin because their economic status and background are known, leaving little room for deception" (1997, 55). Here mothers and daughters generally concur in their ideals, although practices differ.

The emphasis on security—and trust—is certainly prudent under the conditions of Palestinian refugee camp existence but probably holds for other communities in Palestinian society as well. If kinship is considered in the wider framework of an ideology and practice of "sameness," kin marriages may often offer both mothers and daughters enhanced security, family roles, and social meaning (symbolic capital) as well as preserving or producing such symbolic capital for fathers and male kin. This broad generalization should not be read, however, as negating the conflicts and contradictions among family members that are features of actual marriage decisions and arrangements; accounts of girls married against their will to cousins are not infrequent (see Tuastad 1997, 111).

Cousins and Citizens

Palestinian women and men seeking marriage partners—and their mothers, fathers, and other kin members who participate in marriage arrangements—do not contemplate marrying kin because they are bound by normative rules of kinship. Indeed, it would be a gross simplification to say that kin marriages directly flow from the perceived benefits of such marriages because marriage decisions are not necessarily taken in so instrumental a fashion. Nonetheless, the persistence of kin marriage and the prominence of kin and family relations in Palestinian society point to the continued and active importance of a "kinship universe" (Holy 1989, 114), where both domestic and public activities are played out and where social and political identities and meanings are constituted. In the Palestinian context, kinship and place are intertwined in the symbolic economies that produce these identities and where women and men act to realize their hopes for security and better futures in marriage, reproduction and family life. The fact that symbolic economies of kinship are situated locally, however, does not mean that they do not also operate in national (and even transnational) space (see Hilal's chapter in this volume).

The strong operation of kin relations in public life has sometimes been attributed to the weakness of the public sphere and public institutions. In the Arab region, weak and unresponsive states offer scant room for public action, welfare, national identity, or citizen's rights. In the Palestinian case the absence of a state altogether—and the presence of a colonial power—makes the kinship universe an arena for practical action, albeit not uniformly in all places and periods. Israeli military occupation, for example, heightened the

need for family and kinship solidarities for survival and mobility in circumstances dominated by lack of rights and insecurity. Resistance to that occupation, however, generated new collectivities. The flourishing of national
resistance in the form of mass grassroots movements (of students, women,
workers) in the 1980s created new arenas of public activity, interaction and
solidarity, thus diminishing some of the functions of the kin universe. In the
current period of interim Palestinian rule, the situation may be reversed.

Two examples from the different periods are instructive. In the early
1980s, the Israeli military government sponsored the creation of Village
Leagues in the West Bank in an attempt to establish a "native pillar" (Tamari
1989, 603) to thwart rising Palestinian nationalism. The model was simple: re-
actionary peasants, led by family, clan, and village leaders, could be mobilized
against urban-based (and modern) nationalists. The Israeli military government empowered the Village Leagues to grant vital permits and licenses and
funded offices and a newspaper, clearly expecting a "traditional" system of patronage based on kin and rural community ties to function to stem the tide of
nationalist feeling and activity. The most successful Village League, the Hebron organization, was in fact based in a large clan, the Dudin clan, but in
general the Village League project foundered as only the socially marginal,
and even criminal, elements—people who fell outside the moral universe of
kinship and kin solidarities—operated within its organized orbit. When the
first Palestinian intifada erupted in 1987, West Bank villages were the sites of
collective and sustained nationalist resistance, notably including the public
repudiation of members of the Village Leagues. In the interim period, the
Palestinian Authority's own search for political legitimation included an attempt to revive "clan and kin networks" (Jad et al. 2000a, 151), including the
establishment of a presidential office for clan affairs. Opposition to such practices as inhibiting the development of citizens' rights was difficult to mount,
especially because the Palestinian Authority also represented the national
project and a nation struggling to be born.

The fragmentation and the cantonization and closure of the intifada period reinforce the importance of the kinship universe for family and individual survival and welfare but weaken other spheres of public action. However,
kin and family ties are also under threat: restrictions on mobility and siege
conditions negatively affect the ability to mobilize kin and social networks
across localities. One Israeli journalist has observed that "the level of connec-

tion between West Bank cities and villages is fast approaching that of 150 years ago" (Hass 2003, 185).

How do kin and family affiliations relate to contemporary projects of Palestinian nation and state building? Does a "republic of cousins" necessarily hinder the emergence of a "republic of citizens"? Commenting on Palestinian initiatives for reform in the dire circumstances of September 2002—most prominently the Israeli reoccupation of West Bank cities and the closure and siege of all Palestinian communities—one Israeli commentator laid the blame for problems of Palestinian democratization squarely on the Palestinian family, particularly on kin relations and patterns of kin marriage. Writing in the Israeli newspaper *Ha'aretz*, Rubinstein alleged:

> Most Palestinian intellectuals involved in political affairs agree that the main problem hindering development of Palestinian democracy is the traditional nature of society in the West Bank and Gaza. It is a society with tribal elements, where extended family (the hamula, or clan) still represents the main focus of power. Around 50 percent of marriages in Palestinian society, for example, are still within the clan (a substantial portion are marriages between cousins and add to that another 20 percent or so which are marriages arranged by the family). In other words, the Palestinian family denies the individual the most important right of his life—and that is to choose his mate. (2002, 6)

This facile analysis would be easy to dismiss, with its unreflective condemnation of Palestinian society as traditional, Palestinian marriages as backward, and Palestinian families as unequivocally authoritarian, exercising family power against individual freedom and "choice." For example, as this chapter shows, notions of "choice" both are problematic and can be conjoined with kin marriage. However, it is not only the anonymous Palestinian experts consulted by Rubinstein who deploy a tradition/modernization binary to condemn kin marriage; it is echoed in other forms of Palestinian, Arab, and international discourse. Opening a March 2005 conference on "Gender, Displacement, Memory and Agency" on behalf of Palestinian Authority President Mahmoud Abbas, spokesman Ahmed Abdul Rahman called for the participants to address and fight backward practices, identifying these as early marriage and marriage to relatives.[29] In the analysis of the Palestinian Central Bureau of Statistics, marriage to relatives is a negative phenomenon "usually under the control of dominant cultural traditions where women are sometimes forced to marry a relative in order to protect social relations and family fortunes" (PCBS 2002a, 28).

There may well be a genuine concern on the part of Palestinian officials about the concrete issues of birth defects or women forced into unwanted marriages with relatives—and indeed PCBS expresses both concerns—but one senses that a more overriding issue is the perceived imperative of modernizing or remaking Palestinian families in line with the national project of state-building.

A tendency to blame the family for deficiencies in Arab democracy can also be found in the Arab Human Development Report for 2004, which focuses, often with insight and passion, on freedom in the Arab world. Describing the crisis on Arab political structures and the lack of freedom in the Arab world, the Report affirms that "the family, the primary unit of Arab society, is based on clannism, which implants submission and is considered the enemy of personal independence, intellectual daring, and the flowering of a unique and authentic human entity" (UNDP 2005, 17).

But is it really families and kin networks that block Palestinian and Arab democracy?

In the summer of 2002, as unemployment reached about 70 percent in the Gaza Strip (World Bank 2002b), unemployed workers staged a series of spontaneous protests of a scale and kind not previously seen in Palestine, addressed largely to the Palestinian Authority. The message was simply hunger; "Only greens and a dry piece of bread" read one slogan. Among the demands for work and bread was a demand of a different caliber: the workers demanded that the Palestinian Authority exempt their children from school and university fees ("Workers of the Strip" 2002, 7). As the results of the IWS survey demonstrate, Palestinian parents clearly see education of male and female children as both a family imperative and a national right; unemployed work-

29. His remarks were made at the opening session of the conference, sponsored by Al Quds University, the Ministry of Women's Affairs, and York University, which took place 4–6 March 2005 in Ramallah.

ers in Gaza were demanding of their national authority not solely individual rights, but rights embedded both in the family and in notions of national entitlement. The assertion of these rights in one of the most difficult and dark periods in Palestinian history is heartening. In the shadow of occupation and siege, and in light of its internal failures and limited powers, the Palestinian quasi-state may be unable to provide basic security to its "citizens," straining family networks to the breaking point; it is here, however, that any project to "improve" family life must begin. If neo-Rousseauians were to envision a Palestinian republic based on a social contract of citizens, they would do well first to understand the dynamics of a "republic of cousins" and the real needs of its citizens for security and mobility, rather than attempt to manipulate the domain of kinship through encouraging clan politics, as happened in the interim period, or to erase it by polarizing society into modernizing individuals against a "traditional" kinship universe.

3

SIX FAMILIES

Survival and Mobility in Times of Crisis

Lamis Abu Nahleh

Palestinian families are currently experiencing the most serious threat to their existence since the *Nakba* of 1948. The warlike conditions, the prolonged curfews, and the internal and external closures all have created a sustained multidimensional crisis in Palestinian society. One apparent outcome is the severe setback in the economy resulting in either a total loss of or a sharp reduction in household income, creating widespread poverty. The Israeli apartheid policy of cantonization and siege has ripped apart the social fabric of Palestinian society, leaving families more and more dependent on their dwindling resources and frequently cutting them off from potential support coming from kin and social networks. Furthermore, continuous armed assaults on the national leadership and civilians have triggered fear for their safety and that of their homes. Palestinian families thus have to struggle not only to secure their daily livelihoods but to avoid the real threats to their lives.

This chapter examines the lives, living conditions, and strategies of Palestinian families and individuals coping under increasingly abnormal conditions through the narratives of six families in the Ramallah district and in Jerusalem. The focus is on investigating the social, psychological, and material strategies of families and individual members in the context of the daily stresses created by continuing Israeli military occupation and reinvasions and the absence of needed social and material support—how they cope with and negotiate the changes in education, marriage, employment, roles, responsibilities, and relations across age and gender, and how they view their future.

I start out by giving a brief description of how Palestinian daily life has been affected by Israeli policies and military actions in the Palestinian Occupied Territories and setting the current political, social, and economic scene in which Palestinian households and families function and manage their lives, with a focus on how daily life has been affected by Israel's regime of closure and siege. An analysis of the social history of six Palestinian families will follow. The families were interviewed in the summer of 2002, with a view to understanding how their endeavors to adopt and develop strategies for survival and mobility are inevitably linked to assuming different forms of resistance against the Israeli occupation policies restricting their everyday lives.

Palestinian Families in Crisis

It has become clear with time that the crisis facing Palestinian families is not transitory. It did not begin with the outbreak of the second Palestinian intifada on 29 September 2000; rather, the intifada was a consequence of the profound inequalities and apartheid policies rooted in the Oslo years and before, as well as a result of the loss of a horizon of political hope for a solution that meets minimum Palestinian requirements for a viable state. The continuance of this crisis results from the Israeli political and military leadership's sustained commitment to a "Greater Israel." There is also a parallel and very deep crisis in the Palestinian national project. One analysis of the present Palestinian predicament, based on a close reading of Israeli strategic thinking, holds that Palestinians, as long as they remain steadfast in their minimum demands for sovereignty and a viable state, can expect to endure the continuation of the current policy of rapid cantonization, siege, and assault on the national leadership and national institutions.

As noted by Kuttab in this volume, the quality of life and living conditions of Palestinians have not improved, as was expected, but have rather steadily deteriorated. Individuals, families, and communities have experienced economic decline and threats to their personal safety and property through a set of policies designed to pauperize the Palestinians and expand the Jewish presence on their land. In particular, from the signing of the Oslo accords until the outbreak of the second intifada, Israeli settlement activity in the West Bank, the Gaza Strip, and East Jerusalem increased by 52 percent, and the number of settlers rose from 261,000 to 373,000. This is the fastest rate of settlement growth since the Palestinian lands were occupied by Israel in 1967 (Usher 2003, 22). Israeli settlement building has been accomplished by the confiscation of thousands of *dunums* of private and public land; the uprooting of olive, citrus, and other orchards; and the bulldozing of agricultural fields and demolition of homes.

Reinvasion and Destruction

On 29 March 2002, the Israeli army invaded the West Bank and reoccupied all the towns and camps and most villages controlled by the Palestinian National Authority. Entire Palestinian communities were placed under strict and complete curfew. The Israeli army's actions showed a pattern of systematic destruction and vandalism: Palestinian infrastructure was massively damaged; documents, computers, and other equipment were deliberately confiscated or destroyed; and databases and records were irrevocably destroyed.[1] Serious damage and destruction was inflicted on roads, electric poles, water pipes, and private housing, and private and public vehicles were deliberately smashed by Israeli tanks. All sorts of institutions were targeted. Hospitals, clinics, and ambulances were either attacked or completely destroyed; the Ministry of Health medical team was denied access to the city of Qalqilya to vaccinate children (Palestine Monitor 2004). Teachers' and students' lived daily reality was characterized by serious physical difficulties, traumatic events, and humiliation (Giacaman et al. 2002). According to Peter Hansen, Commissioner General of UNRWA, "scores of schools have been used as detention centers, almost 200 have been damaged by gunfire, and 170 students have been arrested" (UNRWA 2003, 4).

Collective Punishment: Assassinations and Home Demolitions

The Israeli policies carried out in the Occupied Palestinian Territories are a deliberate outcome of the strategy of collective punishment, intended to "hit them hard . . . hurt them" and inflict damage and destruction to the whole population (Cook 2004, 19–22). Forms of violence of this sort include extrajudicial "targeted" assassinations in crowded neighborhoods, leading to the death or injury of civilians. Attacks on private homes and work sites resulted in the total destruction of thousands of homes. In the Gaza Strip 661 homes

---

1. For details on the institutional damage caused by the Israeli invasion, see Palestinian NGO Emergency Initiative in Jerusalem (2002a and b).

were destroyed in March and April 2002 (Palestine Monitor 2004). Israeli attacks on houses and homes are attacks on human dignity and violations of human privacy in contravention of international conventions and human rights laws requiring the protection of human life in war conditions. A regular practice of the Israeli army is invading neighborhoods in search of "wanted persons." During the attack, curfew is imposed on the community, and the army conducts searches, accompanied by shooting live ammunition. Even wedding halls, while weddings are in progress, undergo searches and assault.[2]

Immobilizing Palestinians Through Curfews, Checkpoints, and Closures

As forms of collective punishment, curfews, checkpoints, and closures result in the immobilization of Palestinian individuals, families, and whole communities. Curfews put Palestinian daily life on hold and interfere in the planning of social events. Weddings, funerals, and even giving birth or going to the hospital have sometimes to wait until curfew is lifted for a few hours. However, people create their resistance strategies. Shadi Khoury, from Ramallah, was married in July 2002, when the town was under sustained curfew; when it would be lifted or for how long was in the realm of the unknown. His invitation to the wedding and the reception following it was a conventional one. However, it bore evidence of the abnormality and unpredictability of the situation: several alternative dates were handwritten on the outside of the envelope, with the statement, "Due to the current situation, the wedding will be held Saturday, Sunday, or Monday at 11:40 noon. For clarification, call phone number 2950000." Shadi's mother felt victorious; as she said to me, "Thank God. The wedding went very well. We accomplished all the usual rituals and celebrations in two hours."

The Israeli policy of "closures," another expression of collective punish-

---

2. In the last two weeks of May 2004 alone, the Israeli army invaded several neighborhoods in Ramallah-al-Bira at different times. In two incidents, they attacked wedding halls, al-Zayn al-Kubra Hall in Ramallah and Badran Halls in al-Bira, while the wedding party was underway. In the latter case they arrested the groom. The incursion disrupted the wedding ceremony, causing fear and anxiety for the nearby families and preventing several residents of the neighborhood and the wedding guests from returning to their homes before midnight; some had to spend the night away from their homes.

ment, was introduced a few months before the Oslo accords were signed; however, it was systematically and steadily intensified and tightened during the years of the second intifada. Currently, hundreds of military checkpoints block Palestinian mobility in the occupied territories. Movement between the occupied territories and Israel is almost totally banned; it is allowed only for restricted categories of people such as medical personnel, employees of diplomatic or international institutions, workers, and business people, all of whom are required to obtain a permit from the Israeli authorities. However, even permit holders may or may not pass, depending on the political climate or the mood of the soldiers guarding the checkpoints; permits can be declared invalid without warning.

Cantonizing the West Bank Through the Separation Wall and Bypass Roads

Land and people are separated by what one writer termed "a web of bypass roads and military zones" that link Israeli settlements and integrate them into Israel proper. Prior to the second intifada, these served to separate the seven hundred Palestinian towns and villages from each other and to curb any contiguous rural and urban development between them. After the second intifada erupted, roadblocks, settlements, and "outposts" became Israel's new military borders, not only formalizing the separation of the Gaza Strip from the West Bank and East Jerusalem, but also progressively isolating each Palestinian area from its neighbor" (Usher 2003, 22). An Israeli journalist has noted, "the level of connection between West Bank cities and villages is fast approaching that of 150 years ago" (Hass 2003, 185). The construction of the Wall, which includes trenches, sniper posts, patrol roads, and barbed wire, has resulted in the confiscation of even more agricultural land, destroying even more houses, and further tightening the noose on the already besieged Palestinian towns and villages. In the process, it is breaking the social fabric of Palestinian society and separating communities and families from each other, from their homes and land, and from the needed daily services. Palestinian inhabitants of the areas inside and around the Wall cannot get in and out of their villages without a permit; even with a permit, they may be denied entrance if they arrive when the gate is closed by the Israeli soldiers.

Conducting Research under Occupation and War Conditions

This chapter presents an analysis of the lives of six Palestinian families under the sustained crisis resulting from the ongoing Israeli assault on Palestinian society. Analysis is based on a set of narratives and histories recorded with six families in the Ramallah area and East Jerusalem. The family narratives and histories were written not only based on the factual accounts given by the family members, but also on their own views and analyses of their life conditions, the motives behind their acts, and their perceptions of their own status and conditions and that of other family members. This ethnographic study of the families draws on findings of a community-based household survey conducted in 1999 in the West Bank (including East Jerusalem) and the Gaza Strip, as described in the introduction to this volume. Six researchers (five females and one male) participated in the fieldwork carried out from June 2002 to March 2003. The researchers conducted multiple meetings with various female and male household (and family) members ranging in age from thirteen to seventy-seven years. The participants were given the space to narrate and analyze their family histories, experiences, and individual acts. All the meetings were taped, and the outputs were written by the researchers in the form of family histories in the words of the narrators themselves.[3]

Originally, the purpose of this ethnographic study was to investigate in depth some of the issues uncovered by the community-based household survey in order to arrive at a more thorough understanding of the internal dynamics of Palestinian households in the surveyed communities. With the deteriorating political situation and the increasing difficulty in leading a normal daily life, however, the focus and the scope of the study were modified.

3. Here, I wish to acknowledge the lengthy engagement and serious efforts of the five researchers, Nida' Abu Awwad, Riham Barghouti, Rula Abu Duhou, Lina Mi'ari and Yasser Shalabi, who worked with me as a team from spring 2002, when fieldwork started, through spring 2004 when the narratives were completed. This part of the chapter is largely based on the collective work we did as a team. With guidance and supervision from the IWS, they conducted the fieldwork (interviews, recordings, and transcription); they first wrote the findings in report form and then composed the family narratives. It is to be acknowledged here that their contribution to the chapter was not limited to description and narration of the family life events and characters. They also provided insightful points that enriched the analysis. To all of them, I extend my gratitude and appreciation.

The Israeli occupation policies and measures taken against the Palestinian people outlined in the first section of this chapter left their imprint on the research design because the effects of the war conditions and strict closures and restrictions on the life of families could not possibly be overlooked. Although the researchers continued to investigate the issues raised in the survey, the focus shifted to examining them in the context of war and to learning about the families' experiences of living under war conditions. However, severe restrictions on mobility and repeated curfews meant that the range of communities and households to be covered had to be compromised. The seven households chosen for the study were located in communities within a range of twenty to thirty kilometers. As a result, the selected households do not constitute a representative sample from which generalizable statements can be drawn; the purpose here is to attempt to understand the changes in family dynamics and relations in the context of war. Nevertheless, the selection of households considered social class, locale, and household composition and variation in the family's experience of the war; one of the households was in a village, two were in the city, one was in a small town, one was in a refugee camp, and one was in the city of East Jerusalem. The urban and camp households experienced the Israeli invasion and lived for over six months under long periods of curfew imposed by the Israeli military forces on the whole community. However, the households from the small town and village were isolated in their own villages and cut off from work, schools, and medical and other essential services (like water and sanitation) because of strict closures that separated them from the closest city. The Jerusalem household, although not exposed to curfews or armed attacks, was equally affected by the Israeli occupation policies before and during the reinvasion of West Bank cities and towns in the spring of 2002.

Unlike researchers in most parts of the world, the Palestinian researchers faced the same realities as the people they interviewed, and they conducted the research under extremely unusual conditions. Reaching the families, interruption of visits, and postponement of appointments were the simplest difficulties they faced. Like all other Palestinians with no exception, the researchers had to seize the minimal space for the least possible normal life left to them by the military checkposts and roadblocks, long-term and short-term curfews and invasions, military assaults on people and buildings, house-demolitions, assassinations, all committed on a daily basis by the Israeli

Occupation forces against the Palestinians whether living in cities, villages, or refugee camps. Space, time, and location acquired different meanings and associations. One researcher described her experience traveling to visit the family: "I had to spend two hours in the car, at military roadblocks and closures, even though I carry an Israeli identity card, being born in Haifa. Travel time reflects the new geopolitical reality lived by the Palestinians in the 1967 occupied territories" (Lina Mi'ari).

Fieldwork started at a time when the towns and refugee camps were placed under long periods of curfew and siege. On the average, curfews were lifted for a few hours every three or four days, a period used by people to get basic food staples and run urgent errands; some went to work for a few hours during the lifting of the curfew if the worksite was within their area of residence. In the case of the researchers, some managed to drive surreptitiously to the families' homes to conduct the meetings. In one case, the family was generous enough to welcome the researcher to stay over for a few days; hosting relatives, friends, or even strangers was not unique to this family in the prevailing circumstances. Although staying with the family was in one way inconvenient to the researcher, it facilitated participatory observation. Another researcher's connection with the family was interrupted for over two weeks because the village, the location of the household, suffered the killing of one of its young men. Another researcher had to set appointments in the wasted time between curfew time and the lifting of the curfew. However, the family's financial and other difficulties and the daily engagements of the housewife, compounded by actions by the Israeli army, stood in the way of meeting with the family several times.

> While sometimes, when we, who live in the city, "enjoyed" some sort of mobility and freedom for a few hours, the camp where Saber's and Maryam's family live was closed. It was difficult to make appointments with them. No phone could rescue me. . . . I had to visit the family hoping to luck out. . . . Saber utilizes all the hours of the lifting of the curfew to go to the market to work as a porter. . . . Meetings with Maryam also often failed either due to an emergency like getting the [UNRWA] food rations. (Rula Abu Duhou)

Conflict between the research requirements and the safety and survival of the researcher and her family forced her to change the selected family twice.

The first family she chose to work with lived on the opposite end of the town where she lived. However, curfew and total closure of that neighborhood made it impossible to reach the family house. A family that lived in a closer part of town was chosen, yet working with this family failed on the first meeting. Half an hour into the meeting, she received news that Israeli soldiers had broken into her grandmother's house. She had to call off the interview to go home to check on her grandmother, whom she had left alone. On the way home she had to go through some side roads to avoid the soldiers—after all, she was breaking the curfew. When she reached home, she found her grandmother shaking from fear and worry. The soldiers had come to the house and asked for her ID. To get their minds off the subject, she accompanied her grandmother on a visit to the neighbor, Umm Saleh. During this visit Umm Saleh told stories of her family suffering from the nightly bombings and the death of her husband, who had left her with ten children. The researcher writes, "Umm Saleh's story was compelling . . . the reality of the curfew and siege of Ramallah entailed that the family met one of the most important criteria. . . . I could actually conduct all my meetings during the curfew and without fear for my grandmother's safety" (Riham Barghouti).

So far, family and war have been treated as two disconnected themes in the social sciences literature on the Arab region. A telling example is a recent volume, *The New Arab Family* (Hopkins 2003), a collection of studies of various family issues in Arab countries, some of which have recently experienced wars. However, the volume does not touch at all on the issue of war and its effect on the lives and living conditions of the family. A notable exception consists of six case studies presented at a meeting convened by the United Nations organization ESCWA in October 2003, showing the impact of war on the family unit in Arab countries. In general, based on quantitative and qualitative data, the cases present a range of visible effects of war and conflicts on families, including suffering; the death, imprisonment, or disappearance of family members; changes in gender roles; the burden placed on women; changes in social and economic structures; and reproduction, health, education, and domestic violence[4] (ESCWA Center For Women, 2003).

4. Five case studies were presented at the Arab Preparatory Meeting for the Ten Year Review of the International Year of the Family (IYF) 1994 + 10, held at ESCWA Center for Women, Beirut, 7–9 October 2003. The case studies addressed the impact of occupation, war,

On the regional and international levels, studies examining the impact of war and occupation are not different from the kinds referred to above. Theoretical and/or empirical studies conducted from a gender, sociological-anthropological perspective are to my knowledge nonexistent.

What is hoped from the discussion and analysis of the life and living conditions of six families in the following section is to contribute a new perspective for understanding family dynamics, particularly the terms by which men and women, young and old, children and the elderly negotiate the patriarchal contract both in the family and the community, whether in relation to their social or to their political lives.[5]

Six Families: Resistance, Survival, and Mobility

Umm Saleh's Household (originally written by Riham Barghouti)

Umm Saleh's family suffered material damage and psychological trauma, aggravated by the loss of the family patriarch. To them, what appears to be more crucial than the struggle for survival after the death of the father is the social and gender dynamics involved in coping with his absence, as the patriarch provided security and protection. The mother and the children miss the presence of a "man in the house." Two of the children take on agency in negotiating gender roles and extended kin relations and boundaries. Sawsan, the seventeen-year-old girl, resists the extended family interference in her family's affairs and her own personal matters as well as the paternal attempts of her younger brother to control her and her sisters' behavior. Saleh, who is only thirteen years old and the only boy, struggles to fill the shoes of his father and tries to assume responsibility for his mother and sisters.

---

and conflict on the conditions of Arab families from Iraq, Kuwait, Lebanon, Palestine, Sudan, and Yemen.

5. The family narratives, discussed in the following section, were originally written in Arabic, except for one, that of Umm Salem's household, which was written in English. The quotes were extracted from these narratives, which the authors recorded and transcribed; for the purpose of this chapter, I translated the quotes into English and extracted pieces from the original narratives. The Arabic family narratives were thoroughly reviewed by Jamil Hilal, to whom I extend my sincere gratitude for the insightful comments that enriched the analysis here. Currently, the six family narratives are being prepared for publication in an Arabic volume.

Umm Saleh and her family live in the city of al-Bira, a few kilometers from the Israeli settlement of Psagot,[6] illegally built on the opposite hill in the city. The forty-year-old widow cares for seven children: six girls (Sawsan, 17; Tala, 15; Fadwa, 11; Nawal, 7; Dana, 5; Dunia, 4) and 1 boy, Saleh, 13. Jamil, Umm Saleh's husband, was only in his early forties when he died on 31 October 2000, one month after the start of the second intifada. Umm Saleh's family barely had time to grieve his loss when they were trapped in a violent armed confrontation between the Israeli army and settlers on one side and the Palestinian fighters located in Umm Saleh's neighborhood on the other. Although the Palestinian shooting was ineffective, the Israeli soldiers and settlers attacked the neighborhood with guns and heavy artillery, including tank missiles. As a result, the windows of the whole house were shattered and Umm Saleh had to replace them several times, the inside walls were cracked, leakage from the bullet-ridden water-tank deprived the family of running water for several days, and the bullet-ridden washing machine went out of order. Although for her these material losses were considerable, the accounts she and her children gave were of deep psychological trauma, especially because the violent attacks came a few days after the death of her husband. Umm Saleh had to be the father and the mother at the same time; all she hoped for was for her children to survive.

> We were going to prepare dinner. This was seventeen days after [Jamil's death] and the first night we spent alone at home, but death is God's willing. The first missile struck! I had my children all crowded in this room. Then the second missile, I thought, that's it; my children are gone. The electricity was cut off. I started feeling the mouths of my children to see if they were breathing. I said thank God; all but the children. I haven't seen any worse than this. Tala became paralyzed. Fadwa would start screaming like she was insane. I told her, "hold her tight." Fadwa said, crying hysterically, "I now like you, sister. I didn't like you before." I had the younger girls, one on my chest, one on my arm, and one in my lap. The young men from the neighborhood came . . . took us to the neighbors. We all started crying hysterically. Even Saleh, the boy, started crying like women.

6. Psagot is an Israeli colony of around one thousand colonists that was illegally built in 1981 on Palestinian land. The closest Palestinian house is ten meters away from the colony.

This was the first violent night Umm Saleh's family experienced, but it was not the only one. Feeling unsafe in her home, Umm Saleh and her children slept for several days in the basement of a neighbor's house or at her family's home in Qalandia camp and had to come back to their house in the mornings to pursue their daily activities, housework, and school, until one day she decided no more of the moving in and out. The effects of this crisis reflected heavily on the children: one of the younger girls started bed-wetting again; two of them had paralysis fits and loss of appetite for which they had to undergo treatment at the Center for the Victims of Torture and at a private psychiatrist. Sawsan, fifteen at the time, describes her experience:

> I would get up. My sides would be aching. I couldn't move. It would make me cry. I had to take tranquilizers to go to sleep. I almost had a total nervous breakdown. I used to read the Qur'an at night. Then sometimes the shooting would stop. . . . All night I would not get a wink of sleep. How were you supposed to function in school? When the shooting would begin, Tala would turn pale yellow and be paralyzed. . . . Fadwa would totally break down. It was so bad for her; she needed to get see a counselor. . . . I hope to God that those days are never repeated.

Although Jamil died of a heart attack, Umm Saleh and the children strongly believe that it was precipitated by his fear of losing his only son to an Israeli bullet. News about Saleh's going to the checkpoint to engage in rock throwing at the soldiers traveled around among relatives until it reached his parents. About this incident, which she believed caused her husband's death Umm Saleh says:

> Jamil died on the 31st of October. There was nothing wrong with him, he was working normally—he had projects he was working on. The boy, our only son, went to the *mahsoum* [checkpoint]. Usually Saleh doesn't go out. My sister called me and said "while my husband was coming home from work he saw Saleh at the City Inn." I told Jamil and he said, *"Khalas hada al walad rah*—The boy is gone—we will find him in some hospital."

Umm Saleh and her husband rushed to the *mahsoum*,[7] as she calls it, looking for their son. They spent two hours there under the threat of heavy shooting from jeeps and tanks before they could came back home with the son. According to Saleh, he was there because he wanted to write an essay about "stone throwing at the City Inn checkpoint." (These are the excuses some children give to their parents, if their parents think they are too young to confront the soldiers.) That night Jamil had a heart attack, and he died the next day. After his father's death, Saleh had to take a summer job at such an early age to help provide for the family. Umm Saleh's real motivation, however, was not the income but rather to keep him off the streets and away from confrontations with the Israeli army.

The experience of fear that one will lose one's child is not unique to Umm Saleh and her husband because their son is an only son. On the contrary, it is a common worry among Palestinian parents, so contrary to the mythical image that is propagated by Israeli and western media, namely that Palestinian mothers send their children to be killed by Israeli soldiers. In general, Palestinian parents, and particularly mothers, live in constant fear of losing their children. They often cannot prevent their children from engaging in unarmed clashes with the Israeli soldiers, but they are always on the alert, ready to rush to the confrontation site to bring their children back home. It has been well-documented that 85 percent of Palestinian children who have been killed by the Israeli army have not been engaged in clashes.[8]

What is significant about Umm Saleh's family is the way they coped with

7. The word *mahsoum* is the Hebrew word for checkpoint, which has become part of people's daily language. This checkpoint was located in al-Bira near the City Inn; in an area close by, there is an Israeli settlement illegally constructed on Palestinian land and the Israeli military and civil administration headquarters, both known as Beit El. When Palestinians (young and old, males and females) go on demonstrations protesting the Israeli occupation and its measures, they usually head toward the closest checkpoint in their area, the City Inn checkpoint in the case of Ramallah and al-Bira. There Palestinian young men engage in rock throwing, and the Israeli armed soldiers shoot back at them with live and rubber bullets, tear gas grenades, and tank grenades. However, most often the Israeli army initiates the confrontation by shooting at the unarmed demonstrators long before they get close to the checkpoint. A few kilometers to the east lies the Israeli settlement of Psagot.

8. See Cook, Hanieh, and Kay 2004.

the loss of their provider in such difficult and risky circumstances. Umm Saleh and her children felt that they had not lost Jamil as their main provider as much as they had lost him as their main source of social support, protection, and independence.

Umm Saleh expresses the burden of his absence saying, "When there was a man in the house we were never scared of the shooting. Even though he could not do anything we felt more secure with him around." Sawsan also misses his support and encouragement: "If my father hadn't died, all that happened afterwards would not have mattered. He used to take us out on the balcony when there was shooting and tell us to look and not get scared." Of all the family members, the girls felt the emotional loss of their father the most. Unlike the general stereotype of Arab fathers as patriarchs who exercise authority and control, Abu Saleh was described by his daughters as an example of a compassionate, loving, and caring father. According to Umm Saleh, he loved children and wanted to fill the house with them. He never regretted having girls; he named every one of them, and when each was born he would distribute a lot of chocolate such that the nurses at the hospital would think that the newborn baby was his first child. Each of the girls thinks she was his favorite. Sawsan comments:

> When they [her sisters] hit me my father would scold them. . . . Even when Saleh and I used to fight, my father would side with me. You would think that because my father had eight girls[9] and one boy he would side with the boy, but not my father. My father used to like me the most. I used to make him coffee and spoil him.

Although the extended family is often recognized for the social and economic support it provides, it can also be a source of conflict and control. While during his life Abu Saleh established strong ties with extended family kin, his absence seems also to have created a space for kin interference, particularly in gender matters relevant to the girls, which apparently was previously nonexistent. It was not the mother, Umm Saleh, but Sawsan who was

9. Umm Saleh has two other girls who were married at the time of the fieldwork; also, she had a daughter who was killed in a car accident at the age of seven. That is why Sawsan counts eight girls instead of six.

the main agent in negotiating kinship boundaries. While alive, Abu Saleh had close ties established with his own family and with Umm Saleh's. He earned a good income and farmed the land around the house. He often supported both sides of the extended family with cash and domestic produce. His sister appreciated that he managed to send her family food and other supplies during the forty-day curfew imposed on Jalazon camp, where they live. Kin relations were reinforced when he married off two daughters, older than Sawsan, at an early age to two of his nephews. Following his death, these kin ties persisted and were expressed in the support given to Umm Saleh, particularly from her natal family, after his death and during the nightly violent attacks. Furthermore, her house often accommodates Jamil's sister, who is her daughter's mother-in-law, and the daughter and her husband, who, because of closures, cannot always return home in the camp after work. In fact, kin interference in Umm Saleh's family affairs came more from her natal family.

Umm Saleh and her children are religious and observe religious duties. Saleh, the only son, goes to a school run by the *awqaf* (religious endowments), and he likes it because "the school has an Islamic culture and there is a lot of emphasis on the Hadith of the Prophet." As a mother of orphans, Umm Saleh rejects the idea of engaging in paid work. She is burdened with raising seven young children; she states: "These are orphans. I must raise them well. I will get rewarded in the afterlife by God for this good deed." The religiosity of Umm Saleh's family helped them cope with Abu Saleh's death and with the fear and anxiety caused by the military assaults on their neighborhood. At the time of constant shooting and bombing, Sawsan, who almost had a nervous breakdown, used to read the Qur'an to calm herself and get some peace. Umm Saleh comments on how she coped with her husband's untimely death:

> It's amazing how strong the heart of a believer is. I am a patient woman. I kept reading the Qur'an and praying to God. I was shocked but I held on to my senses. His sister came, she went crazy—the whole neighborhood heard her screams. . . . I had lost everything, my husband, the father of my children, everything. But I was calmer than she was. What is one to do? God gives patience.

Umm Saleh's family, however, is neither conservatively nor fanatically religious. Sawsan perceives the difference between her family and her mother's father and brothers and rejects their blind conservatism, which they use to control her and her sisters. She complains about having to spend nights and days at her grandparents' or uncles' homes after the death of her father because she felt the pressure and the control exercised on her:

> My grandfather gives us lessons in morality and behavior. I hate it. He always repeats the same thing. If we weren't raised right then it would be fine, but we were raised right. . . . Uncle Nasir, the eldest of my uncles, he goes crazy over everything. If he sees a girl talking to a guy, just talking, is there anything wrong with that? It's normal, he goes crazy. He is jealous over his wife more than his daughters. They all have to wear full *shar'i* (Islamic dress) all the time. I can't stay in his house. I don't like his ways. Also, my uncle Ali always complains about the way we dress and us going out. He always seems to catch us going out.

Sawsan's uncles took the right to supervise her and her sisters' social behavior and were keen on getting Sawsan married even without her consent. At the age of fifteen, a next-door neighbor asked for her hand and she refused him. She complains, "My uncles were pressuring me. They promised to buy me stuff if I agreed. I couldn't stand the pressure that my family was putting on me. . . . I know my father would have supported me." At the end, Umm Saleh resolved the issue by refusing to force her daughter into a marriage she did not desire. But worse than that for Sawsan was being sexually harassed by one of her maternal uncles. However, for a teenager, she was courageous enough to inform her mother about the incident and instigate a family boycott of the immoral uncle.

> He harassed me several times. I stayed quiet after the first time and the second time, and then when he did it a third time I said enough. I told my mother. She went crazy. She told him, "my brother, I depended on you. I leave my girls with you because I think they are safe and you do this." She kicked him out of the house. We totally cut off our relations with this uncle.

To provide for her family after her husband's death, Umm Saleh depends on different sources of formal and informal assistance. Although her deceased husband had a business of his own and made a good income, neither one had saved for the future. She sold the car, which her husband used for work, and the status of the shop he owned was still pending, not having been sold. She has all her children in school free of charge and does not have rent to pay because the house she lives in is owned by her in-laws, and they have never claimed it. As a mother of orphans she is entitled to assistance from the Ministry of Social Affairs and from other sources, like *zakat* committees and charitable societies. However, she feels too proud to ask for the assistance.

It was never clear why Umm Saleh was neither open about how she managed financially with seven children nor interested in discussing the matter, and it was unethical to pressure her to do so. Her main concern was psychologically coping with her husband's loss and the violent events surrounding the time of his death. As a believer, she even thinks that God takes care of it: "God gave us these problems with the intifada, to help us get over Jamil's death. We were so devastated by Jamil's death but when we had all of these problems we had to deal with them."

A more important concern for her is the social upbringing and protection of the children, which she uses to justify not working for pay, in addition to her being unskilled and unaccustomed to working. Moreover, she is not convinced that she can do men's work to replace her husband in his workshop: "you need a man to take measurements of windows and walls; also a [male] subcontractor would not contract a woman to take a curtain-making project." For her the main reason for not working outside the house is supervising the children, particularly the girls. She explains:

> I really have no time to work outside. I have children and teenage girls . . . in a critical period and they need attention and supervision. My husband's shop is still unoccupied, and if I want I can use it to sell anything from it. But my problem if I work outside is that I will neglect my children and the girls. If I had given birth to boys it would not make a difference to me. But the girls are teenagers and require a lot of attention. You know it's difficult to leave the girls alone; a friend here, a friend there, you know. . . . I do not want to "lose" my girls. I am always there with my eyes wide open and barely can manage. I do not allow them to go anywhere. This is a difficult time.

Saleh also sees his sisters' behavior as one of his responsibilities. As the "man of the house," Saleh tried to assume several responsibilities, but he was too young to have his efforts recognized or appreciated: "I have to take care of my sisters. Make sure they don't argue or fight or upset each other. Except for Sawsan, we are always fighting. In the end, only my mother can resolve the differences between us."

Saleh's words were always apologetic, as if he felt unrecognized; on taking a summer job, he commented, "It's not because I am a boy. It's just that I was the one to find a job. I used to work with my father and now I work with my neighbor." In several instances, Umm Saleh's family members explained that the absence of Abu Saleh encouraged the Palestinian fighters to take their backyard as a base from which to shoot at the Israeli army and the soldiers. Saleh tried to turn them away but still felt unappreciated.

> Also, the men [Palestinian fighters] used to shoot from our house because there wasn't any man in the house. They used to take advantage of the fact that we were alone. I tried to scream at them once and tell them to go away but they would not listen to me. . . . When the house got shot at several times, we went to talk to the Tanzim [10] in the camp. They told us to find a house and that they would pay the rent, but they never came through. No one could stop those youth shooting from here. . . .

The only incident Saleh's family could not but appreciate was related to his courageous act in facing the Israeli soldiers. One of Saleh's important ventures on the path of assuming the role of the "man of the family" was facing the soldiers when they came to the house, especially when he ended up being taken as a human shield. In the words of a grown-up man who is not scared, he recounts the event:

> It's just that I am not scared. My sisters get scared of them and can't talk back to the soldiers. I don't know why they get scared. Like when there used to be shooting, all of them would get scared even though there was nothing to be scared of. It doesn't scare me. . . . [That day, the neighbor across the street]

---

10. Al-Tanzim is a regional branch of Fatah that took on the responsibility for order and discipline, and engaged in solving social and political disputes and conflicts in the community.

gave me the keys to the house in the morning.[11] At around four in the afternoon, I heard them trying to break down the garage door. I ran out and told them to stop because I had the keys. He [the soldier] told me to open the garage door and the other door and I did. Then the soldier put an M-16 to my head. He asked me if I was scared. I told him that I wasn't scared. He pulled me by the arm and went to my mother and took her ID. They told my mother that they wanted to take me with them. My mother told him, no, he is my only son. . . . They took me from house to house to get people's ID and they kept asking me about specific people. I made like I didn't know anything. When they asked about one particular guy over and over again, I told them that everyone knew that there was something mentally wrong with him, although there really isn't. They took me inside the jeep and showed me a map of the houses in the neighborhood. They said "this is your house, this is so and so's house . . ." I saw that all the houses had numbers on them and next to each one they had put the ID numbers of the household members and their telephone numbers. I told him that I was tired and I wanted to go home. I had been with them for almost two hours. He told me to go. I just went home.

In this adventure, not only did Saleh risk going around with the Israeli soldiers with an M-16 pointed to his head, but he also risked giving them wrong information to their inquiries. If by chance the soldiers had discovered that he had lied to them, he would not have escaped being arrested, seriously injured, or possibly even killed. But that is how a "real man" would behave.

Umm Nathem's Household: Three Sons and Loss of Work (originally written by Nida' Abu Awwad)

Like many Palestinian families, Umm Nathem's family had been hard hit by the current intifada conditions, particularly those resulting from the Israeli policy of closures. After the family picked up the pieces following the death of the head of the household, Abu Nathem, which coincided with the first in-

---

11. A common practice of the Israeli army is breaking into houses using explosives to open the outside door when the residents are away. To avoid damage to their houses, Palestinian leave the house key with the neighbors when they plan to be away overnight.

tifada (late 1980s), accumulated resources, and started investment in construction and marriage arrangements, three of the sons lost their jobs in Israel and joined the ranks of the unemployed. The eldest son suffered the male-breadwinner's crisis while the eldest daughter had to bear the ramifications of the sharp decline in the household income while keeping up with providing for two households.

Umm Nathem lives with her family in a small town eight kilometers to the north of Ramallah. Her husband died in 1990, leaving her with nine children, the eldest nineteen and the youngest less than a year. During his sickness, which coincided with the first intifada, Abu Nathem had to sell his business partly because of the difficult economic conditions of the intifada and partly because of his ill health. Selling the business was necessary in order to provide for the family and to pay for medical expenses (although they were partly covered by UNRWA). When he died, Nathem, the eldest son, nineteen at the time, had already withdrawn from school to work to help his sick father. The eldest daughter, Suhaila, seventeen at the time, had to quit school, because even the free UNRWA education was beyond the family's means. Her labor was needed, so she had to seek low-paying work at a sewing workshop; she was unskilled and was hired as a trainee. Umm Nathem justifies withdrawing Suhaila from school: "then, we had no provider and all the income we earned was insufficient to meet the household needs." She herself was both unskilled and burdened with care for the children and the housework, which did not allow her to work for pay. However, she carried out different kinds of home production, baking *taboun* bread, cultivating the house garden, and raising some chickens and a goat. The family thus had to make ends meet depending on multiple resources: Nathem's income, Suhaila's low pay, home subsistence, and irregular assistance in cash and produce from Umm Nathem's natal family, who lives in Jericho. In addition, as a registered refugee family, they were entitled to UNRWA rations, free education for the girls, and some medical coverage. As the mother of orphans, Umm Nathem received a monthly allowance from the *zakat* committee, but only for the youngest of her children. However, although her family can be classified as a hardship case, she was denied assistance from the PNA Ministry of Social Affairs because she had "an able-bodied male." In the meantime, two of her daughters got married after completing two years of college education at an UNRWA institution. Benefiting from UNRWA free education, the girls were able to continue their schooling, while the boys, having work opportunities in Israel and doing poorly at school, quit and joined the labor force.

Between 1995 and 2000, Umm Nathem's household had five members working. Two of the sons, Zaidan and Hamdan, quit school and joined their older brother, Nathem, in work in Israel. Suhaila got a better-paying job in a factory, and Umm Nathem started a home-based child-care service for neighborhood families and pursued vegetable gardening and home production. The combined income enabled the family to live comfortably. The younger girls were more advantaged than Suhaila. Two of them got married after graduating from a two-year college. Today, the three youngest girls are all enrolled in UNRWA schools. Umm Nathem's intention is to get them to finish their education like her other daughters.

> I like it that all my children, boys and girls, get educated. I do not discriminate between a boy and a girl. It is true that our economic conditions did not allow Suhaila to stay at school. I try my best to give all my children education as long as they want it.

None of her sons completed school because they had no interest in education and had access to well-paying jobs. Except for Suhaila, all the other daughters got more education than their brothers. Although Umm Nathem believes in girls' education, she thinks that marriage provides them future security, while work becomes important for them only in case of need: "Education is important especially for girls. Even if she does not work after graduation, an educated girl would not need anyone if her living conditions turn bad. She can go out to work." However, would the youngest three girls continue their education if the household resources get more limited? Or would practical reality force them to quit school and seek work, like Suhaila?

Nathem built a career as a Caterpillar driver and was able to earn a good income and to be the primary provider for Umm Nathem's family. He got married and stayed in the family house until he had four children. He explains why he did not start his own household:

> My father died before I got married and I had to provide for the family. I could not afford to build my own house, and also I could not leave my mother and my siblings; I have to be a father to them. I broke up with my fi-

ancée, my maternal aunt's daughter, when she refused to live with my family
to avoid problems. When I broke up with my second fiancée upon her request and for the same reason, my mother immediately found me a bride.
She was afraid I would be affected psychologically and would decide to emigrate and leave her. One week after the second engagement broke up I was
already married.

Although Nathem's account of his marriage shows his inability to start his
own household, it also emphasizes the outcome of the dynamics of the patriarchal family system. Umm Nathem played a major role in keeping her eldest
son close to her. The family needs a male provider and the mother stops or
supports a marriage to accommodate her needs. Nathem was willing to respond to her needs and requests.

In the prosperous stage of their lives, Umm Nathem's family started thinking of the sons' future, their settling down in marriage and establishing their
own households in separate apartments, though attached to the mother's
house. All family members cooperated and pooled their resources to build a
flat on the second floor for Nathem and his family and to prepare for the marriage of his younger brothers. This scheme excluded Suhaila, who was close to
her thirties. She was expected to cooperate and pool her resources, but her future options were not considered, as if her life opportunity was already decided upon.

To build the flat, they borrowed money from relatives and bought construction materials on credit, counting on their multiple incomes for paying
back the debt. Kifaya, Nathem's wife, sold her gold (which was all she owned)
to cover some of the expenses. Suhaila continued to work and to contribute to
the well-being of the family. The one positive aspect in her condition is that
she was free to allocate her resources as she saw fit; what she "chose" to do was
to improve the house and furnishings, buy gifts for her nephews and nieces,
and travel to Jericho to visit her maternal relatives. By the year 2000, Nathem
and his family had moved into the apartment, which had electrical equipment (a refrigerator, a television, a satellite dish, and a microwave oven) and
one furnished bedroom. The rest of the flat had neither furniture nor heating.
The family started their post-intifada life cycle immersed in debt.

With the outbreak of the second intifada, Umm Nathem's family went through a harsh life cycle. All three sons lost their work in Israel. Nathem describes his condition:

> I lost my job and my family's income when it became impossible for me to reach my work inside the Green Line. I used to take the risk and sleep at work away from the family and go home only once a week; sometimes I came home only once a month. To go back to work or home I had to walk eight to ten kilometers in the mountains to get around the Israeli checkpoints. While at work, I was always tense, living at the edge of my nerves, especially when I heard that the Israeli army raided my area of residence or imposed a strict curfew. I was always worried that one of my brothers would be arrested. The most important reason is that the Israeli authorities refused to give me a pass to go to my work and refused to renew my magnetic card, without which it is impossible to travel from the West Bank to areas inside the Green Line.

Umm Nathem lost her source of income, too; no one could afford to send children to her child-care center. The family income dropped from NIS15,000 (around US$3,000) a month to less than a third of that. Suhaila, who earns a regular monthly salary, was left with the burden of providing for both families, her own and her brother's. UNRWA rations have gotten tighter, now that most of the children are over eighteen. They still cannot access other formal sources of assistance, like the grants from the Ministry of Social Affairs, because they do not meet the conditions for assistance. Closures and mobility restrictions imposed by the Israeli occupation deprived them of assistance from and communication with Umm Nathem's natal family. In the course of coping with their new status, the two families (Umm Nathem's and Nathem's) combined their resources. Umm Nathem comments:

> It is not possible that my children and I eat and drink while my son and his family are hungry or cannot get medical care because they have no money. So instead of making two meals, my daughter-in-law and I started cooking one on the same stove and sharing it to save the expenses. . . . We are better off [than Nathem's family], we can buy the household needs at the beginning of every month from Suhaila's salary. Buying things in large quantities is cheaper and this way we can give my son's family their own needs.

Although Umm Nathem is entitled to an inheritance from her natal family, she refuses to claim it. "I do not think of claiming my right to inheritance. . . . My relation with them [her natal family] is good and if they think of giving me my share, I will take it. Otherwise, all I want for them is their well-being."

Umm Nathem and the rest of the family members had to deploy all the different kinds of coping strategies people in harsh economic conditions and in crises would utilize, ranging from cutting down on food to giving gifts. Kifaya depended on her mother to give her money to buy gifts for her brothers or sisters. Umm Nathem, who cooks for twelve members, sees her priority as providing food, yet of lower quality and in smaller quantities.

> You know, we cannot live without food. But we had to change our style. We stopped cooking meat. Instead of two chickens, I use one and cut it into small pieces. Chicken is cheaper than meat. These days we depend more on vegetarian food like lentils and fried vegetables. We buy fruit less and only vegetables in season; it is cheaper this way.

Seeking other sources of income was a kind of disguised employment for Umm Nathem's unemployed sons. Nathem and his brother fall in the category of "day-to-day strugglers" identified by Sletten and Pedersen (2003). Not hopeful of finding a regular or well-paying job, they engaged in low-income informal enterprises. Nathem and Kifaya entered into partnership with someone from the town to raise two cows and make dairy products to sell. However, this attempt failed. Nathem explains: "We did more work than we earned. I felt that my wife and I were paid laborers while my partner had all the income, the milk and the cheese without any effort." His younger brother, Hamdan, started another business with a partner selling used car parts, but the income he earned was very slim. All the family members, males and females, usually get something in kind (oil and olives) during the olive harvest as they usually rent an olive orchard and harvest it. They continue to do so, irrespective of how profitable the season is and how dangerous it has become to harvest olives. (Palestinian harvesters are routinely attacked and prevented from picking olives by Israeli settlers and soldiers alike.)

Umm Nathem's family had to give up their dreams of advancement and mobility. The boys' future marriages and independent homes and flats had to be put off. Kifaya, Nathem's wife, who lost her gold, her future security resource, had to compromise for a less costly and lower level of preschool education for her children:

> The previous kindergarten was better than this one, but I have a good relationship with the principal who might waive part of the fees for me. I may also have to send them on foot to save the cost of transportation.

Suhaila, who is thirty now, "had no dream" except how to manage to make the two families get by; she may have the chance to secure her old age pension through work. She laments losing her pre-intifada freedoms:

> Before the intifada, I spent my salary as I wished, without pressure. I used to buy things for myself, getting gifts for my brothers, sisters, and nephews, renewing the furniture with no pressure. Now, I am deprived of all these things. My only concern is how to distribute my salary according to priorities. . . . Work at the factory is exhausting, and when I return home, I never go out. My only chance for rest and entertainment was visiting my aunts and grandparents in Jericho for a few days. This was good for me because of my rheumatism. Now, I can't even do that because of the closures.

Suffering the crisis of losing his job and turning from a provider to a dependent, Nathem's only practical strategies were to seek alternatives in informal enterprise, which failed, and to cut down on smoking from three packs to one pack a day. While out of work, he showed an aversion to borrowing, an attitude he did not have when he earned an income and relied on borrowing to build his house and furnish it. Nathem expresses his feeling of humiliation with regard to the debt he could not repay: "When I moved in, the flat had only the electrical equipment, which I bought on credit. I could not pay back the credit, so the shopkeeper took back the refrigerator from the heart of my house."

At present, he feels that borrowing or accepting assistance is not a manly thing and thus refuses to borrow. "A man does not open his hand and beg from women or people or strangers." To deal with his crisis he isolated himself.

> I am going to go crazy without work and without money. I became very nervous and lost interest in seeing people. I would sleep during the day and stay

up all night to avoid seeing people. I am used to working and having plenty
of money and to buy whatever I need or desire, but now . . .

This crisis was reflected in the internal gender dynamics of the family and
was heavily felt by Kifaya, his wife. Because of her young age at marriage and
low level of education, she occupied a low status in the patriarchal family system and could neither negotiate nor defy the system. Before and during the
crisis Kifaya was marginalized in her in-laws' family by her husband, even in
matters most relevant to her. Aware of her weak position, she states:

My husband did not consult with me on going into business partnership
[keeping the two cows]. He did not discuss with me anything or tell me what
my role in the business was. . . . He decided everything when we built the
house. . . . He consulted his mother because he thinks she is more experienced than me and has better understanding and better taste. Although I
would have liked to participate in selecting things and furniture for my
house, when he told me to stay aside and not to interfere, I just kept aside. I
did not even have the chance to name my children.

Her status got worse after the crisis, and she had to suffer the psychological burden of her husband's loss of work and was controlled rather than supported by his mother or sister:

He [Nathem] changed a lot after he lost his work and income. He became
very tense. He would not want to see the children or have them around him.
. . . Staying continuously at home he became more demanding and began to
interfere in everything and object to everything. . . . This increased my work
burden and put more pressure on me. He even got to beat me one time and
I wanted to leave the house, but his mother and sister followed me to the
street and brought me back home.

Suhaila justifies Nathem's behavior:

With the intifada, my brothers became more nervous. I do not blame them
for that especially since they became penniless after they had earned high
income that was more than we needed. When we ask them to buy anything

for the house they get nervous, they scream and curse. They have no money to provide for us and to go out with their friends; so they stay alone around the house.

At the same time, she had to be more practical and more reasonable than Nathem, because she bore the responsibility for both families' well-being and could not afford to suffer a psychological trauma. Although she took two loans in advance on her paycheck, she refused to borrow from relatives, friends, or shopkeepers because no one has money to lend and because she would not be able to pay them back.

Umm Nathem's case as outlined above represents an average Palestinian household that does not plan for the long-term future. The family underwent enormous changes in three life cycles between the first and second intifadas; however, they were responding to conditions as they came. This is consistent with the IWS survey finding that when economic conditions were more re-laxed and Palestinians had relatively more hope for the future, households in general neither planned nor saved for the future.[12] Instead of planning or sav-ing for the future, Umm Nathem's household reacted and interacted with the conditions surrounding it, like the death of the head of the household, access to work and accumulation of resources, and the loss of the male breadwinner's work. Family and gender dynamics reflect how household members accom-modate and even reinforce the patriarchal family system in crisis and even in more relaxed situations. Umm Nathem gained her status after the death of her husband and through creating a bond with her eldest son, and she is actively involved in reinforcing patriarchal norms and codes. This attitude apparently accommodates her needs and is rewarding for her to cope and survive or attain social mobility. She was an agent in Nathem's marriage and housing arrange-

12. Examining parents' aspirations for the education of 1,036 female and 1,010 male chil-dren revealed that though the majority of parents intend to give their children higher education, they do not have plans for how to finance it: 87 percent of interviewed mothers and fathers claimed that they would draw on the household income; only 8 percent reported using personal savings (for both girls and boys), which may or may have not existed at the time; only 3 percent saw the possibility for a loan or borrowing from relatives to educate girls and 2 percent to educate boys; only 2 percent saw that boys could work and study; and none saw that possibility for girls (Abu Nahleh and Johnson 2002).

ment to keep him close to her. So, for similar reasons, she could not abandon him and his family when he was out of work. To sustain her ties with her natal family, upon whom she relied for social and financial support, she could not afford to defy them and claim her inheritance. It was her decision to take in Nathem and his family although Suhaila was the provider.

Nathem also had to accommodate his mother's requests and needs, as he was the eldest son and was still young when his father died. Although he assumed the role of the family patriarch, his authority did not go beyond the boundaries set by his mother. Facing the crisis of losing his job and status as a provider, he continued to occupy the head of the household, trying to maintain his masculine authority with his wife and children, and in this, he was supported by his mother and sister. Suhaila, on her part, could not avoid accommodating the needs of the new family structure and seemed to have no choice other than observing duty and obligation toward her family, especially because she is unmarried and lives in the family house. Like her mother, she is probably interested in strengthening her kin ties to secure her future. Kifaya is the weakest link in the whole system because of her age, lack of education, early marriage, and gender status in the family. She recognizes she had to contribute and compromise, without having the right to be rewarded.

Abu Khaled's Household: Three Daughters and Marriage Arrangements (originally written by Yasser Shalabi)

Abu Khaled, forty-seven years old, provides for a family of ten: Umm Khaled his wife, thirty-eight; four daughters between the ages of twelve and eighteen; three sons between the ages of nine and thirteen; and a ninety-five-year-old father. The family lives in a small town twenty kilometers from Ramallah. Although the town is considered an agricultural rural locale, its inhabitants rely primarily on labor in Israel and remittances from abroad, because a large number of families emigrated to the United States and Latin America. Before the current intifada, Abu Khaled was a construction contractor in the Israeli labor market. However, as he explained, mobility restrictions, the rising cost of building materials, as well the difficulty incurred in transporting the material and the financial and psychological cost of transportation through unpaved, lengthy, and dangerous roads, all contributed to a reduction of market demand on the skills of workers like him. He lost his job as a building contractor in Israel and became unemployed. However, he had some savings and, like the majority of households in rural areas, he owned his home; furthermore, his children were all under seventeen and were all enrolled in public schools in their place of residence.

Abu Khaled's household can be classified in the category of hibernators. After losing his job as a contractor in Israel, he had to choose between using the household savings and waiting for the situation to improve or resuming work and starting a small business to provide for the family in the meantime. He was convinced, though, that the latter choice was not possible: "The situation has been changing so rapidly and so unexpectedly that I could not afford to use my savings to start a business." In less than a year, the family used up the savings and were left without any income. Their socioeconomic status reversed, turning them from a family that could assist relatives and friends to one dependent on assistance and borrowing.

A quantitative study may list someone like Abu Khaled's family as selling assets, when in fact the single asset he had was his mobile telephone, which he gave up using to save money. He had a car. He tried to economize by not renewing his license, but when he found that he couldn't sell it unlicensed, he decided to sell its engine, which was all he owned. Unlike Nathem, who sank into psychological crisis, Abu Khaled had practical saving mechanisms.

> I quit smoking mainly to save and not for health purposes. This allows me to save NIS 20 [about US$4] daily for myself and my family. . . . I stopped going to the coffee shop as I used to daily. This saves me the embarrassment of inviting friends for coffee or tea [which I cannot afford at the present] . . . I stopped my activities in the club and the community. I believe being active in social institutions requires you to be well-off or at least be able to provide for the family needs and give donations for the public good. If you are well-off economically, it strengthens your position in giving your opinion and defending it, especially when you have no education.

While Abu Khaled's coping strategies represent reduction in spending on unnecessary items, Umm Khaled's strategies reflect reducing expenditure on basic food items. Being in charge of managing the household's limited resources, she had to rely on reducing expenditure and consumption of daily basic needs. She describes cutting down on food.

> At present, I count my money before I go into the butcher's shop and buy
> with what I have. I used to buy the best quality vegetables. Now I consider
> the price not the quality. I don't buy fruit, period. We have to save [on every-
> thing] . . . to make ends meet.

But even reducing expenditure and consumption was not sufficient to
sustain the family. They had no alternative but to depend on assistance and
borrowing. Abu Khaled accepted kin assistance and borrowed from friends
and acquaintances. Abu Khaled's family had no option but to depend partly
on semiregular and one-time assistance from his brothers, sisters, relatives,
and friends and from Umm Khaled's natal family, all living abroad, to keep a
line of credit at the shops.

Abu Khaled borrowed to avoid social embarrassment.

> When my daughter got engaged to a relative, I had to buy her a gold bracelet
> on loan from a friend to present to her in public. I cannot afford getting em-
> barrassed in front of people. But when my other daughter got engaged to my
> brother's son, my brother took care of all the expenses including the gift I had
> to give her.

Abu Khaled's and Umm Khaled's coping mechanisms went beyond material saving of reducing expenditure and consumption to affect the children's
education and marriage opportunities. Salma, their eldest daughter, was deprived of secondary education. The reason, from her parents' perspective, was
mobility and cost. To continue school she would have had to travel to another
town because their town does not have a secondary school; this was costly
when her father had no income. Her parents regret having to withdraw her
from school but see no other alternative. Salma says:

> I would like to continue my education but my parents did not favor it. It is
> true that my grades are not so good, but I am interested in finishing my edu-
> cation. I had to accommodate my parents' desire and quit school.

Abu Khaled's justification for withdrawing his daughter from school contradicts the general and common attitude toward withdrawing girls from
school, referred to earlier in this study. He states:

If her academic status had been good we wouldn't have withdrawn her from school. Frankly speaking, if our financial status had been better we would have kept her at school, and she might have improved.

She understood this and expressed the belief that it was her "obligation to feel with him especially that I am the eldest of his children and can have an influence on my younger sisters and brothers." Both parents were aware she had needs that she was denied because she felt the responsibility for not burdening them. Umm Khaled comments:

We know my daughter does not burden us with her needs like clothes and other personal stuff because she feels with us. This attitude bothers us! Not only were Salma's education and other needs compromised, but also her opportunity to get married was affected.

Living in a community with most families dependent on strong kin relations and on emigration to the United States and remittances from emigrant relatives, Abu Khaled and Umm Khaled saw in strengthening kin relations through their daughters' marriage a mechanism for coping and securing their living and the future of their children, primarily the sons. The parents compromised their aspirations for their girls' future in favor of kin ties and access to emigration. Although they were not on good terms with Abu Khaled's brother living in the United States, Umm Khaled encouraged reconciliation through approving the engagement of her daughter Maryam, who was only fourteen years old, to his son.

Abu Khaled and I thought we would not accept to have our daughters marry before they turn eighteen. But sometimes life conditions impose things on you. When family reconciliation can help us improve our conditions, with Abu Khaled without an income and with a large family requiring a great deal of expenses, I convinced him to accept because I felt this engagement will lift us from our present situation. We wanted to have Salma, our eldest daughter, get married first, because marriage of the younger girls would affect her future chances and people's perception of her. But the suitors asked for her sister's hand, and everything in the end is decided by one's fate.

Abu Khaled:

I was hesitant to agree to Maryam's engagement. She is only fourteen. My wife convinced me; she felt it would improve our kin relations and give us and give our sons better future opportunities. My nephew has American citizenship, and through him my daughter can get citizenship; then I will have the chance to have it through her.

Having approved of Maryam's marriage at such a young age meant that they had no reason to object to the marriage of Hind, sixteen years old, to a distant relative in the town, although they had previously refused the suitor. Umm Khaled explains:

I was not convinced of the marriage arrangement for my daughter. But sometimes one falls under social pressure. Earlier, my relatives asked for Hind's hand, and I refused, saying she was too young and should not marry before her older sister. Now that I agreed to let her younger sister get married I have no excuse. Refusing their offer can create problems and we do not need such problems these days. Besides, my relatives are well off and my daughter would have a good life with them. If I refuse their request, they would look for another girl.

The strategies undertaken by Abu Khaled and Umm Khaled have affected the future of the girls and were also an attempt to secure the boys' future. Marriage at an early age will deprive them of their education and other future options. "Finishing school after marriage will be difficult. One will have a husband and children and it will not be easy to study," Hind says. Maryam believes, "When I get married, I will travel with my husband to America. Definitely, I will have to quit school." However, Abu Khaled sees their responsibility will be transferred to their husbands. "Others [husbands] will bear responsibility for my daughters but my sons I am responsible for."

The family narratives of Umm Nathem and Abu Khaled are similar in that both households were prosperous in the pre-intifada period but became nearly impoverished following the second intifada. In both households the male breadwinners lost their work in Israel as a result of the Israeli policy of closures and restriction of mobility. Moreover, the process household members went through to reorganize their priorities and reallocate household resources entailed similar gender consequences for members of both households. In both cases, women and men, particularly the mothers, were agents in the process of household decision making and enactment of the patriarchal family codes and norms; however, women and girls were at greater disadvantage than men and boys, particularly in education, marriage, and bearing the brunt of the shock. Abu Khaled's family, though, offers a more profound case of gender disparities in which his girls had to pay a higher price than Suhaila. In both households, the family members struggle in similar and different ways to cope economically and socially with the impact. While Nathem's loss of work and income created a psychological crisis for him that was enacted on the gender and family dynamics, Abu Khaled was able to absorb the shock because he had alternatives to seek, such as savings and emigration, although at the expense of his young daughters' life opportunities. The case of Abu Khaled's household indicates that family and social networks in his town can still provide support to the needy, unlike in the case of Umm Nathem's family, where Suhaila expressed her worry that all families around her were going through economic hardship, making it impossible for them to assist or lend to others; some usual coping strategies are eroding in their town. Borrowing and assistance options were available to both households, but the heads of the households reacted differently to these options. Abu Khaled benefited from them to avoid social embarrassment while Nathem refused to lean on them to maintain his social status. Such negative social attitudes appear to rise strongly against borrowing when family members perceive other means are possibly available or when people, particularly males, are hard-hit in their identity as a source of support and protection.

The Dar Salem Household: Cooperation and Conflict for Unity and Separation (originally written by Lamis Abu Nahleh)

The Dar Salem household represents the case of a Palestinian family who had to grapple with the impact of the Israeli occupation in three stages of its life. The Israeli occupation deprived them of their home and land and demoted them to wage laborers. Throughout three decades, the patriarchal head of the household struggled for upward mobility to regain some of what the family had lost. In the 1990s, with his death and the curfews and strict limitations of mobility accompanying the eruption of the second intifada, the family was

struck again. The consequences were rough. In the course of coping for survival and striving for mobility, the family members had to accommodate the
changes the family underwent through submission, cooperation, and conflict.
This dimension of Dar Salem is analyzed below in two regimes, that of Abdel-
Qader, the father, and that of Salem, the son.

The account of the first patriarchal regime of Dar Salem represents the
rise and fall of the patriarch, Abdel-Qader. Abdel-Qader and Safiyya, Salem's
parents, who were paternal cousins, got married in 1956, and by 1966 they
had four children, three daughters and a son. Both descend from feudal families that come from a small Palestinian town bordering Jerusalem. Before
1948, their families were settled in a village within the borders of the Ramallah district where they established homes and owned agricultural land. However, they maintained their property and strong ties with their extended kin in
their town of origin. In 1948, when Israel annexed their home town of origin
they lost their right to return to it and also lost their land, but they kept the title
proving their ownership of it. Having settled for years in the village and established a family home and life, earning their living from their agricultural
fields, they were uprooted again from their village, which was completely demolished by the Israeli army in the course of the 1967 war. Safiyya, seventy-
seven years old, recalls the incident with pain: "We did not choose to leave. I
swear to God, they forcibly threw us all out under the threat of arms . . . everybody, men, women, children, the elderly, that some left barefooted and some
without food or clothes for the children." Like all the village families, they lost
their home, their belongings, and official documents, including their land
title, under the rubble. Forced to flee, the families were dispersed as refugees
in different locations in the West Bank. Safiyya and her young children had to
manage independently until 1969, when they got reunited with Abdel-Qader
and started a new life in the city. Like several other families, they were
refugees without official refugee status and became laborers.

As the head of the household, Abdel-Qader struggled against all these
losses with two main strategies: establishing a prosperous privately owned
business and creating a firm patriarchal family system. He moved across job
boundaries, starting as a construction worker, then becoming a contractor for
the Israeli construction business, and ending up in 1977 running his private
construction business. Through these years he was able to maintain a decent
standard of living and a recognized social status in the community. He ran his

business and made his decisions totally independently and was able to accumulate material resources. Until his death he was the main source of social and economic support for the members of his household and other extended kin. According to family members, his character played a major role in his success. Munira, his daughter-in-law, fondly describes his character saying, "My aunt was engaged to him and waited ten years to get married. No one dared to break up their engagement. Known to be bold, determined, and never to compromise or give up, no one could say no to him."

At the household level, Abdel-Qader was the sole decision maker and the primary actor who defined the boundaries within which the household members could move and act without disrupting the patriarchal system he set. Accordingly, their roles and responsibilities were defined, and so were the children's opportunities in education, marriage, and work. Endogamous marriage formed a fundamental strategy to sustain continuity of the family line, which got ruptured by the Israeli war and occupation, and to maintain and strengthen kin relations and contacts. Kin marriage started with his own marriage in 1956 and was followed in 1971 by the marriage of his eldest daughter, Huda, who had not yet turned fifteen at the time, to his sister's son, who was a refugee in Jordan. Safiyya said, "The girl cried when she heard the news of her engagement because she was too young and understood nothing. I did not interfere. The decision was her father's and my uncle's." They saw in Huda's marriage her only future opportunity, since she had already quit school, and a way to avoid conflict with her aunt. Her husband was then taken in by Abdel-Qader's family; he joined his wife in the West Bank by family reunion procedures, worked with his uncle, and was treated as a son. Huda's sisters and brother all finished their postsecondary studies before they got married. Safiyya, their illiterate mother, encouraged their education "I have no objection to any field they chose to study. Nothing is better than education; it's a weapon. Do you want them to be illiterate like me? Is this better? Of course, it is not." And Abdel-Qader did not object because that did not seem to defy his familial system. In addition, university education grew and spread in the Palestinian occupied lands in the 1970s, and getting higher education became a common practice for that generation.

Salem's marriage in 1988 strengthened Abdel-Qader's patriarchal family system. His marriage to his cousin, Munira, also a refugee in Jordan, was arranged by his father and her father. On this matter, Safiyya did not interfere:

He was staying with his uncle while completing his college education. They [his father and uncle] told him, "here is your cousin; she is better than a stranger [a non-kin]." Salem himself accommodated the marriage arrangement saying, *"ibn-il-'amm la bint il-'am"* [the cousin is for his cousin in marriage]; it's our tradition, and our families encouraged it.

Munira, though seventeen at the time, was against the arranged marriage: "I wanted to refuse Salem, not for any deficiency in him. I was against kin marriage. . . . But my father said, 'do you want to kill me?' " Salem's and Munira's marriage happened as arranged.

With their marriage, the nuclear household was transformed into an extended household. Abdel-Qader insisted that Salem and Munira live with the family although he rented an apartment attached to his own and furnished it for them. In addition to keeping Salem within the extended family, he kept him economically dependent on him. He gave him a job in his private business and treated him like any other worker; although Salem had a degree in business administration, his father did not give him the opportunity to use his education and marginalized him in running the business and the decision-making process.

Abdel-Qader defined for Salem and Munira the spatial and material confines of living within an extended family that would guarantee their inability to seek separation from his household. The apartment he rented and furnished for them had no proper kitchen but only had appliances enough to make a cup of coffee or tea for themselves or to serve their guests. Living with the extended family meant having all their meals and major social events in Abdel-Qader's house and leaving for Abdel-Qader enough space to pursue his lifestyle away from noise and interference. Salem, as an only son, accepted and believed in the idea of being part of the extended family and marginal in his father's business; as a worker, he received a fixed monthly salary from his father, which he and Munira were free to spend as they wished. He did not attempt to launch battles with his father but simply and peacefully lived with the household rules and norms he set. Munira, on the other hand, made a few unsuccessful attempts to defy his control. Regarding living with the extended family, she said, "We had no choice but to respect my uncle's desire and decision." Although she knew that separating from the family was not negotiable, she still tried twice:

Once I suggested that I start cooking for my family and living within our limited budget but my uncle strictly opposed the idea. . . . Another time I proposed moving to a vacant apartment a few meters from this house that was
larger and better for the girls once they are grown up. Salem was convinced
of and supported the idea, but my uncle was determinedly against it.

Munira's battle with Abdel-Qader never reached the stage of conflict. She
was more successful in her other attempts to resist the patriarchal family system, in matters related to her work and the kind of education she desired for
her daughters. He detached himself from these disputes, which she had to resolve with her husband and the other women in the family; they were matters
that did not defy the terms acceptable to him. In general, he was not opposed
to women's education, work, or mobility. His youngest daughter, Laila, had
finished her undergraduate studies, had a job, was mobile, spent her salary as
she wished, and did not get married until she was twenty-six. According to her,
he never interfered or pressured her. In her marriage and her divorce one year
later, she said she had full freedom of choice, although her ex-husband was
the son of one of her father's friends. She was supported by her father to file for
divorce, and after the divorce she brought her infant daughter to stay in her
natal family house. Like Munira, she was aware that living in Abdel-Qader's
home, though beneficial to her as a divorced woman, also meant the lack of
privacy and independence, yet she could not challenge the conditions of life
there. She describes her experience:

The catastrophe is not the divorce but what follows it. If you did not have a
strong personality, independence, and a sufficient income, you're in trouble.
Even if you did, you need to have a supportive family to allow you this independence; otherwise it is catastrophic. . . . [However] in this house, you cannot live at comfort or in privacy. The house has an elderly person [the father]
who is in control of everything. . . . My child and I had to accommodate to
his lifestyle and not intrude on his quiet evenings or afternoons at home. We
had to wait until he went to bed to sleep or else sleep in the guest room on
the floor because we had no room of our own.

Up to that point in the family's life, Abdel-Qader's household could fit the
"principal-agent" in the noncooperative household model in which "one

partner has a clear advantage in determining intra-household resource allocation by virtue of his ownership of the means of production" (Katz 1997, 35).
However, Abdel-Qader's power and control were not derived only from his
being the owner of the business and the main household provider. In many
contexts, control and power are derived from access to other extrahousehold
resources that may be social, cultural, and ideological. In the Palestinian context, affiliation with a political party and involvement in the national struggle
forms a major source of power. It is true that his patriarchal power and system
could not be resisted or shaken up to a point. However, his patriarchal control
faced major challenges when Siham, his second daughter, grew up to be a
secondary student and thus eligible to enter the arena of political and national
struggle. All the family members agreed that Siham was the only member
who dared to challenge him because she took after him, yet of all members
she gained his greatest love and fondness; he always said, "this daughter of
mine is worth one hundred men." Siham describes her rebellion: "At that
time I knew nothing. I could not even reach the center of town by myself." In
the mid-seventies, she joined a leftist party and became active in the student
movement:

> I developed an ideological outlook, which was in my father's view too revo-
> lutionary; this created a serious conflict between us. My mother indirectly
> encouraged me to join the party, when she explained to me that they were
> good and patriotic people. She tried to forbid me from going out on the
> streets to demonstrate or clash with the soldiers; she was worried I'd be shot
> or arrested.

At that time, Siham was not the only one who had a progressive leftist ideology or who got involved in the national struggle against the Israeli occupation. She and all other family members showed nostalgia for that period when
all the community around them, men and women, including extended kin,
neighbors, friends, and acquaintances, went along the same path. But she did
not let her father know about her political activism because he thought that it
would get him arrested or attacked by the Israeli army; he repeatedly warned
her saying, "Don't force me to confront the occupation. I have a home and a
family to care for." Although he was proud of her political stand and argu-
mentative ability and often called her to debate politics with the Israelis he did

business with, he sometimes used physical force to stop her activism and get her "off the path she chose," as she put it. Upon completing secondary school, Siham was offered a scholarship to study abroad, which aggravated the conflict with her father. The mother, Safiyya, claims she stayed out of this matter. In this endeavor, Siham said she was supported by Salem. Salem analyzed his father's position:

> My father never consulted with anybody on any decision he took except when he doubted the consequences of his decision. He wanted someone to blame in case the decision turned out to be wrong. That was the first time he consulted with me, but I know [now], in practice the decision was his and his orders were to be obeyed.

Siham went abroad without the explicit approval of her father.

> It is true he paid the fees for my scholarship but did not accompany me to Jordan to put me on the plane and wish me farewell like fathers do. . . . In his mind, my political activism did not ruin my social reputation so he can depend on me living abroad. . . . Later I understood that he was forced to approve thinking that he would avoid political dangers by sending me away.

To her father's surprise, Siham came back with the outbreak of the first intifada and rejoined the ranks of the national struggle. She had also chosen a marriage partner while abroad. When she refused all other suitors, her father gave up: "My daughter made it easy for me; she brought her future husband with her." Siham remembers him saying: "my daughter is a hopeless case; no way can I convince her to change her mind."

Only in the last year of his life did Abdel-Qader's children defy him and his decisions. In the last stage of his life, he made a number of decisions that alienated the entire family: he sold the land he owned for a cheap price, he was planning to start a business abroad, and there were rumors about him planning a second marriage. Laila describes her father's last days:

> Though he never consulted with us, this time we went nuts. All of us, Siham, Salem and myself, stood together and succeeded in preventing him from going abroad. That period was miserable for us. . . . In the last few days he

was in so much pain. We're used to him always being strong. I was in so much pain too. He died and I did not know whether I was sad for him or over him. . . . However, the real catastrophe began after he died. . . . Acting on his own, my brother Salem took a few decisions, which destroyed him and destroyed us.

Salem, who never objected to his father or challenged his power, was aware of how his father limited his opportunities.

My father lived under specific conditions that affected his character. He was strict not knowing mercy. He was strict with me because he wanted me to be firm. . . . He was very kind, compassionate, and generous, but more with outsiders than with us. He could not distinguish friends from nonfriends. After his death, the friends remained and the opportunists disappeared. There is nothing I could have learned from him. Each of us is a different personality. I took his generous character, but our conditions are different. I gained power and control through him. When he went, the social and economic prosperity went with him.

Munira expresses the extent of the loss of Abdel-Qader:

I doubt if anyone his age had lived his life. He was in full control of his life and decisions. He was both powerful and passionate. We lost a lot by his death. We never thought of observing how he dealt with the issues of life. We never benefited from his presence nor questioned where from he derived his power, respect, and status. Everything was under his control. And we let the boat sail!

The death of Abdel-Qader in 1997 started the second patriarchal regime of Dar Salem when Salem, the son, assumed control of the family business and the extended household. At the age of forty-one, he became the head of the household, which consisted of himself and seven females: his mother Safiyya (77); his wife Munira (36); his three daughters, Nawal (13), Yara (10), and Zaynab (8); his divorced sister (36); and her daughter, Nadia (8). For the first year, the family continued as before. Munira had a job and was in control of her salary, and her three daughters were enrolled in a private school. Laila also had a regular job and was in control of her salary. The housing arrangement remained as it had been, two living spaces but one extended household. Safiyya occupied the status of the elder of the house but was not in full control. Her new status opened space for paternal and maternal relatives, not only to visit all the time but to interfere in family matters, a condition that was never acceptable when Abdel-Qader was alive. As the head of the household, Salem took charge of providing for the family from the income earned by the family business. Knowing that he was not the sole heir to the family business, he had to get the approval of his mother and sisters to use the assets his father had left to develop his business. Laila said that she and her sisters gave up their right to claim their inheritance: "We gave up our right to him because he was our only brother. Our only condition was that he would maintain the business." Following in his father's footsteps, he ran the business independently, without consulting with anyone. He tried to establish his own regime by modernizing the production equipment; however, not being used to decision making and lacking experience in business deals, he led the business into bankruptcy. The family was shocked when the debtors started knocking on the door.

This business crisis brought about a lot of conflicts among the household members and between them and their relatives. To understand what caused the crisis, Salem's sisters threatened to claim their share in the business. Munira's natal family was accused of causing part of the crisis. Munira acted fast to rescue her husband and asked the assistance of her natal family in Jordan to pay some of the debt. In this crisis, Munira the cousin was considered a sister-in-law/daughter-in-law and, instead of being appreciated, was blamed for acting independently. However, all of Salem's immediate and distant relatives agreed that he had to bear the consequences of his mistakes. With the eruption of the intifada, accompanied by the Israeli invasion, closures, and mobility restrictions, the status of the business worsened; Salem had to lay off his staff, yet the revenues were too slim to pay back any debt. He emphasized that "if it were not for the intifada and the closures, which prevented us from accessing our output markets, we would have been in a better position at least to pay back our debts." Irrespective of their conflicts, the end result was the same: the business was sinking in debt, and Laila and Munira had no option but to cooperate to bear the brunt of the shock. Laila secretly sold some of her gold; Munira and Laila pooled their monthly income. Munira had to do overtime work for pay, and Laila did Palestinian embroidery to earn extra income. Laila was given the responsibility of managing the tight household resources;

she and the rest of the members employed all possible household coping strategies to make ends meet. Evaluating their socioeconomic status at this stage, Salem says: "We abandoned the tradition of living luxuriously and went back to the families we originally belonged to," referring to the 1967 era when he was a child. As Munira put it, "I can say we are now living on the poverty line in economic terms when we used to be classified as a middle-class family." Laila, however, expresses nostalgia and determination to revive the golden age of the family, "I have never dreamt in my life that we would accept welfare assistance. . . . We never experienced debt during my father's lifetime. Abu Salem's household must maintain its decent status."

The repercussions caused dramatic changes in gender roles, mostly afflicting Salem. Losing his main source of income and his ability to provide for the family, he suffered the crisis of the failed male breadwinner. Although Salem believed there was nothing he could learn from his father, he did inherit his patriarchal culture. On turning from a provider to a dependent, he expressed doubts about his self-worth:

> It is known that the head of the household provides for his family, and when one is used to being the provider and then his wife and sister provide for him, he becomes dependent. I am considered a dependent. . . . For a whole year I have contributed very little to the household income. I felt belittled. You know, we have experienced a great deal of humiliation from the occupation and from people, but there is nothing worse than being humiliated with debt.

Munira saw that seeking an alternative income would help Salem regain his status: "I encouraged him to find work, even as a worker; a job would give him an income and that way he would be independent and in control; then he wouldn't need anyone." But Salem believed that the only strategy that would rescue him was to devote himself and his time to the business. The only thing that would bring back his pride and status was to recover the glory of the family business. Most of the time he was under pressure and tension, and to avoid conflict with household members and to save himself "the embarrassment of looking her [his wife] straight into the eye," he spent most of his waking hours at work. He was determined not to seek any alternative to earning an income and insisted on taking the challenge, which had no potential considering the worsening of the economic situation and the tightening of mobility restrictions.

Being job-holders, Laila and Munira became the main providers for the family, and they also occupied the status of the decision makers regarding almost all decisions concerning allocation of household resources. Although they all agree that the three consult before a decision is made, in practice Laila is the main decision maker, and Salem and Munira accommodate her decision and appreciate her financial and managerial assistance, without which they would have not managed. Munira confirmed that she and Laila often make the decision and then ask Salem for his opinion, "although we know he would agree but only to maintain respect for his status." The relations of the household members also showed conflicts on various matters such as the household division of labor, Munira's work outside, kin interference, and so forth. The conflict that Munira and Laila constantly had to deal with was creating a balance between the benefits of living within an extended family and the longing for separation and privacy. However, both are conscious of the force of the patriarchal family norm. Munira stresses, "Even if we were financially well-off we cannot leave my aunt [Salem's mother]; we feel she is our responsibility." Munira feels that Safiyya is not a mother-in-law but a mother to her and says, "I promised myself that if she got sick—God forbid—I shall cooperate with Laila to take care of her, even if that meant leaving my work." Laila, who always complains about the burden of housework and accuses her brother's family of causing this burden, says, "I sometimes tell them jokingly, you are settlers, occupiers, go home. But I won't leave my elderly mother alone, and I cannot deprive her of her only son. I understand her need for him to be close to her."

The socioeconomic and political conditions that prevailed during Abdel-Qader's lifetime differed from those that prevailed after his death. Toward the end of the 1990s, economic conditions started worsening and deteriorated with the disruption of the peace process and the eruption of the intifada. The leftist, progressive, and secular political forces that prevailed in the 1980s retreated from the political public arena, while the religious and Islamic forces spread and expanded. In the process, as is the case in other societies under conflict and economic hardships, the current living conditions in Palestine, characterized by deteriorating economic conditions, unpredictability, insecurity, and constant tension, along with the rise and expansion of Islamic radical movements that have been actively involved in mobilization and service provision both in Palestine and the whole region, led to a rigid, ritualistic, and politicized religiosity.

This new trend created constant overt disputes between Munira and Salem and covert negotiations between Munira and Laila, which were enacted on their dynamics with the children, particularly the eldest of the daughters, Nawal, who was thirteen. Winning the battle over issues related to Nawal meant winning the battles with the three younger girls. In 1997, following the death of her father, and like the majority of women relatives and friends, Laila donned *shar'i* dress and started observing all the duties of a Muslim. The young generation was affected earlier by the spread of political Islam. Young men joined the Islamic movements and young girls started wearing the *hijab* (head cover). Men and women from the community also increasingly became religious and adopted an Islamist outlook that guided their interaction with others. One year before the current intifada, Salem quit drinking alcohol, he started praying and fasting, and he also joined the crowd of men in the mosque every evening to attend religious sessions after prayers. At present he is socially conservative and tries to influence Nawal's (and his younger daughters') outlook. Most were highly affected by the Islamist surge, except for Munira and Siham (and Siham's husband), both of whom are among the very few women in the extended family and the local community who do not observe Islamic dress. The conflicts in Dar Salem emerge mostly on issues related to thirteen-year-old Nawal: should she wear the *hijab*? Should she quit dancing with the *dabkeh* (folklore dance) group? Should she travel abroad with the *dabkeh* group? Should she continue higher education? Should it be here or abroad?

Now that Salem has turned into a "real Muslim believer" as he identifies himself, he holds a different social outlook than Munira does regarding Nawal's education, work, and marriage. He does not mind her education to any level she desires, as long as she stays home. Referring to his earlier position regarding his sister Siham's education, he clarifies, "This is my daughter. I am worried about her and cannot ensure she'll be safe abroad." According to him, she can choose any field of study, except "what is not acceptable in our Islamic society, like acting. This I will firmly oppose." As for her marriage, he encourages marriage at the age of eighteen for girls and boys and does not mind if

Nawal chooses to get married before finishing her education. As for her wearing the *hijab* and leaving the *dabkeh* group, he states:

> Nawal wants to wear the *hijab,* and this is my desire too. I do not approve of her dancing with the *dabkeh* group. I want her to quit but she should be convinced and should approve of that. I do insist and nag her on that. . . . That a girl dances hand in hand with a boy is not only wrong but *haram*. It is *haram* both by the *shari'a* and religion.

Laila has a similar perspective but claims that she does not interfere:

> I know that Nawal is an outstanding performer in the *dabkeh*. Believe me, I cried from joy when I saw her on the stage that I even made my daughter join a *dabkeh* group. . . . I agree that she should quit, but if her mother and her father approve of her staying in the group I don't interfere. We try. . . . I try but the decision is her parents' decision.

Nawal's mother has a totally different view of Nawal's opportunities and outlook. She insists on higher education for all three girls; she wants them to get at least their BA before they get married and will not compromise on that; she also encourages her daughters to work. Regarding her position on religious beliefs and practices, Munira stresses that she is a believer but that religious beliefs should not lead people to become blindly conservative; to her, people should make decisions out of free will, but first they have to be aware and well-informed. Her view reflected in bringing up Nawal:

> I suffer a lot in raising my daughter [Nawal]. I cannot reach her. This religiosity trend cropped up all of a sudden, and she accommodates to it without reasoning. She is so confused. One time it's her father, another the school. . . . One day she wants the *dabkeh* and another she doesn't. Her cousin wears the *hijab,* she wants to wear it, too. This idea of religion, that everything is

haram, haram, haram. I tell her you should not hold on to the idea without being informed.

Concerning Nawal's wearing the *hijab*, Munira is determined that she should not make a decision before she is eighteen. After that she cannot force her to do anything one way or the other.

Nawal herself reflects all the contradictions and conflicts in Dar Salem, the school, and the neighborhood. She is internalizing nationalist, religious, secular, and modern values all at the same time. Nawal aspires to become an astronomer; however, she would compromise and study sociology, a field of interest to her, if the Palestinian universities do not offer astronomy. She justifies her compromise with a nationalist argument, "If we study abroad, we are tempted not to return to our country. Our country needs all the educated Palestinians to develop it." Although she is ambitious enough to finish university education, she does not seem to mind getting married earlier; she says: "If I had a good chance for marriage, I don't know, my ambition might change." Regarding work, she would want to work because she doesn't like staying at home. But she is ready to compromise because, as she says, "I don't want work to stand between me and my husband. I can always engage in activities in the house." She goes on and repeats her mother's view: "Sometimes a woman works for her self-worth, and when she is determined to work she will decide to do that when she turns eighteen." On the issue of *hijab*, Nawal says, "I wanted to wear it. My father approved, but I knew my mother was against it before I turn eighteen." The teachers at school seem to encourage it, and some scold and punish those girls who don't wear it. Nawal said that at school she learned that "the *hijab* gives a girl self-confidence and protects her from being harassed on the street." She adds that several girls wear the *hijab* out of jealousy and not "as our religion instructs us," as she put it. Then she adds: "as my mother says, some girls wear the *hijab* but do not have morals." She is willing to stay in the *dabkeh* group until she turns sixteen and her "body matures and looks like a grown-up woman."

Munira thinks her guidance and education will help Nawal sort out her conflicts as she grows up. She states:

> I try to instill in my daughter that she should learn to be able to decide on her own. Not to imitate others . . . to live her life as it comes. . . . In my opinion,

the decision in the end is hers. You provide her with education and the proper conditions. Then she can decide for herself.

Throughout the three stages of their lives, the Dar Salem family has been in constant interaction with the local community to which they belong and the larger Palestinian community in resistance and struggle against the Israeli occupation. What is significant about this family, although not unique to it, is how the changes and interactions it underwent were enacted on the internal gender dynamics, primarily represented in ideological conflict among the family members. During Abdel-Qader's regime, the family members largely accommodated his control. However, at various points in time, conflict over intrahousehold power relations prevailed through covert and overt negotiation mechanisms; the latter was mostly expressed in Siham's relationship with her father. Although she was young and still economically dependent on her father, she had access to nonmaterial sources beyond the household (the community and the political party) that empowered her to launch a battle with her father, whom no family member could defy. The loss of patriarchal authority at the end of Abdel-Qader's regime could not be redressed during Salem's regime. Not very long after he assumed his father's position, Salem suffered the psychological impact of the male breadwinner's loss of work and income. Unlike in the cases of Abu Khaled and Nathem, both of whom also lost their jobs and incomes, he suffered his crisis silently, placing his efforts in a challenge he was aware he had no chance of winning. Also, loss of his work and income caused major changes in the household relations and gender roles: not only did Munira and Laila become the primary providers, but they also assumed decision-making status. In contrast with his father's regime, early on in Salem's regime, overt conflict surfaced in intrahousehold relations and dynamics, particularly when the family members analyzed the economic crisis that he caused. With the negotiations reaching the practical level of dealing with the crisis, intrahousehold cooperation overruled conflict. However, that does not mean that conflict over power relations disappeared; in fact, it surfaced in a different way as the household members attempted to promote their ideology through the socialization of the young daughters.

What is puzzling about Dar Salem is that the ideological conflict has not extended to the issue of Salem, the only son, who does not have a son to secure the family's continuity. Both Saffiya and Salem expressed a strong desire to have a boy born to Salem. Munira reported that if Salem wasn't an only son, she would have been satisfied with the three girls; she wanted to have a baby boy just to get rid of the social and familial pressure. However, at present since she cannot have more children, her health has priority over giving birth to a boy; this attitude is shared by Salem, his mother, and his sister, Laila. Munira strongly believes that Salem would never take a second wife to bear him a son. However, would this position of Salem's be maintained regarding all the changes he has been undergoing? That is for the future to decide.

The Al-Ayyoubi Household: Struggle with Occupation, Poverty, and Culture (originally written by Rula Abu Duhou)

While families like Abu Khaled's and Umm Nathem's, discussed above, have options that may allow them to survive and maintain their integrity, destitute families like those living in refugee camps are more at risk. Poor families in camps are large, with several children below the age of work, or if they are eligible for work, they are often not skilled or educated enough to find jobs. Data collected in 1999 in the IWS survey indicate that in general, Palestinian households depend largely on wage labor; the highest unemployment rates are prevalent among refugees and those with low education. Refugees have slightly larger families, and they also have a higher rate of unemployment. In particular, camp households are not only highest in unemployment, their household heads are most disadvantaged as managers and professionals; they have the lowest level of home amenities, have fewer rooms, and are poorer according to wealth and socioeconomic status indices (Giacaman and Johnson 2002a, 48, 51). With a low educational level and almost no income, poor camp families are often classified among the poorest of the poor. They struggle to be part of the labor force and often fail to do so; as such, they are eligible to receive humanitarian assistance in cash or kind from various sources, but this barely helps them. Generation after generation, they start and live their lives in refugee camps and do not have the opportunity to leave it; and if they do for the purpose of marriage or kin reunion, it is mostly to another camp. At the same time, those individuals and families who become relatively well-off move out to the nearby city or to the outskirts of the camp; however, they remain strongly tied to the community there and some express a longing to go back to the camp. The strong ties that connect former refugee camp residents to camp life are the topic of ongoing research.[13]

In general, and particularly for poor families, life in a refugee camp is confining because camps are crowded and restricted in physical and social space and mobility. UNRWA provides educational, medical, and social service facilities inside the camp; these services paradoxically improve the lives of camp residents and at the same time restrict their mobility, particularly for girls and women. Poor camp families are left to struggle for survival and mobility without proper support or protection, which is one reason for their loyalty and commitment to the community in which they are located. The community in a refugee camp consists of subcommunities formed of families tied by kinship and place of origin from before the 1948 *Nakba*. Camp families and individuals obtain community support and engage in collective and solidarity activities, most apparent among women. However, at the same time they are highly constrained by community norms and codes that they rarely can defy and thus make no attempt to exit the community. If they do they would not only be socially isolated but also lose their identity because they have no option to leave the camp or join another community. Although most camp families live in nuclear households, the housing arrangements, restricted by physical space, bring public space into close proximity with private space. In their own houses, camp families hear and see and are heard and seen by the neighboring families, who may or may not be kin.

The importance of the refugee camp community for individuals and families has been reinforced by living under the Israeli occupation for decades, in the absence of a state. Furthermore, the establishment of the PNA under the terms of the Oslo accords and its limited jurisdiction in issuing legal codes and laws contributed to the dependence of individuals on extended families, kin relations and networks, and communities. In addition, the PNA did not invest in establishing the rule of law. Instead, it tended to revive social norms and social traditions of tribalism, patriarchal family system, and religious identities, which was most apparent in the quotas defined in the first Palestinian election

13. Some colleagues and I are at present conducting an ethnographic study in three communities in the Ramallah area, one of which is a refugee camp. These preliminary remarks come from the initial ethnographic data collected for the purpose of that study.

law of 1994 and in the appointment of municipalities and village councils. To gain legitimacy and support and to promote its authority, the PNA encouraged the use of and dependence on customary law to manage communities and to provide social order.[14] In such a political socioeconomic context, how are poor camp families expected to lead their lives?

The al-Ayyoubi family lives in an urban refugee camp. It is a large family of ten: Saber (42 years old), the head of the household; Maryam, his wife, 40; and four girls and four boys (Muhammad, 21; Amal, 19; Mahmoud, 17; Maysa', 14; the twins Ahmad and Sana', 12; Wafa', 8; and Amjad, 3). Both Saber and Maryam originally came from the Palestinian town of al-Lidd before their families were forced out of their homes and town in the course of the 1948 war and became residents of a refugee camp. Saber recalls his family history, which expresses how refugee communities were formed:

> In 1948 my father, along with several other people, was forced out of al-Lidd and fled to Gaza, when the Jewish 'isabat [gangs] invaded the town and started killing people. He was newly married to my mother, and they went to live in a refugee camp in Gaza. The living conditions there were very difficult, so his brother decided to move to the West Bank. For the same reason, my father also moved there. At that time a lot of people from al-Lidd also came to the West Bank. My father settled in this camp, and I was born here. Since then I have been living with some of my brothers and sisters in the same neighborhood. My wife is from the same camp but we are not related.

Both Maryam and Saber were born in the refugee camp where they currently live and have not left it since then. Neither completed elementary school, and they married at an early age. Maryam has felt the burden of the political situation since the day she was married.

> I got married on the day of the Sabra and Shatila massacre in 1982, a day I can never forget. Even in our weddings politics is present. I quit school at fourteen to get engaged. I was too young and could not read the alphabet. I

---

14. See Hillel Frisch 1997 for a more detailed discussion of the PNA's relation with extended families and its involvement in customary reconciliation, the application of customary law, the motives behind it, and its consequences and implications for state building.

went to a sewing workshop for one year until I got married. Saber also quit
school to marry me. He was two years older than I was.

Maryam and Saber and their eight children live in a poorly furnished
house in the camp that is owned by his paternal uncle, who is a refugee in Jordan. Although the house has four rooms, only two are suitable for occupancy.
After their marriage, they lived with Saber's family in a two-room house. The
family tradition is to accommodate each son who gets married until the next
son marries, then he and his family have to move out to make space for the
newlywed brother. Saber was the last of the boys to get married; when his family grew larger, his parents moved out. Saber and Maryam renovated the second room for the children paid for by Maryam's gold. She professed not to
care: "Gold is not important. What is important is that we have a good room."
Selling gold or women's jewelry is a common household strategy to cope with
a financial crisis. However, most often, it is women's strategy, which expresses
altruistic behavior in favor of the family's well-being.[15] One of the two rooms
in the al-Ayyoubi household is multipurpose; it functions as the bedroom, the
living room, and the kitchen all at the same time. Not only are the rooms
poorly furnished, they are separated by curtains; the floor has no tiles, and the
inside walls lack finishing and paint. The other two rooms are currently unin-
habited because the family cannot afford to repair them. Unable to afford
their own electricity gauge, they draw their supply illegally from Saber's
uncle's shop.

As an unskilled laborer, Saber, the main provider for his family, had a job
at an Israeli bakery for a few years. However, two years before the first intifada,
he was imprisoned by the Israeli authorities for three years and consequently
lost his job. Between the first and second intifadas, as an unskilled worker, he
had no stable job or regular income. Since the second intifada, he has been
earning a daily income when there is demand for his unskilled labor as a porter

15. Gold selling appears in two other family narratives here. In one case the divorced sister
sells some of her gold without the knowledge of other family members to pay back some of her
brother's debt; in the second case, the wife sells her gold to support some of the expenses incurred in the construction of the family's house. See the cases of Umm Nathem and Salem.

at the vegetable market and as a house cleaner. His daily wage ranges from NIS20–50 (US$5–10) depending on the market demand. Saber complains:

> There are no work opportunities. These days I work one day and ten days I go without work. My daily income is very low, much lower than before the intifada; we can barely survive. Our debt increased and with the new scholastic year and now during the feast [al-Fitr], I am unable to cope with the expenses.

Amal, the nineteen-year-old daughter, was not allowed to continue her secondary education outside the camp; instead, she was instructed to do a one-year vocational training course in hairdressing. However, upon completing the training, her parents did not allow her to work outside the house, nor could she attract clients to her home. Saber justifies his decision: "I do not mind if she works, but now she has to help her mother at home especially after she got sick. She has to do the housework in place of her mother." Maryam agrees and adds, "In our culture, it is disgraceful to let a girl work; people would ridicule us and would say you cannot afford to buy a meal so you send your daughter to work."

Although Maryam and Saber are destitute, and Amal and Muhammad could increase the household income if both are encouraged to engage in paid work, they are anxious about getting their children married. To ensure Amal's marriage, both parents, particularly her father, do not let her leave the boundaries of the camp. Her mother is concerned about buying her a few items of bridal clothing and saving them for her marriage even if that means borrowing money. Here is how she sees her daughter's future:

> A girl should marry at an early age, and it is better if she marries someone from the camp, then we would know more about him. And now with the closures during the intifada, it will be difficult to visit her and check on her if she marries outside the camp.

On the other hand, Maryam and Saber perceive of their sons' education and work as a path to marriage, rather than as a path to future security and social mobility. Amal's brother Muhammad has an irregular job at a restaurant; he is paid on a daily basis and is deprived of his meager daily pay in the case of curfew or an Israeli incursion of the town or a general strike ordered by the Palestinian resistance. Muhammad is encouraged by his parents to save his meager daily pay, which does not exceed NIS20 (US$5), to construct a flat on the "second floor" of the house in preparation for his marriage. Maryam explains: "he keeps his income at the bank because he knows if he brings it home it will be spent on our needs, and he has to secure his future." The parents, and particularly Saber, are more flexible with him and allow him to make his choices, as long as that leads to his marriage. Saber states, "I do not care; he can chose what he likes; what I care for is that he studies and works, so that he can get married."

Saber and Maryam do not seem to be able to provide their children with much better education than they had. Being a registered refugee family, the children can get free education until grade nine and vocational education at any school or vocational center run by UNRWA. The five youngest children are enrolled in elementary school. Amal finished ninth grade at the UNRWA school in the camp; her only option for secondary school was to enroll in a public school outside the camp in the nearby city. Her father, however, would not allow her to go. Her mother says, "She is a grown-up now. And a grown-up girl usually becomes subject to gossip" However, she is determined to get her brothers educated. Unlike Amal, seventeen-year-old Mahmoud finished ninth grade at the UNRWA school in the camp and was sent to a public school in the nearby city. However, he quit two days after school started. He felt that his life was threatened by the settlers from the Israeli settlement located on a hill opposite the school. Students are always at risk of being shot at, injured, or arrested;[16] often they are provoked by the settlers (who are protected by the army) and are forced to engage in confrontations with them, which exposes them to danger. The older son, Muhammad, finished high school, and after two attempts he obtained the general examination certificate; however, he was not admitted to the vocational college run by UNRWA, his only alternative. "We would like him to go to al-Quds Open University; but where do we

16. On 16 November 1993, the Hashimiyya Secondary Boys' School was invaded by the Israeli settlers and army, and in the attack a sixteen-year-old student, Rami Izzat al-Ghazzawi, was shot dead as he was trying to rescue his schoolmates who were injured by live bullets, rubber bullets, and tear-gas canisters. His parents still keep his blood-stained school uniform and school bag. I personally witnessed the details of the consequences of the event.

get the money to pay the fees?" The efforts of the mother are focused on getting one of the two sons admitted to the UNRWA vocational school, which she
considers their right as refugees.

> It is not possible that my two sons remain in front of me day and night, and I
> am sitting still allowing their future to be lost. I went to see the principal at
> the [UNRWA] vocational college and I insisted. . . . One of them at least
> must have an education. . . . I also went to see the refugee camp director
> here in the camp and he promised to help me . . .

Maryam's and Saber's attitude toward their children's marriage, education, and work are in line with the findings of the IWS household survey. The
survey showed that preference for kin marriages was reported by less than 20
percent of the households surveyed; refugee parents seemed to have a slightly
greater preference than urban or rural parents for relative marriages (Abu
Nahleh 2002a, 111–12). The reasons given by those against kin marriages reflect class differences: the wealthier households were more concerned about
genetic problems while the poorer (which include camp households) were
worried about social problems (Abu Nahleh 2002a, 119). Regarding work and
education, the same survey showed that, in general, parents were in favor of
their daughters' work even after marriage (Abu Nahleh 2002b, 135); in particular, camp households had the highest intentions for their daughters' education (Abu Nahleh and Johnson 2002, 103). However, in practice, parents
withdrew boys from school or transferred them to other schools primarily because of scholastic failure; in contrast, they withdrew girls predominantly for
marriage plans and domestic responsibilities and transferred them to other
schools that were closer to home (Abu Nahleh and Johnson 2002, 101, 98).
Both findings are confirmed in Saber's and Maryam's attitudes and practices
toward their daughter, whose study and work opportunities were hindered by
their restricting her mobility and working toward her early marriage.

Children's marriage and education are not Saber's and Maryam's only
worries; clothing and pocket money are some of their other daily worries. Both
agree that the older children's clothes are the item most costly for them.
Maryam complains, "Every month, the girls want new and fashionable
clothes, either a blouse or a scarf; they do not accept any pair of pants. Clothes
are becoming a big burden for us; they have grown now and they know what

they want." This attitude reflects the difference between parents' perceptions and their realities regarding their children; though they see young children as more costly, in reality youth who want to be fashionable and imitate peers seem to be more expensive. The IWS household survey revealed that parents perceived older children as most costly among existing children but that most camp and poorer households perceived children under five as the most expensive; the rate of those who made this choice shows a significant difference among communities controlled by whether they are urban, camp, or rural respondents, with camp respondents ranking the highest (Johnson 2002).[17] In addition, Saber's daily expenses while at work and the children's daily pocket money to buy snacks and sweets are another burden, primarily felt by Maryam:

> Every day my husband goes to work, he needs to buy food, soft drinks, and cigarettes. This, added to the children's pocket money when they go to school, means that Saber's daily pay is gone. . . . Whenever I ask for some money, he says he does not have any. . . . The children do not understand and keep asking for money. . . . The intifada conditions are making it difficult. . . . Our debts have increased and Saber doesn't find work like before. I have to constantly borrow from my [women] neighbors, and when I get assistance, my husband doesn't ask for it because he knows I use it to pay the debt back.

The family has accumulated unpaid electricity and water bills and a bank loan, which they used to pay in monthly installments before the intifada. Saber says, "my brother-in-law helped us and the electricity company did not cut off the current. My uncle asks us to pay the bill or he will cut off the sup-

17. The IWS household study revealed that children are most costly for households who have three age groups among their existing children. When mothers' and fathers' perceptions are examined by socioeconomic status (SES), 35 percent of low SES and 34 percent of medium SES households in contrast with only 30 percent of the high SES households perceive children aged under five as most expensive (Johnson 2002, 86). Controlling parents' perceptions by region (urban, camp, or rural) reveals that although in all three communities parents perceive children under five the most expensive, there are significant differences among them; camp households ranked the highest at 40 percent, followed by village households at 34 percent, and urban households scored the lowest rate at 30 percent.(Johnson 2002, 84)

ply. If they want to do so, they can go ahead. I couldn't care less. We'll go back to the oil lamp." Before the second intifada, they took a loan from the bank to maintain the house; since then they have been unable to pay it back. Maryam's father, their guarantor for the loan, had to repay it. "My father had no choice but to pay back the loan. The bank deducts the amount from his salary every month. Every day, he comes to the house and screams at us. What can I do? Where can I get the money to pay it back?"

Increasing dependence on assistance was their second primary alternative. Because they are refugees, they are entitled to receive assistance in cash, monthly food rations, and basic medical insurance from UNRWA. Maryam usually sells the UNRWA monthly rations in order to meet other necessary needs. She had to undergo surgery that had been postponed for several years. Although her medical expenses are covered by UNRWA, she needed to buy a supporting belt at her own expense, which she could not afford: "I had to sell the food ration we received from UNRWA to buy the belt. I had to do the surgery a long time ago but we had no money." Apparently, the belt was not as much a problem as the expenses that followed the surgery. Maryam complains, "After the surgery our expenses rose. Every day I had to spend money on buying fruit, snacks, and juice to entertain the guests, my neighbors and relatives [who visited her after the surgery], and sometimes I had to cook meals."

As a destitute household, the al-Ayyoubi family gets on every formal and informal list for assistance. Characterized as a "social case" family, they are entitled to about US$70 per month from the Ministry of Social Affairs; however, they have been receiving it intermittently because the ministry was short of finances. In addition, they receive irregular emergency humanitarian aid donated by groups or NGOs, which are distributed by the camp's Popular Committee to all the families regardless of their need. They always get Ramadan *futra* [alms]. Both Saber and Maryam mentioned, "any person or any organization who has Ramadan *futra* to donate to the needy goes to the mosque, and there they always refer them to us." Saber's family also depends on informal assistance and loans from neighbors or acquaintances and from relatives, particularly Saber's father and Maryam's brothers. During Ramadan and special occasions, Saber borrows from his father to give his sisters money gifts for the '*id* (feast). Maryam's several brothers, who are, relatively speaking, well-off, give her and her children money for the 'id. Although Saber sees Ramadan as a burden, Maryam sees it an opportunity to pay back her debts.

Although Palestinian society has relatively positive attitudes toward women's work outside the house, Maryam's interpretation of her own situation and that of her daughter blames cultural traditions and norms that she does not believe she can defy. However, as her family gets more and more destitute, she realizes the need for paid work. All her married life, Maryam has been a housewife in charge of caring for the family. Her attempts to earn some income are in her view impeded by cultural traditions; her words express her lack of skills. While Saber was in prison, Maryam and her children lived on his allowance as a prisoner. Maryam justifies not seeking paid work by referring to cultural traditions: "I was a prisoner's wife and all people had their eyes on me. According to our traditions, it is shameful for a woman to go out to work when her husband is away." However, the reality is that several women from Maryam's neighborhood engaged in home-based informal small enterprise, which they promoted through the all-women network in the neighborhood and local community. Small enterprise is one of the several aspects of the camp women's social relations and network.

The women's social relations and networks in Maryam's neighborhood are similar to those described by Shami in her study of two urban, refugee, and low-income communities in Jordan. In these communities, social integration or separation among households sharing the same courtyard is recognized by an imaginary line that is crossed only by children without impunity; household boundaries and private and public space distinctions are defined by family networks and mutual help, as well as the social relations women create on the basis of cooperation and division of reproductive and productive responsibilities in the household, the neighborhood, or the city. These, rather than kinship or physical parameters, are the basis that shape their social identity and give meaning to their relationship and sustenance in times of hardship and insecurity (1996, 17–18). Rula Abu Duhou, the researcher who worked with Saber and Maryam to write their narrative, provides insightful commentaries on camp women's networking and relations through her observations of camp life during her repeated visits to Maryam. Overwhelmed by the fact that Maryam's house was in constant motion, she describes it as "more like a popular club or a coffeehouse accommodating women's gatherings of as many as ten women at a time of various ages and marital statuses, despite its small size and run-down condition."[18] During the women's gatherings, their conversations encompass all sorts of themes, ranging from those socially accepted to those banned, starting with sexual issues and ending with politics. Their conversations may include news about who got married, who got divorced, who visited whom, what the Israelis did that day or what might happen on the political scene, and what the latest developments in Abu 'Ammar's [Arafat's] siege are, and so on; at that point, they were not reluctant to discuss the private matters of a public figure, such as Abu 'Ammar's wife and the mysterious reason behind her staying abroad. Another important issue that gets into the exchanges is who bought what, what the prices of goods are and where the best deals are found, where to get food or cash assistance and how to do that, and who got UNRWA assistance while she is not entitled to it. The most recurrent subject in their gatherings is discussions of their sexual life and an examination of who has sexual problems with her husband and why, and how they can be solved; who went out bare-headed and without a scarf; who stays long on the roof of the house or sitting on the balcony. The theme of girls' reputation and security and how the Tanzim follows up on these issues in the camp overwhelms their conversations and is associated with the subject of getting their daughters married. All this takes place in the presence of girls of various ages, who are banned from leaving the boundaries of the camp and sometimes the house. These discussions may be seen as a kind of orientation for the girls in preparation for future marriage.

Women neighbors' visits to Maryam's house are never made on notice; they may stop by on their way to or back from the market to share that day's adventures or experience. A neighbor may stop by to borrow a cooking pot or a scarf to wear on her way to visit someone in the camp or her trip to the town, and visit with Maryam; the visit may be long depending on whether other neighborhood women are there. In one of my visits to Maryam, I had to wait for hours to meet with her because of these social and networking visits; Maryam commented, "this is how we live here. You want to visit us, you have to bear with us." Exchange and borrowing among women may extend to boil-

18. The rest of the description of the social relations and networking Maryam and her women neighbors engaged in is based on Abu Dahou's commentaries written in Arabic, which I extracted, translated into English, and composed into one text.

ing one's cup of tea on the neighbor's stove, bringing the laundry to be washed, or cooking for the neighbor and taking care of her children if she is on a visit to the town or sick at the hospital, as happened during Maryam's illness. A very significant form of establishing their network of cooperation and exchange is represented in the collective visits or the running of errands that they take on inside or outside the camp, such as shopping for the best prices, paying utility bills, collecting the UNRWA food rations, or selling them to local shopkeepers to get good deals. During the Israeli reoccupation of the camp, women took up solidarity activities collectively.

Maryam explains the important role she and the neighborhood women had in supplying each other with food, such as flour, bread, sugar, and other provisions and in extending solidarity to families in the camp:

> We are all brothers [and sisters] and Muslims and we all help each other. I took from my neighbors more than they took from me because their husbands work, and they're better off than me. We always gathered ourselves in the neighborhood and paid solidarity visits to the families of the injured, imprisoned, and martyrs. It was more difficult for men to move around because the army is all over the camp. We women can manage better.

The visits of women in Maryam's neighborhood are also utilized by some to promote their own small businesses, selling their neighbors clothing and household items. In one of these visits, Maryam borrowed to buy bridal clothes for her daughter and household items. However, she also wanted to have her own business to make some money. To do so, she borrowed seed money from a neighbor. Her repeated attempts to sell small products from her house failed because she could not separate her small home project from the household's needs.

> I don't think of the loan I got from my neighbor. I used to sell the detergents and spend the money on our daily needs. I also used some of the detergents in the house. All the supply ran out and I had no money to buy more or to pay back the loan. . . . I will never repeat this. It is enough that the neighbor keeps asking me to pay her back the money and I have no idea how to do that.

Although earlier Maryam had professed that "their culture" prevents women from seeking outside work, in the struggle against the difficulties of daily demands, she finds it inevitable to negotiate with Saber on the possibility of working for pay. Her services are required by a family in the nearby city outside the camp, caring for an elderly woman. Saber does not agree.

> My husband says no, but I want to work. If we have money we can construct another room. . . . The boys and the girls are grown up now and they should not all sleep in the same room. If my husband insists that I do not work, we shall remain as we are . . . it is not disgraceful to work if one can help improve the house condition.

Coping with daily living, the unending demands of the children, the worry about their future, and the social and political pressure and constraints and maintaining loyalty to and integration into the supportive community in the absence of public support systems and the rule of law, Saber sees his only chance of social status in being nationalist and patriotic and in protecting family honor. Maryam also has similar aspirations but engages herself in more practical concerns, like her sons' education and her eldest daughter's marriage.

During the current intifada, Mahmoud was shot in the foot by an Israeli soldier or settler, disabling him for around two months. Having had this experience, he insisted on not returning to the school in the vicinity of the settlement, the only inexpensive school available to him. The boy is currently out of school, out of work, and suffers from depression. Because Mahmoud was injured, the family received assistance. As they did for all those injured in the camp, the rehabilitation committee rebuilt the bathroom in the house, which now constitutes the most modern-looking part of it. They also received some financial allowance from other sources. Saber feels honored by this incident, considering himself a descendant of a patriotic family involved in the struggle against the occupation, several members of which, including himself, got arrested or are still imprisoned. Maryam feels the pain: "I was crying, and my husband was laughing at me telling me, 'now you have to be happy your son is like all the young men in the family.' "

The researcher working with the al-Ayyoubi family was surprised to discover an incident of honor killing in the family that took place between her two visits to them. Amal, the eldest daughter, volunteered the whole story. On her way home, the researcher stopped by a center at the camp to ask about the matter and found out that it was the topic engaging everybody there. Saber regards the honor incident and his son's injury by an Israeli bullet as ways to attain social status and social approval. He explains how he felt honored by taking a lead in the planning and killing of his widowed and illegitimately pregnant sister. He sees that by "washing away the dishonor of the family" he is a respectable person again.

> The period before the killing happened was very difficult for me. I did not go to work. I could not leave the house. The killing was an end to the problem. The dishonor is not a problem as long as we do our duty and "wash" it. The people are pleased with us because they think we behaved right. All the family helped us, even those living in other camps, to collect the bail money and get my father out of jail. Now I am very happy. Nothing is as serious as honor. It is a difficult and big issue. Now I can go out with confidence because the dishonor has been "washed away." Everyone is happy; the family, the neighbors, even our in-laws, the family of my sister's husband and her children are all happy. Her eldest son, nineteen years old, was upset at the beginning, but then he understood and felt that it was a burden and we got rid of it. All the people shake hands with us and congratulate us because they saw that we are "men." Our in-laws have strengthened their relation with us. Now all the family can raise their heads high in pride. Everybody in the camp is pleased with us.

Such an incident can happen in any Palestinian locality and cannot be considered specific to camps only. People commit such crimes motivated by various reasons. In the case of Saber, he and his father and brothers planned and executed the killing. Each had a role, but Saber, being the most destitute of all, either truly or pretentiously, took it upon himself to execute the killing. His father, an old man, was to take the official responsibility when the police investigated the crime to save his sons, who have large families to feed. The rationale was that he was too old to be kept in prison and would be released on bail. This act was based on an understanding that honor killing does not receive a high sentence and more important, that customary law replaces the rule of law. Although Maryam approves of the honor crime, she worries about the financial, psychological, and social burdens.

We have been subject to psychological and financial pressures [to pay the
bail for releasing Saber's father from jail]. The worst is the social scandal the
girls in the family will bear. The last suitor for Amal backed off after he heard
her aunt was killed. She destroyed us and all the girls in the family. Can you
imagine forty-five girls of marriage age having their futures destroyed? The
scandal will chase us all our life.

Examining the living conditions of the al-Ayyoubi case, one would expect
that being responsible for a destitute family whose only resource is labor
power, Saber and Maryam's main concern should be the allocation and reallocation of labor to cope and survive. However, for political, economic, and
cultural reasons, they seem to be hopeless in managing their labor resources,
and thus perceive of securing their children's marriage as a strategy to secure
the family's continuity and persistence.

Saber and Maryam's views of their children's current and future options
are based on their perception of the present reality of their living conditions
and extrahousehold restrictions. Regarding women's paid work, Maryam justifies her reluctance in seeking outside paid work in her repeated expression,
"in our culture. . . ," blaming it on the social and cultural traditions that she
does not see herself able to violate. As a prisoner's wife, she could not engage
in paid work because "according to 'our' traditions, it is shameful for a woman
to go out to work when her husband is away." Maryam's perception of cultural
traditions and norms are not to be generalized. The case of Farha discussed
below shows the triple burden prisoners' wives often have to bear, one of
which is engaging in paid work. Similarly, according to Maryam, the community would ridicule her and her husband if their daughters went out to work,
accusing them of being incapable of providing for the family. However, in
these cases, Maryam seems to refer here to the specificity of the community in
her camp, and more specifically, to the kin and social network to which she
belongs as well as within particular conditions. Although she claimed that her
community's social and cultural traditions do not favor women's work outside
the home, restrict the mobility of women whose husbands are away, and con-
fine young girls like her daughter, and perhaps other women, she and several
women in her neighborhood are mobile and active as a neighborhood group.
Part of their activities includes using their gatherings to pursue their home-
based small businesses. Lately, Maryam is thinking of seeking outside work

and seems to be ready to negotiate and defy in the face of severe need and hopelessness.

Maryam's perception of women's work, which may sound contradictory or confused, is in line with some research findings on attitudes toward Palestinian women's work. Public opinion polls show that support for women's work outside the home rises in periods of relative security (Hammami 2004) and support is strongest for "respectable" employment in white-collar and professional positions (teaching in particular), work which is largely inaccessible to most poor women. Male conservative attitudes may well play a part— and indeed may harden with the humiliation of unemployment. However, opposition to women's outside work may be real fear at the dangers and insecurities of public spaces, particularly for young women. This fear may vary in different localities: refugee camp women and girls seem particularly vulnerable to both fears and community sanctions, yet are in most need of income (Abu Nahleh and Johnson 2003).

The complex and inevitable constant interaction of households and individuals with the larger local community, the neighborhood in particular and the camp in general, is reflected in the al-Ayyoubis' familial and social dynamics and relations. The importance of the community in the Palestinian context supports Agarwal's argument regarding individual choice, that the ability to exit the community is constrained by social and economic factors and that noncooperation or conflict with the community can be over shared economic resources, political status, and norms for social behavior. Individuals can more easily exit the community than the family because the harm (loss of economic support or social sanctions) in exiting the community would be less. In this case, the individual can emigrate or join another community because communities, unlike families, are not based on strong consumption and production relations; a community is not a unit for consumption, production, and investment, and the individual's relation with it is not based on day-to-day contact as is the case with the family (Agarwal 1997, 29–30). This may be true if relations within a community are based on economic relations only. However, the camp context here provides a challenge to the part of Agarwal's argument regarding the critical differences between the household and the community in relation to the individual: first, that the community is larger and the cost of individual noncooperation can be minimal; and second, that the community is not necessarily a joint economic unit. Both of these points are not supported here. In the case of refugee camps, the role of the community is more fundamental in both economic and social relations to individuals' social and national identity and their sense of belonging. Individuals and families are highly integrated in their own community, which provides social cohesion, economic support, and a sense of national belonging, which makes it almost impossible to be defied. Exiting it means suffering a total loss in a context that provides no other alternatives.

In particular, the case of the al-Ayyoubi family shows how the Israeli occupation and the community and family patriarchal system militate against all attempts by the couple to break out of the circle of poverty or to improve the life opportunities of their children. Plagued by lack of a decent and regular income, unable to cope with the daily demands of a large family, and torn between cultural constraints, lack of the rule of law and formal state support and the restrictions of the Israeli occupation, the family goes deeper and deeper into poverty and debt, which jeopardizes the children's education and marriage opportunities. The impact on Saber's masculinity and social status is so immense that he hopelessly struggles to maintain the minimum level of human dignity. His individual acts and negotiations with the family and the community codes and norms are based on his perceptions of what qualifies him to stay integrated in his community and gain some social status. According to his idiosyncratic judgment, these are expressed in supporting the national struggle and protecting family honor. On the other hand, Maryam, his wife, though she also seeks community integration and respect and attempts not to cross its boundaries, is overwhelmed by her struggle on more practical matters such as managing the household and guaranteeing the children's education and marriage.

The Maqdisi Household: Prison and Privileges in Jerusalem (originally written by Lina Mi'ari)

This family history considers a Jerusalemite family whose residency and legal status[19] are different from those of West Bank families but whose experience of

19. Following the Israeli occupation of the West Bank (including East Jerusalem) and the Gaza Strip in 1967, Israel annexed East Jerusalem to the state of Israel in violation of the Fourth Geneva Convention. In 1970 the Israeli Knesset issued administrative laws to define the status of

the impact of prison is representative of a Palestinian prisoner's family. As Jerusalem residents, Palestinians living in East Jerusalem pay full taxes and in return receive social security and health insurance benefits; they can seek work in Israeli administered establishments and are in theory allowed to move freely within Israeli borders without a permit. In fact, however, they have been subject to the full spectrum of Israeli occupation measures throughout the nearly forty years of occupation. They get arrested, tortured, placed under house arrest, beaten up, prevented from traveling; their homes are invaded, searched, or demolished by the Israeli army; and their land is expropriated for Israeli settlement construction. Although they have not been subjected to curfews and military shelling and bombing, they have suffered the impact of the war conditions and tightened closures created by Israeli polices. For one thing, strict mobility restrictions impinge on their communication and contact with their extended families, friends, and acquaintances as well as on their economic and living conditions. Although East Jerusalem Palestinians have a legally different status from Palestinians in the West Bank, almost all are connected to the West Bank through social and professional networks. A large number of Jerusalem families have been living in West Bank cities where the provider works and where their children go to school.

The Maqdisi household depicts the crisis and changes a prisoner's family undergoes. Their social history reflects changes in family dynamics, gender relations, and the status and role of the family and other support networks.

Farha and Kan'an got married in 1977. Upon their marriage, Farha (now forty-seven years old) had just completed school and started college; Kan'an (fifty-two years old) was the household provider employed at the Israeli-administered municipality in Jerusalem and was a clandestine political activist. In the first fifteen years of marriage, Kan'an spent ten years in Israeli prisons. Seven months following the marriage, he was arrested by the Israeli occupation forces and sentenced to four and a half years in prison. In 1985, after spending three years out of prison, he was arrested again and was sentenced to five and a half years in prison. As a result, family life and relations

---

the Palestinians living in East Jerusalem. Accordingly, they came to be considered permanent residents but not citizens of Israel. They can vote in the municipal elections but they are not allowed to vote or run for the Israeli Knesset; they are required to pay full dues and taxes in return for some social and legal benefits.

did not develop normally. Farha had to cope as a single mother and the wife of a prisoner during her husband's absence from home; by age thirteen her eldest daughter was assuming the role of caregiver. Later she and the children had to adjust to Kan'an's return. Kan'an, on the other hand, had to struggle to regain his status as family head, husband, and father in control of his wife and children.

The interaction between family dynamics and political affiliation and national struggle was crucial in the life of Farha and Kan'an, but more significantly in Farha's outlook and practices, particularly during her husband's imprisonment. Farha and Kan'an got married the traditional way after two months of engagement in 1977. In this period, the mid-1970s, Palestinian political parties and factions were actively recruiting youth to the national struggle and gradually assumed a role (and sometime supplanted the family's role) in children's upbringing, social and educational support, and even marriage arrangements. This encouraged youth to challenge and achieve some degree of separation from their families and largely their extended kin. Farha's reflection on her marriage choice exemplifies the attitude of the youth then:

> In my extended family, I was known to be a rebel. I was among the first few girls who obtained a diploma. I worked and had a strong independent personality. I had open-minded friends from well-known families in the village. My parents allowed me the space to be open, although my uncles were very traditional. I did not want to marry within the family, and that is why I agreed to marry Kan'an. All my uncles and relatives strongly opposed this marriage. Getting married to a nonrelative was a challenge to them as this was not a family tradition . . .

In some instances, young men's and women's choice of marriage partners is politically induced. For women, getting married to a patriotic nationalist leader or a political activist represents a strong national belief and ethos; for men, looking for a partner who is politically committed or has a nationalistic bent improves the likelihood that she will be able to cope with their imprisonment or going underground. However, when faced with practical realities, women sometimes are shocked, particularly when they discover that their husbands' progressive political beliefs conflict with their conservative social outlook. Farha expresses her disappointment:

In the early days of our marriage, I realized that Kan'an was always tense and nervous. This was because of his secret political activism, which he informed me of three days after our marriage. Then I was fascinated by the idea that he was patriotic, especially since I, myself, participated as a student in the demonstrations without my parents' knowledge. . . . My husband's family is a traditional conservative family with tribal heritage. It is closed onto itself. They believed that the role of the daughter-in-law is to serve them. . . . I suffered a lot but I could not complain to my family because I decided to marry outside the family. Kan'an had the same social attitude as his family. In general, Kan'an does not like to have a modern wife; he wants a wife like his mother, a housewife who does the housework and raises the children. He was against my college education. He did not see a need for it. I insisted and explained to him that I should have an income to depend on in case he got arrested. He kept silent though he disapproved, and I continued my education. But whenever he met me on the street near the college, he would pretend he did not see me so that people would not know that his wife studied there.

Like many newlywed Palestinian couples unable to afford a home of their own, Farha and Kan'an started their life with the extended family. For Farha, who had a different social outlook than that of Kan'an and his family, living with her in-laws was burdensome. However, the extended family formed her major social and economic support system, particularly in the first round of Kan'an's imprisonment. Family support, coming from the natal family or the in-laws or both, was a common practice for the majority of prisoners' wives and children. As Kan'an explains:

While [I was] in prison, my wife was living with my family, and my father provided for the household. He was well-off. Also, there were many other prisoners like me who had families, and I was not any different. I was not worried about Farha and Tahrir [his daughter]. They visited me every two weeks.

During this period, Farha describes the change in her relations with her in-laws as positive.

Before Kan'an was arrested, his mother tried to control my movement. After he was arrested she changed and said it was none of her business. None of them interfered in what I did or where I went. Perhaps they sympathized with me that Kan'an was arrested when we had just been married. They knew why I went out. I was going to college and later to the kindergarten where I worked; other than that, I went out either to visit my family or to visit Kan'an in prison. . . . They also took care of my daughter, Tahrir, while I was at work. When she was eighteen months, I left her with them and with my family when the society that employs me sent me to Jordan to attend a training course. Nobody opposed my travel. No one doubted my behavior.

Holding "Jerusalem residency" was not of much benefit to Farha and Kan'an in this phase of their life. Kan'an was an employee at the Israeli-controlled Municipality of Jerusalem and was fired upon his arrest. Unlike wives of other Palestinian prisoners employed by Palestinian institutions, Farha was deprived of her husband's salary. They had only one child who was legally entitled to receive the child allowance from the Israeli national security office. However, Farha could not make use of this because it was automatically used to pay back social security dues that her husband had failed to pay for several years. As a Palestinian prisoner's wife, she was eligible for support from the political party with which her husband was affiliated. She received a small monthly allowance, which required a lot of paperwork and travel to Jordan to obtain. Farha also could keep her child at a nursery run by a society that supported children of prisoners free of charge. Later and after her graduation from college, she was given a modestly paid job at a kindergarten run by the same society.

After Kan'an was released from prison in 1982, he pursued his political activism. Although financially they were not much better off than before, depending only on Farha's salary, he decided to live separately with her and the child in an apartment below his parents' house to have some privacy. Farha, on the other hand, wanted to wait until they had their own house and live totally separately from her in-laws. Kan'an prevailed; they moved into the new apartment. However, that renewed the family conflict and affected Farha's relations with her in-laws. Farha explains:

> The decision to live in a separate apartment in the same house was Kan'an's decision. I would have preferred to move to a separate house. He decided we

should move out of the family house fast because he was still politically active, and he did not want his father to see his comrades meeting at his house. His father was opposed to his political involvement especially after he was arrested. . . . My relation with my in-laws was affected when we moved out, especially my relation with Kan'an's mother. We became a bit distant because she felt that I took her son away from her, although I was not behind the idea of leaving the family. She was also upset because now I had my own house and I stopped doing the housework for her.

When Kan'an was imprisoned in 1985, Farha had to face more challenging living conditions. Her burden was heavier because she was caring for three children, expecting her fourth child, and living independently of her in-laws. As soon as she gave birth, instead of giving her a maternity leave, the society laid her off and she was unemployed for two years before she was rehired by the same society. Again she had to depend on various sources to make a living. This time she received the Israeli social security allowance for four children, and for two years she also received the welfare allowance that unemployed Jerusalem residents are entitled to. In addition, she was also eligible for the allowance allocated to a Palestinian prisoner's family provided by the political party.

In the five years of Kan'an's imprisonment, Farha's time was consumed by the different responsibilities and roles of mothering, paid work, and political activism. In addition to bearing the burden of raising the children, providing for them, and caring for the house, she was actively involved in the national struggle when the first intifada erupted in 1987. Farha perceives major changes at the family and community levels. She explains:

> The first intifada was a period of constant action and activism. I was continuously engaged in activities in support of the intifada such as organizing the neighborhood women in the women's group affiliated with the political party. At night, I secretly embroidered Palestinian flags. During that period women's mobility outside the house was accepted and justified. Some women could even sleep outside their homes because of their activism. Kan'an's family was very supportive. They sympathized with me, and also they were affected by the general political environment and the social appreciation the prisoners received during that period. They changed from being very

conservative and reserved into becoming more open socially. They gained social status and appreciation because their sons had an active political role, and they established strong relations with the families of other prisoners.

Because they had residency status in Jerusalem, were affiliated with a political party, and had a supportive family system, Farha and Kan'an enjoyed relatively more privileges than households of other Palestinian prisoners. Therefore, the ten-year period that Kan'an spent in prison did not have a major economic impact on the household. However, his imprisonment had a much deeper impact on intimate marital and intrahousehold relations. As a newlywed couple whose marriage was traditional, Farha and Kan'an were deprived of the opportunity to establish any kind of marital relationship. The one-hour visit at prison every two weeks was not sufficient for the couple to get acquainted with each other, to discover conflicts in tastes and interests, or to discuss family matters, especially when the visit used to take place from behind bars under the close scrutiny of armed security personnel. In the three years they spent together after his first release, they were busy having children; Kan'an was also engaged in political activism, which took him away from home. During the ten years of imprisonment, Kan'an and his prison mates kept busy struggling for better prison living conditions and getting self-educated on political issues. To start with, Kan'an's secret activism forced him to keep a low profile, which with time made him more and more socially withdrawn. Spending ten years in prison added to his isolation. His reserved attitude toward others was a main reason for expressing reluctance to be interviewed during fieldwork; during the meetings, he was not as outspoken and as expressive as was Farha, which did not give him enough voice in the family narrative. Farha, on the other hand, was mobile and active and managed all the family's private and public affairs relatively independently, as well as participating in the national struggle. This condition, which is a common condition of a prisoner and his wife, was reflected on by the couple later on after Kan'an was released.

After he was released from prison the first time and we lived separate from his family, he appreciated my efforts and was considerate. He helped me in the housework, cleaned the house and washed the dishes and cared for the children. That was when he was out of work, but after he got a job, he stopped helping me. After his release the second time, he was exhausted and his health was worn out. He slept long hours and that made him more isolated from the rest of the family. He has always been unsociable and did not mix with others. He rarely visited my family and visited his brothers and sisters only on occasions. Lately, he comes home late after work. My relationship with him is very distant. He does not share with me his concerns; he does not appreciate the hard work I do. We do not have an intimate relationship; and the three daughters we had after his release were accidental.

Kanʿan also has complaints about his relationship with Farha; though he expresses them briefly, his words are charged with anger about losing his status as the man of the house. He emphasizes his role as the father, the decision maker:

Farha and I usually discuss matters and reach a common understanding. However, Farha is very tense and emotional and I avoid arguments with her. In my opinion, at the end the decision should be made, and it is the father who should decide.

Having had to manage on her own, Farha seems to have established some sort of independence that makes Kanʿan uncomfortable. Currently, Kanʿan and Farha keep separate budgets. Kanʿan states:

I know nothing about Farha's income or how much she gets from the National Security.[20] But she knows how much I make. I decide on how to spend my income, and she decides on what to do with hers. I pay the bills and expenses and sometimes we pay the phone bill from the National Security allowance we get for the children.

This conflict is not limited to Kanʿan and Farha but extends to involve the children and Kanʿan. By incarcerating Kanʿan for ten years, the Israeli occupation imposed on Farha and Kanʿan obligatory spacing between children. A few months following his first arrest, they had their first (girl) child, Tahrir,

20. The subsidy minor children receive from the state as Jerusalem residents.

who was twenty-five years old at the time of the interviews. Between his first release and his second arrest, they had two boys and a girl (19, 18, and 17 years respectively). After his second release in 1991, they had three girls (10, 9, and 8). This forced spacing between the children created a generation gap among them and affected their relations with their parents. The first four children feel that they are closer to their mother and are distant from their father. Farha had to manage the household and the children and thus established her own system of household relations and responsibilities. Owing to years of forceful separation from his family and the impact of spending years in prison, Kan'an became more and more withdrawn and grew further and further away from his family, yet he tried to maintain his status as the head of the household.

The eldest daughter, Tahrir, was the most affected of all the children and had to assume responsibility for her siblings and share worries and concerns with her mother at a young age. She describes her experience and her relation with her parents:

> I have a very close relationship with my mother since I am the eldest daughter in the family. There is an age gap between me and the rest of my brothers and sisters. For several years I was an only child. While my father was in prison, and when my two brothers and sister were born, I had to grow up early. I did not live my childhood. My relation with my younger brothers and sisters is that of a caregiver. . . . At home we [my mother and I] were two "heads." There was always conflict between us over who could impose her opinion. . . . My relation with my father was limited to the one-hour visit at prison. After his first release, I could not get used to referring to him when I needed something. I continued asking my mother for permission or advice. My mother is very attached to me, and I can gain her on my side when there is an argument or a conflict at home. . . . This caused problems with my father. We [my father and I] always fight over matters that concern me, like going out and wearing makeup; even simple things like using the hair dryer, he considers them to be shameful. My father boycotts anyone who disagrees with him. . . . When I wanted to go to Egypt, he was against it. I prepared all my travel papers and left. Unwillingly, though, he kept silent.

The other three younger children have similar feelings toward their parents; among them they have established strong sister-brother relationships.

They do not understand why their father is distant from them or why he struggles to control them. Samer (eighteen years old) says:

> I developed good relations with my brother Nathem and wanted to go with him to Egypt to continue my studies. I also have good relations with my sister Sama, who is one year younger than me. The three of us are close in age and we spent a lot of time together at home during the holidays. When my mother was at work, each of us was responsible for caring for one of our three small sisters. My relation with my mother is close and special. I share with her my private matters. I am not on good terms with my father. I spend most of the time with him at the shop but we do not get along well. I wanted to work to earn some pocket money and help my mother, who supports my brother's education. My father says, "Why do you want to work? I take care of your expenses." He does not agree and does not discuss the matter with me.

Sama (seventeen years old):

> I almost have no relations with my father. He is not close to us. He does not allow me to do things, like going out with my friends. I stopped asking him. I feel my mother is responsible for deciding for me and my siblings. When I need permission or advice I go to my mother and she tells my father. . . . We are not used to consulting with my father, and he does not interfere much. He also does not communicate with other people. My relations with my mother are not so good. I feel she is closer to my older sister and brothers. They share with her their private matters. I don't. I have a good relation with my older brother, Samer; we think alike. Tahrir and I got closer only when we moved to this house and started sharing a room. My three small sisters get along well together. They go to the same school and play together. I have a special relationship with my small sister Sireen. I took care of her [during the holidays when my mother was at work].

Kan'an denies that his imprisonment was primarily responsible for this unhealthy relationship with his children and wife. He also does not explicitly blame the Israeli occupation because then he would also have to blame himself for struggling against it. Instead, he throws the blame on Farha, whom he feels has drawn his "natural" role and status away from him.

The prison did not affect my relations with my children. Their visits with me while I was in prison created a basic understanding between us. The problem I see is that they were spoiled while I was in prison, which is usually the case when the father who represents firmness is away from the house. I am not satisfied with how Farha raised the children while I was away, especially in spoiling them, and I think that the upbringing of the children by the mother alone remains insufficient. The mother and the father complement each other.

On the issue of the children's education and marriage he holds a conservative opinion, which reflects his negative reaction to the conflict he has with his eldest daughter, Tahrir. He thinks that she is a negative influence on her younger sister.

God willing, I would like to educate all my children, boys and girls. But this does not prevent the girls from getting married if they get the right chance before they finish their education. Early marriage and settling down is better for the girls in the difficult conditions we live under, especially because we feel insecure because of the Israeli occupation measures. [Referring to his eldest daughter Tahrir] I believe it is important for the girl to get married first and then finish her higher education because when the girl is educated she becomes condescending and would not accept those men who ask for her hand, and then she regrets when it is too late. I prefer for Sama to get married now if a suitable man proposes to marry her.

Kanʿan's fears are confirmed by Sama's outlook for her future

I hope that I can finish my studies and then get a job and be self-dependent like my sister Tahrir. I like the way my sister lives. She is independent; she bought a car and can buy anything she wants because she has an income.

As a result of his imprisonment, Kanʿan suffers the crisis of the male head of a household and struggles with keeping his patriarchal image. This is the case not only because he was deprived of sharing in the upbringing of the children, most of whom grew up while he was confined in prison, but also because he is unable to assume the status of the main provider for his family. After he was released from prison the second time he was weak and could not find regular well-paying work. He was hired by the PNA for a relatively low salary, and in the afternoons he works for his brother in a grocery shop. He tried to run an independent business but failed because he needed the seed money to complete building the family house. One of the projects he started and thought was a potential success was hindered by the Israeli policies against Palestinian house construction in East Jerusalem and the suburbs inside its municipal borders. Kan'an explains why he could not start a business that would bring him a relatively good income:

> When I bought the land in Abu Dis, I was thinking of investment. Since the land is located near the university, I thought I would build an apartment building to rent apartments to university students. I never planned to settle in Abu Dis. I wanted to build my own house on the half acre that my father gave us in Jabal al-Mukabbir [the same residential area where his parents lived and that is within the borders of East Jerusalem]. But the complex and intricate difficulties involved in obtaining a building license from the Israeli authorities, the extremely high fees we were required to pay, and the complicated regulations that restricted house construction and expansion in Jerusalem forced me to change my plans. I decided to build my house in Abu Dis. At that time several families moved to Abu Dis for the same reason.

Where imprisonment created a male crisis for Kan'an, it helped Farha develop independence and self-worth. Negotiating kinship relations within a family patriarchal system, which she refers to as "tribal," she was successful to a certain extent, particularly in matters relevant to the family's living, well-being, and social status as a prisoner's family. However, in matters that are gender-specific, she failed to win her battle. On the personal level, Farha perceives herself as not being rewarded although she has contributed a lot to the well-being of the family. She has tried to fight for some of her rights; she won her dispute with her husband but not those with her in-laws.

> All my life I have been working but I never felt that my income is my own or that I have a personal bank account. Since I started earning an income, I have been spending it on the needs of the household and the children. When we were building the house, I used to get my salary and hand it directly to the contractor. After that I spent all my income to meet the household needs until I took charge of paying for my son's education. Now I keep

all my salary to pay his fees in Egypt. Before that, Kan'an told me all my salary was mine and that I could spend it as I liked. But I use it to buy household needs. In theory the salary is mine but in fact I do not own anything. . . . I thought of retiring but I realized I do not have one penny saved. I wish I could retire, but we cannot do without my income. . . . When Kan'an was in prison the second time, I thought of obtaining a building license to start the house, and I suggested that we register the land title in my name so that I could start the paperwork. Kan'an's father refused the idea. All his relatives tried to convince me that this was not acceptable behavior, and I had to give up the idea. Kan'an also refused the idea. I felt that it was my right to register the land in my name especially since I shared in paying for it. I was very upset and left the house for a few days. But then I had to come back. . . . When I received a sum of money, my share from a piece of land we inherited from my father, Kan'an suggested that I deposit the money in his bank account, and I agreed. After a while, the idea bothered me, and I asked him to give me the money back because I felt it was my right, especially since I contributed a lot financially to the house. After a long argument, he gave it back to me. I saved it to pay for the education of one of the children.

Her daughter Tahrir gives her own perception of her mother's outlook and character, which is biased as a result of the conflict they both had over Tahrir's choice of a marriage partner.

My mother is a modern woman. She is very aware of a lot of [modern] progressive and gender concepts. She got educated, raised us, and supported us. She encourages us to get educated, and she stood up for her rights. At the same time she is affected by the surrounding environment, and often takes a socially conservative position, such as her position regarding my marriage.

Farha objected to Tahrir's choice of spouse although he was a relative of hers. She thought he was not the proper future spouse for her daughter because he had bypassed her parents and started a relation with her when he still held strong emotions for his ex-fiancée.

The case of this family shows the serious impact of imprisonment on intrahouseholds roles, relations, and dynamics, which did not allow the family members to live at an acceptable level of harmony. Kan'an's imprisonment made him suffer a crisis as the male head of the household, and he struggled with keeping his patriarchal image. On the other hand, it allowed Farha space to develop independence and self-worth. In the absence of Kan'an from the household, she set up her own household management system and division of roles, and thus created a network of relations between her and the children and among the children themselves. Tahrir, the eldest daughter, assumed a caring role and shared with her mother in decision making at an early age, contributing to her developing a strong and independent character. Furthermore, she gained status because for the past few years she has been a major income earner in the family and has helped support her siblings' education and cover the family's expenses. Not having grown up under the authority of her father and having established a sisterly and friendly relationship with her mother allowed her to challenge her father's role as the decision maker. Kan'an was not an integral part of this whole network, nor did he have the chance to contribute to forming it. When he returned to join the family, he was not well accommodated. Kan'an denies that his imprisonment has affected his relationship with his children and wife. And he does not blame the Israeli occupation, to avoid blaming himself for struggling against it. In the case of the children, who could not recognize his "intrusion" in their family system, their behavior with him was not unusual for prisoners' children. In general, it is unclear why children like Tahrir and her siblings behave negatively toward parents who are politically active. Is it their feeling of being neglected and deserted? Are they blaming their father because they were too young to blame the Israeli occupation?

Conclusion

"The family is a big heart that holds and accommodates everybody" (Munira).

But how long can the Palestinian family sustain its function and role as a "big heart"?

Palestinian families live under conditions characterized by increasing insecurity, vulnerability, and cantonization. The consequences of this sustained crisis are not only represented in loss of jobs and a sharp decline in household income, but also in placing more and more families at risk of losing their lives and of suffering serious physical and psychological ill effects; basic services and systems (like sanitation, medical care, education, labor market) have been fragmented, and the whole social and cultural fabric of Palestinian society has been ruptured. In such a context, how long can the Palestinian family sustain itself and respond to the escalating demands placed upon it if its resources are stretched to the limits; if seeking alternative income is hopeless and the usual household coping strategies are eroding; if poverty is generalized in the local community and the society as a whole; if the formal welfare support system is directed to the poorest of the poor, favoring widows and orphans, or the pre-intifada poor; if the formal support system provided by the PNA is limited to monthly salaries and a tight budget for welfare assistance and is mostly dependent on donor assistance; if the possibilities for job creation are almost nonexistent; and if increasingly families are unable to access medical and educational facilities? Undoubtedly, in such conditions, Palestinian families are left almost totally unprotected in the absence of any sort of support, whether in securing their daily bread or in attaining their basic legal human rights; they are left alone to resist and struggle for survival even as they strive for mobility.

The socioeconomic trends and dynamics of the intifada, war conditions, and Israeli policies confining Palestinians and preventing any semblance of normal life are all enacted in the arena of intrahousehold relations and dynamics across gender and generation. The family narratives presented and analyzed in this chapter do not reflect the dramatic side of the political conditions in terms of physical loss of lives or material damage but do provide an initial understanding of the invisible yet deeper impact of the long-standing Israeli occupation. In the course of struggling for survival and mobility, the individual household and family members are constantly in dynamic interaction within the boundaries of the familial patriarchal system and the extrahousehold dynamics of the Israeli occupation policies, the formal and informal support institutions, and the local community in which their families and households are located

Loss of work and decline in household income has strong resonance in the gendered reallocation of household material and labor resources and reflects the gendered reaction of dealing with the dilemma. As documented in quantitative and rapid appraisal qualitative research on the impact of the intifada, male breadwinners suffer the crisis of job and income loss and women "absorb the shock," carrying the burden of providing for the family. As documented in the literature, in general men do not compromise on their previous socioeconomic status and look or wait for opportunities; women, on the other hand, are more practical and seek opportunities that enable them to maintain the family living and integrity. Hammami shows how Palestinian refugee rural women are more flexible in adjusting to the new context, taking up various productive roles they were not used to, while their men, unable to find what the rural culture terms as "decent and respectable" work, assume one role (holding the refugee ration card) and, according to their wives, sit there doing nothing for the rest of their lives (1998, 308–9). Our family narratives support existing research. Dealing with his dilemma of turning from a provider to a dependent, the male breadwinner's response varies with his particular circumstances. The few who can live on savings or have opportunities to immigrate or receive remittances from abroad can deal with their crises, whether they try to seek additional income alternatives or just hibernate. Others, and these are increasingly becoming the majority, very often employ the strategies of isolation, avoidance, aggression, assistance refusal, and striving to maintain their status as heads of the household and primary decision makers. Women, as secondary providers for the family, take the role of primary providers by contributing their income and taking overtime work or seeking a source of income if they are homemakers, in addition to their management roles involving tighter household budgets and resources. That women assume the role of primary providers makes the common case that women's work is key to family survival; however, in other cases the practice of women's paid work is restricted to minimal home-based income generation or conditioned by circumstances specific to the local community. Women's reactions to the male breadwinner crisis vary by circumstances; they may accommodate it, sympathize with it, bear the burden of its consequences, or struggle against and resist it.

The narratives here go beyond what quantitative indicators or coping strategy studies reveal. The coping strategies of the families included here seem to go beyond pooling of resources, reallocation of labor and material resources, reducing expenditures and consumption, and depending on assistance and borrowing; they show that marriage is central to survival and mobility whether in times of sustained crisis or in more relaxed times. Furthermore, coping strategy studies reveal intrahousehold cooperation and cannot capture intricate and hidden conflicts inside the household. In the process of household reorganization of priorities to maintain integrity and to seek better future options where possible, individuals are forced to compromise their aspirations. Whether the compromise is on parents' hopes for better education and marriage opportunities for children, individual or parental desire for establishing separate households and living arrangements for their children, or individual adults' aspirations to be independent and in control of their resources or secure their future, the consequences often disadvantage women. In the Palestinian context, marriage arrangements for women and for men, too, appear central to the family's coping for survival and striving for mobility, whether in times of crisis or in more relaxed conditions. However, in the case of coping with the dilemma, marriage as a parental strategy can often be impacted by gender, placing future opportunities in education, work, or free choice at stake, particularly for young girls. In the case of marriage as a mobility strategy, girls are sometimes either excluded or at a disadvantage. In the marriage arrangement process men and women, particularly some mothers, are active agents.

The intrahousehold relations and dynamics in the family narratives reveal that women and men are both victimized within the family patriarchal system and agents in reinforcing it, accommodating its norms and codes, or negotiating and resisting its restrictions and boundaries. Some girls as young as seventeen are active in negotiating kinship boundaries and restraints on their own and their family's private matters, and others of the same age accommodate parental choice to marry them young and deprive them of education and the opportunity to grow up to exercise free choice. Adult or older women follow a similar path; some may negotiate and resist on varying issues, winning some of their battles while losing others; some women reinforce patriarchal norms sometimes out of altruism and at other times in pursuit of individual interests in survival or future security and mobility. Men, on the other hand, show a greater tendency to protect and maintain the patriarchal family system. In the absence of the family patriarch, boys as young as thirteen feel pressured to earn an income, discipline sisters, and risk confronting the Israeli occupation army and the consequences of its restraining policies, although they may be ridiculed or unrecognized because of their youth. Adult men are also concerned with maintaining their masculine roles and protecting their patriarchal image, which the Israeli occupation in a variety of ways had a major role in destroying.

The impact of the Israeli occupation and the rise and development of the Palestinian national movement in resistance to the occupation has had both

visible and invisible consequences for the patriarchal family system and its interaction with the local community and the formal and informal institutions
of the Palestinian national resistance movement. Consequences like girls'
early marriage out of parental concern to avoid risking the occupation's ability
to compromise their future or the separation of wives and children from their
husbands and fathers are visible and can be quantified. However, the impact
of imprisonment on the most intimate and private marital relations, such as
forced spacing between children, sexual and marital relations, and parent-
children relations, are invisible and highly damaging to family integrity. Another significant impact of the interaction of family dynamics and extrafamily
dynamics with the Israeli occupation is the ebb and flow in the ability of individuals, particularly girls and women, to negotiate and resist kinship boundaries and constraints on their gender roles, relations, and rights. The spread of
progressive, leftist, and secular ideologies at one stage in the history of Palestinian society under the Israeli occupation, or its regression and the expansion
and spread of active Islamist movements at another stage are enacted on the
internal gender dynamics of the Palestinian family. In both cases the Palestinian family is a vehicle through which national, cultural, patriarchal, and/or religious ethos and morality are transmitted and perpetuated. In the former
stage, men but especially women had opportunities to negotiate gender-
power relations and patriarchal control. Their success was most often related
to issues tied to nationalism and patriotism and in disputes with husbands and
other females in the family; however, they lost those highly gendered and cultural disputes. In the later stage, negotiations and conflicts have not disappeared but have become more invisible and abstract, becoming more
complex and more difficult to pursue with the increasing economic hardships, unpredictability, and loss of horizon for a just political solution.

Palestinian families are sometimes victims of the conditions that Palestinian society is currently undergoing. When aspects like male aggression, the
protection of family honor, and women's victimization are quantified, they
may be interpreted as widespread phenomena, emerging from "the old chest-
nut of 'adat wa taqalid [customs and traditions]" (Abu Nahleh and Johnson
2003, 45), particularly in the rural areas and refugee camps. However, the narratives have revealed a different interpretation. Destitute families like those
living in refugee camps are more at risk. Poor families in camps are large, job-
less and incomeless, living on various but slim sources of assistance, confined

within a narrow physical and social space, and unprotected in the absence of proper and or sufficient public support systems and the lack of the rule of law or an effective legal system. Such a context can provide a better understanding of the extent of pride and honor felt by a hopeless destitute male, deprived of masculinity and social recognition and confined in all ways by the Israeli occupation.

Cooperative and noncooperative household models have been helpful in providing insight in the analysis of family narratives in this study; however, they are inadequate by themselves in the analysis of Palestinian families in a context shaped by a history of dispossession and occupation. In addition, a significant finding revealed by the camp narrative and others contradicts some of the findings of these studies. In the Palestinian context, the local community has proved to be of such high significance to the survival and mobility of families and individuals that it does not allow them to negotiate exiting it. Unlike other contexts, the Palestinian local community provides social cohesion, in addition to economic support, and plays a major supportive role for individuals and families who are in daily if not hourly contact with it, although it confines them and pressures them in many ways.

A final note concerns the representativeness of the cases and narratives presented and analyzed in this chapter. The narratives are not a representative sample from which I can draw generalizable conclusions. Such conclusions require more investigation of issues and matters that have arisen in this study and other studies focusing on similar themes. However, the narratives help us identify family prototypes, and their analysis contributes insights that can be added to the existing literature on the impact of the intifada, war conditions, and the occupation and reoccupation of Palestinian communities and the policies of Israeli cantonization and siege. I hope that this investigation can also contribute to the international literature on families in the context of war, conflicts, and hardships.

4

EMIGRATION, CONSERVATISM, AND CLASS FORMATION IN WEST BANK AND GAZA STRIP COMMUNITIES

Jamil Hilal

This chapter attempts to analyze emigration data collected through a household survey designed by the Institute of Women's Studies at Birzeit University and executed by the Palestinian Central Bureau of Statistics (PCBS) in 1999, as well as other relevant data published by PCBS and a number of studies.[1] The analysis deals with two related aspects of the emigration process. The first pertains to the extent, patterns, and features of the phenomenon as it emerged in the West Bank and Gaza Strip soon after the shattering of Palestinian society in 1948. The second attempts to read the social processes and consequences of the phenomenon.

Two themes are pursued within the context of settler colonialism, daily border crossing for work inside Israel, large-scale work emigration to the Gulf states and Jordan, arrested urbanization, and the impact of political regional changes in the last three decades of the last century. The first theme concerns the ways in which emigration fostered social "conservatism." The second examines the relationship between emigration and the formation of a Palestinian middle class. In the West Bank and Gaza Strip, this class formation took place outside a "national" economy and outside the usual relations with other social classes. The two Palestinian areas witnessed the growth of a significant section of a Palestinian working class through employment in Israel, again outside a "national" economy and in the absence of a sovereign Palestinian state. In the Palestinian case, and probably in the case of other migrations to

---

1. I was involved in the questionnaire design, fieldworker training, and analysis of some of the data other than those related to emigration.

oil-producing Gulf states of professionals and individuals with advanced education and skills, we witness a "conservative" impact on the mother society.

Sources and Consequences of Palestinian Emigration

Socioeconomic and Political Background

Emigration has been a salient and persistent feature of the life of Palestinian communities in the West Bank and Gaza Strip since 1948. The shattering of Palestinian society in 1948 (which Palestinians call *Nakba* or catastrophe) paved the way for emigration to become a prominent feature of Palestinian life. Palestinian communities have experienced eviction, as happened in 1948 and at specific times since. Internal migration, particularly from rural to urban centers, was known to Palestinian society during the British Mandate (1917–48). After 1948 the eastern area of Palestine (known later as the West Bank) and the southern area on the Mediterranean coast (known later as the Gaza Strip) that remained in Arab hands became two of the main destinations for Palestinian refugees driven out from areas occupied by Zionist forces and declared as Israel in May 1948.

The destruction, in 1948, of the "cosmopolitan" coastal Palestinian cities of Jaffa, Haifa, and 'Akka (Acre) that had emerged as growing urban centers during the British Mandate, left for Palestinians inland towns (such as Hebron, Nablus, East Jerusalem, and Gaza City) that were, and continue to be, dominated by presumed kinship networks (known as *hamula*, *'a'ila*, and occasionally *'ashira*) of differing size, sometimes counting in the thousands. The Israeli occupation in 1967 and before that Jordanian and Egyptian rule (in the West Bank and Gaza Strip, respectively) effectively arrested urbanization and failed to produce the necessary economic development to halt or slow down the pace of out-migration.

Two general features of Palestinian communities in the West Bank and Gaza Strip need be identified from the outset: emigration, which formed an integral dynamic of Palestinian communities from 1948 to the early 1990s;[2]

2. There have been a number of estimates of the magnitude of emigration from the West Bank and Gaza Strip after the 1948 war and the June 1967 war. Among the early attempts was that of Abu Shukr (1990) in the mid-1980s. On the basis of a survey of 1,186 households, he

and an ongoing renewal or reconstruction of family relations. Both in fact have been decisive in forming strategies aimed at enhancing life chances in highly risky and precarious socioeconomic and political conditions.

Improving life chances means attempting to secure or advance income, employment, savings, or the accumulation of wealth; higher status; access to health, education, and better living conditions; general welfare; and freedom from repression. It also means minimizing risk that ranges from guarding against unemployment to escaping being jailed, to guarding against injury, to reducing the risk of one's property being destroyed or confiscated. Kinship solidarity or identity of the kind referred to locally as *hamula* or *'a'ila* solidarity acquired new relevance for Palestinian households as their communities faced major political shifts, social dislocations, and economic uncertainties and as land ownership was privatized and wage labor became the dominant source of income.[3]

These two features—discontinuity with the past (leaving home and crossing borders to new places and cultural spaces) and continuity, real or imagined, with the past (reinvesting in kinship solidarities as a form of social capital)—must be viewed against the background of major socioeconomic and political processes that have reshaped the various Palestinian communities since the *Nakba*, particularly those in the West Bank and Gaza Strip since their coming under military occupation in 1967. An anthropologist studying a refugee camp in the West Bank (Dahayasha camp) has observed that while labor migration of professionals to the Gulf enhanced their economic position, the fact of their being denied rights and freedoms in the countries of migration prevented the translation of this gain into social independence and mobility. The contradictory situation of the professional migrant in the Gulf state "fostered a twofold dependency: on the one hand, that of the family on

---

noted that 40 percent of families in the West Bank and 39 percent in the Gaza Strip reported having emigrant members; 65 percent were sons or daughters and another 17 percent were brothers and sisters of the household head. Nearly two thirds (65.5 percent) of emigrants were between twenty-one and thirty-five years of age (Abu Shukr 1990, 53, 56, 57). See also Salim Tamari's review (1983, 185–92) of other studies on out-migration from the West Bank during the 1960s and 1970s.

3. For a review of literature on the role kinship in Palestinian society, see Rothenberg 1998/1999.

the economic support of their migrant sons and daughters; on the other that of migrants on the familial social ties and connections in the household. One of the results of this is the prolonged preservation of traditional patriarchal relations within the family despite the physical separation of young family members and despite the latter's economic advantages" (Rosenfeld 2004, 163).

Since the middle of the last century, the West Bank and Gaza Strip have been undergoing a process of rapid marginalization of agriculture and the increasing dominance of wage labor as the source of income for the majority of households. The two areas have had increasing access to Palestinian secular education, including education at the university level. High rates of emigration and the redefining of kinship solidarity have been taking place within the political context of imposed external rule and colonial occupation, together with the absence of statehood. The beginning of Israeli occupation coincided with the emergence of the PLO as institutions and as a political discourse defining (in secular terms) the Palestinian national political field and mobilizing Palestinians for independent statehood.

In the 1980s, the Palestinian national political field saw the appearance, from outside the ranks of the PLO, of political Islam represented by Islamic Jihad and Hamas. Both these movements stood in opposition to the secularism that prevailed within the PLO. Political Islam did advocate and observe a strict code regarding gender relations, and this is part of the agenda of the Islamization of society. Social conservatism, although it covers the field of gender relations, is not confined to it nor does it position it within a political agenda as political Islam does.[4]

The second Gulf war in 1991 placed the PLO in political and financial isolation as Arab and regional support was diverted to organizations of political Islam, including Hamas and Islamic Jihad. Such organizations were investing much of their efforts in redefining political culture and building up their constituencies.[5] Thus they succeeded to a large extent, particularly in the second

4. It may be worth mentioning that the Arabic term for conservatism does not have the political connotations of the English term. It stresses social conduct and behavior in the public space and sphere.

5. See for example, poll no. 6 conducted by the Development Studies Programme at Birzeit University in February 2002 (DSP 2002). Hamas and Islamic Jihad showed higher popular support than Fatah, the ruling party in the Palestinian National Authority (PNA); more than

intifada, in replacing the traditional Palestinian embroidered dress (that varied by region and even by village) with the uniform "Islamic" dress; imposing the use of the green "Islamic" banner instead of the national flag; and replacing the Palestinian male headdress *(kufiyya)* that PLO fighters used to cover their faces, with a black mask. In the summer of 2005 one municipality in the West Bank that was dominated by Hamas supporters banned a cultural festival that was to take place in that municipality, declaring that such activities (music, signing, feature films, and dancing) were in conflict with Islamic values.

Emigration and Social Conservatism

The idea that emigration has reinforced conservatism in village communities of the West Bank was suggested by Tamari (1993, 26). What I am proposing here, however, is that the impact of emigration on Palestinian communities was more generalized. That is, emigration acted as a factor in promoting social conservatism not only in villages, but also in towns and refugee camps. Commuting to work in Israel and emigration to the Gulf states and Jordan have affected sections of the working class and a section of the middle class.

Social conservatism stresses the significance and importance of local traditions, local identities and kinship solidarities *('a'ila, hamula,* or *'ashira)*.[6] Such significance is not granted by political Islam, which tends to distrust local identities and local traditions, as they tend to open the possibility for the reconstruction and reinvention of tradition.[7] Nevertheless there is an overlapping between political Islam and social conservatism. The most obvious areas of the overlapping between the two appear in the area of gender relations and in the reassertion of male control over the sexuality and reproductive functions of women.

---

40 percent of those polled supported Fatah in 1996 and 1997, but that support dropped to less than 25 percent in the early months of 2002, whereas support for Hamas, which was about 12 percent in 2000 (before the second intifada), rose above 20 percent by early 2002, and to 30 percent in June 2005. In the Legislative Council elections in January 2006, Hamas won a majority of seats, moving from the main opposition party to the ruling party of the PNA.

6. Local and kinship identities and solidarities are behind much of what is labeled *wasta* (mediation), which means exercising favoritism in job, business, and service allocation on the basis of local, family, or political connections.

7. In the sense used by Eric Hobsbawm (Hobsbawm and Ranger 1983).

Political Islam generally distrusts popular culture, and tends to undermine the role of women as guardians of local traditions and customs. The latter role was emphasized as males' commuting to work in Israel during the 1960s, 1970s, and 1980s left women in charge of defining local traditions and customs. Men's religious radicalism seemed to reinforce their social conservatism as indicated by the results of a large-scale survey conducted in the West Bank and Gaza Strip in the early 1990s (Heiberg and Ovensen 1993, 263). However religious radicalism should be distinguished from the popular religiosity that often is integrated with local traditions (veneration of local shrines, local religious festivals, and the like).

Endogamous marriage, for example, cannot be explained simply as an attempt to keep property within the kinship group or as adherence to inheritance norms, because propertyless households practice cousin marriage no less than propertied ones. In the 1960s, 1970s, and 1980s the political and socioeconomic dynamics promoting endogamous marriage included providing assistance to new arrivals (as emigrants seeking work or as students seeking higher education), as well as playing the "crucial role in the recruitment process and mobility of the peasant-workers within the Israeli economy" (Tamari 1983, 389).

The general motive of most Palestinians in crossing borders has not been to change their lifestyle, customs, or identity, but rather to improve their life chances. As such Palestinian emigration can be classified as a form of "conservative" migration in contrast to "innovative" migration, which seeks a new lifestyle and mode of living (Boyle, Halfacree, and Robinson 1998, 37). Palestinian emigrants found the best employment opportunities in the oil-producing Arab states, despite the fact that these countries were known to have very restrictive social and cultural fields and that the state acted as the guardian of morals, using religion as a tool of control and legitimation and for the enforcement of a strict code of behavior. In most of these states, civil society (political parties, trade unions, mass and professional organizations, and social movements) is practically nonexistent or simply confined to religious associations and institutions. In the 1970s and 1980s these states experienced an upsurge of radical Islamic movements, some with an absolutist interpretation of Islam. This milieu affected immigrant Palestinian communities in the Gulf states, as well those in Jordan, which until the late 1980s shared many of the features of the authoritarian state. Furthermore in these states the political and organizational expressions of Palestinian national identity were either suppressed or viewed with suspicion. Palestinian immigrants were denied not only rights to citizenship but also rights to permanent residency regardless of how many years they had lived or worked in the countries in which they resided. Even those born in these countries were not granted citizenship rights.

The usual pattern of out-migration in the 1960s and 1970s was phased. Males went first, to be followed, at a later stage, by their families. In the first stage, women who were left behind came under the control of their husbands' families or (if the latter were absent) their own natal families. In the second stage, women joined their husbands as dependants (as associate rather than autonomous emigrants) with no or little chance of paid employment outside the home. Thus, emigration strengthened the traditional conception of male as provider and female as housekeeper. Here a link can be seen between emigration and social conservatism. Inside the West Bank and Gaza Strip, customary restrictions on female inheritance and the predominance of wage labor (which excluded, to a large extent, women) gave additional weight to this ideology (Glavanis and Glavanis 1989; Moors 1995), particularly as more and more men in villages and camps joined the labor force, employed in Israel and later by the Palestinian National Authority.

Available data suggest that no more than 12 percent of Arab emigrant women, including Palestinian women in the Gulf countries, were gainfully employed in the 1980s;[8] this percentage is similar to employment rates in the West Bank and Gaza Strip in the 1990s. That means that the bulk of women emigrants were dependent (or considered as such) on their husbands or nearest of kin. Thus gender relations and attitudes were reproduced and reasserted as a consequence of the process of emigration itself.

Israeli colonialism did deliberately diminish Palestinian public space (as represented by cinemas, theaters, cafés, hotels, clubs, parks, places of outdoor entertainment, and political gatherings) and obstructed the emergence of a free and active public sphere where political and professional organizations and the mass media could operate (apart from East Jerusalem, which was an-

8. In the mid-1980s some 5.1 million immigrants resided in the six Gulf states, constituting 72 percent of the total labor force in these countries. The labor force participation rate for migrant Arab women was 12 percent (Russell 1995, 259).

nexed by Israel soon after its occupation; there, some space for cultural activities and for the publication of newspapers and journals was allowed). The
scope of the public sphere was reduced further during periods of tension and
militant resistance, as happened in the first and second intifadas (with curfews, blockades, sieges, and other restrictions). Israel, as a colonial power, out-
lawed political organizations and imposed censorship on the Palestinian
press. This restriction, it has been argued, gave more prominence to private
space and the private sphere.[9] The suffering and repression that were intensified during both intifadas have reinforced a kind of puritanical ethic, which
frowned on some public activities, especially in the cultural sphere.

Palestinian migrants who went to the oil-producing Gulf states in the
1950s soon formed a community that was identified by its national origin, and
to which new emigrants were drawn. Lacking the protection of their own
state, Palestinians felt, probably more than other migrant communities, that
they were under the political and social scrutiny of the host state. Like other
immigrants to these states, Palestinians were excluded from the usual forms of
social integration with host societies (close friendship, marriage, home visiting, and so on).

The socioeconomic, cultural, and political boundaries that immigrant
communities map for themselves are expressions of a heavily tilted balance of
forces within the state in favor of the locals as against the immigrants. Similarly, a skewed balance of forces exists in the case of Palestinian commuters
who work in Israel: residence is not permitted, integration is not accepted, and
equal status with Israeli workers is not acknowledged.[10] Thus most Palestinians in the West Bank and Gaza Strip know Israelis simply as occupiers, and a
minority knows them as bosses. In the Gulf states Palestinians experienced
their residence in the host country mainly as foreign employees working for an
indigenous stratum of state and private employers.

9. This phenomenon was noted by Marianne Heiberg with emphasis on the Palestinian
housing unit as a private domain signaling the prominence of the nuclear family in Palestinian
society (Heiberg and Ovensen 1993, chap. 3).

10. Wages earned by Palestinians were considerably lower than those earned by Israelis
doing the same jobs. West Bank and Gaza Strip workers in Israel were barred from becoming
members of the Histadrut (the general trade union of Israeli workers) and from residing in Israel.

The discrimination felt by emigrant Palestinians (in terms of wages, rights, legal status and standing, and dependence on the goodwill of a local sponsor or *wakil* for the continuation of work and business) promoted reliance on kinship networks, both at home and in the host country, as a form of social security. Palestinian identity was reconstructed through intermarriage within the community or with partners from home, by celebrating national days and events, and by supporting the PLO or one of its political factions. In the late 1960s and in the 1970s, a national political tradition was created with rituals, language, and symbols that were familiar to most Palestinian communities inside and outside Palestine, as much as the state which they lived and worked allowed.

Palestinians emigrating to Gulf states and Jordan entered political fields that did not allow criticism of the host regimes. In North America, Europe, and Australia, emigration meant crossing cultural fields that required a process of negotiation by emigrants of their cultural and national identity. A majority of Palestinians found refuge in celebrating their national (often territorially specific) customs, which they viewed as existing at the time of leaving their home *(il-iblad)*. The process of identity reconstruction often involved (among other things) family reunions and marrying from the emigrant community or returning home to marry. It also involved making visits to home communities and occasionally investing in land, real estate, and business there. The spread of village and town associations among Palestinian emigrant communities in Arab and American cities is an example of how solidarity on the basis of localities is reconstructed as a way to reassert local identities and links to the homeland. Such associations are formed to keep alive traditions that in some cases have been abandoned in the home communities.

Social conservatism, like the popular religiosity that is widespread in Palestinian society as in many other societies in the region and elsewhere, does not carry a specific political agenda, as does political Islam. Political Islam seeks political and societal change invoking a vision drawn from a specific interpretation of Islam. Palestinian villages and camps, where most Palestinians who commuted to work in Israel came from, were turned into dormitories for the men; this arrangement did not help in promoting a radical outlook. In fact, the Israeli colonial-settler occupation turned the whole West Bank and Gaza Strip into a suburb of Tel Aviv and other Israeli urban centers.

As mentioned earlier, Israel's colonialism deliberately obstructed Palestinian self-propelled urbanization and the cultural and organizational forms associated normally with urbanization.[11]

Jordanian and Egyptian rule, and the subsequent Israeli military colonial occupation, encouraged *hamula* or kinship cleavages, as they were seen as facilitating central control and delegitimized or weakened (it was thought) Palestinian nationalism. Thus, kinship solidarities did help to maintain a kind of social conservatism, in the sense of maintaining patriarchal relations. It is true that membership in political organizations and other nonterritorial associations did grow in the 1960s, 1970s, and 1980s. But the main input of these organizations was understandably nationalistic, with an orientation to the establishment of an independent Palestinian state and not sociocultural change as such.

Furthermore, the political economies of the West Bank and Gaza Strip did indeed hinder the emergence of class-related solidarities, as a result of a highly fragmented working class, a localized and weak capitalist class, and the dominance of small family business in the informal sector of the economy, among other factors. Thus it is not *hamula* or clan identities as such that kept class identities from developing among villagers, as has been suggested (Tamari 1981, 60) or made them underdeveloped in refugee camps in West Bank and Gaza Strip (Heiberg and Ovensen 1993, 258). It is the political economy of the West Bank and Gaza Strip and the colonial situation that have kept social class in an embryonic state (Hilal 1999, 70–77).

The absence of a Palestinian territorial state and its attendant attributes of citizenship with its sets of rights and obligations is a factor that promoted a reliance on other structures for socioeconomic support. Such structures were provided by kinship and locality affiliations, as well as by political organizations, those belonging to the PLO and to the Islamic movement. Often, depending on the strength of each at any particular moment, each of the two types of affiliations utilized the other to strengthen its influence.

---

11. Higher wages from work in Israel and its settlements did promote some upward mobility because it helped working class families send their children to local universities in the 1980s and 1990s. The fact that university education was largely free also helped in the making of the new middle class in these areas.

The Political Economy of Palestinian Emigration

The socioeconomic and political situation following the *Nakba* encouraged Palestinian communities in the West Bank and Gaza Strip to adopt emigration as much as wider kinship solidarities as household strategies. Among these processes are those that restructured, in major ways, local and regional labor markets creating uneven economic development and differential labor markets (capital intensive and labor intensive, as well as the creation of a vacuum for jobs that could not be filled by local labor). In other words, demand for labor was created—during the 1960s, 1970s, and to a degree in the 1980s—in the Gulf states, Israel, North America, Europe, and Australia to which Palestinians in the West Bank and Gaza Strip could respond. This led both to speculative and to contractual emigration and in some places to the formation of "chain" migrations or migration "streams" (to the Gulf states and the Americas, and to Jordan in the 1950s and 1960s). Contractual migration applied more in the Gulf states, whereas many Palestinian emigrants to North and South American relied more on help from relatives who were already there.[12]

Rather than viewing emigration within a functionalist framework of social adaptation (Hovdenak, Pedersen, Tuastad, and Zureik 1997), it is more fruitful analytically to view it as "enterprise creation" through which individuals and families seek to change their circumstances by opting out of risk situations created by wars, occupation, repression, economic stagnation, or discrimination. It should be noted that the availability of opportunities for opting out is crucial and that these opportunities are differentially accessible as they vary by class position, educational level, age, and gender. Strategies do not end with the arrival of emigrants in their country of destination; rather, strategies evolve as emigrants attempt to improve or change life circumstances and create new households and family structures.

Emigration as a matter of household strategy involves questions of timing, logistics, use of resources, and scenarios of possible outcomes. Thus, it is likely to involve all the adults of the household even if only one member is an emi-

12. For a discussion of these terms and approaches to migration, see Boyle, Halfacree, and Robinson 1998.

grant, as is often the case in the initial stages of emigration. Like marriage and higher education, emigration involves the use of household resources, expectations of the use of resources upon the return of the emigrant (e.g., remittances, investment, house-building), regular visits or permanent return or permanent settlement abroad, the consequences on the internal relations within the household, and emerging new family formations. In fact, marriage and emigration are often interrelated as male emigrants return to seek wives from their original communities. It is generally known, for example, that those who have U.S. passports (men or women) are regarded as desirable marriage partners who can help to improve the life chances of other members of the household.

By looking at emigration as a household enterprise (where household members have unequal decision-making powers), one avoids entanglement in the structure-versus-agency theoretical debate. Emigration is usually planned, negotiated, and enacted by household members within the context of specific socioeconomic and political processes. However, emigration cannot be reduced to a process of "individual and household adaptation to a complex social world" (Pedersen 1997, 7), because it is not clear to what the individual or household is "adapting." Moreover, it is an ongoing process that involves different strategies at different periods and as situations and circumstances change. It takes place within a context of structured socioeconomic and political changes, and the agency of individuals or households is not simply passive adaptation but involves active intervention with the intention of changing the individual's or household's life chances or socioeconomic situation.

Typically, emigrant groups engage in various cultural or ideological forms of resistance, assimilation, conformity, or escape in the host country. Mechanisms for such engagements take the form of reproduction of identity (national, ethnic, religious), citizenship (a demand to acquire the full rights of citizenship), or interest politics or a combination of these. Thus the Palestinian communities in the Gulf states tended to assert, in nonconfrontational forms, their Palestinian identity; in states like Kuwait, they formed a kind of "ghetto" (Abu-Bakr 1999, 35). Palestinians who migrated and settled in Jordan tended to combine a strategy of socioeconomic integration with the maintenance of their Palestinian identity and links particularly with relatives in the West Bank. In North and South America, probably a more complex interplay between interest and identity politics took place with emphasis, perhaps, on Arab and religious identities.

The Oslo accords and the establishment of the PNA (as an embryonic territorial state) in 1994 reversed trends in the population movement in the West Bank and Gaza Strip by allowing the return of some 130,000 Palestinians within the four years following the establishment of the PNA.[13] However, the continuation of a colonial-settler situation (as evidenced by the reoccupation in 2002 of the PNA-controlled areas) has not significantly reduced the push factors toward emigration, particularly among the young, the ambitious, and the educated.[14]

Emigration as a Mechanism of Middle-Class Construction

Emigration has provided an important channel for the construction and reconstruction of the Palestinian middle class.[15] But the bulk of this new middle class, insofar as the West Bank and Gaza Strip were concerned, was made in the Gulf states and in Jordan. In these states, the Palestinian middle class had to be accepted by the dominant institutions of a "conservative" nature. Emigrants to Europe and to the Americas had multiple routes in the formations of their class identities. Decisive among these are level of education and type of employment. Successful integration of educated Palestinians into the new countries (including citizenship) often reduced their interaction with their home communities. As early as the 1950s, researchers were noticing the consequences of emigration for the class structure of Palestinian villages. The construction of an "American quarter" in Baytin, a Palestinian village in the

13. At the end of 1997, when a population census was carried out, slightly more than 267,000 (10.5 percent of the population) were recorded as returnees. Of these, 48.5 percent were returnees after the establishment of the PNA (Malki and Shalabi 2000, 53–55).

14. In poll no. 6 mentioned earlier (see footnote 5, page 188), two-thirds of the respondents (68 percent) in February 2002 said that they did not feel safe (personally) because of the confrontation that has been developing with the Israeli occupation. Nearly 22 percent of respondents said that they would emigrate if they had the chance. The percentage among the very young (i.e., between the ages of eighteen and twenty-two) rose to 39 percent.

15. For an interesting account of emigration and its relation to the construction of the Lebanese middle class, see Khater 2001.

West Bank, is an early illustration of the formation of a middle class through emigration. Modern and spacious houses in this quarter were built by families that had at least one member who had emigrated to the United States and who had been successful in business and had sent money to build a family house or had himself returned to build a house for himself and his family (Lutfiyya 1966, 13–14). The same patterns can be found in other villages and towns in the West Bank and Gaza Strip, thanks to successful emigrants to the Arab Gulf states. Thus, emigration for Palestinians has often involved movement from one class position to another.

The demise of agriculture (and thus agricultural land as a source of wealth) and the collapse of the old Palestinian national movement in 1948 (which was dominated by landowning and merchant families) was followed in the 1960s by the emergence of a new national movement. This movement was led by a political elite that was composed mainly of college-educated middle- and working-class individuals. This change undermined the landowner-merchant class of the Mandate period (Hilal 2002, 39–58).

Large sectors of the new Palestinian middle class were formed as part of an emigrant community, without the ongoing interaction in their society with other social classes. The interaction, in the Gulf states, was with the "indigenous" elite who maintained its distance, and with a "lower" class of immigrants from Asian countries. The "conservative" attitudes the Palestinian middle class adopted were also consistent with their high concentration in the service sector of the oil-producing economies (as well as in Jordan), the marginality of the migrant in the political systems of these states, and a state-controlled cultural space (dominated by a state-sponsored version of Islam geared to control rather than the promotion of democratic values).

"Conservative" attitudes were not merely externally induced. Most emigrants from the West Bank and Gaza Strip came from small urban and village communities with a remembered peasant past and strong kinship loyalties and patriarchal gender identities. They hailed from communities that had little experience with urbanization or urbanism with its distinctive and multiple styles of life and forms of association. The pervasiveness of such village and provincial styles of life is reflected in high rates of kinship marriage within these communities as well as among their middle-class emigrants, reproducing patriarchal relations. The geographic proximity of the Gulf states to the West Bank and Gaza Strip gave emigrants the chance to return periodically to their home communities and disseminate attitudes and norms acquired in the host countries. This has been especially true of West Bankers and their emigrant relatives in Jordan, with whom they had regular contact.

The continual loss, through emigration, of skilled and educated individuals from the West Bank and Gaza Strip communities has deprived these communities "of their more innovative members" (Ammons 1979, 224), or more accurately, of those who possess what Bourdieu calls cultural capital (Bourdieu 1994). In addition, hundreds of highly qualified individuals with political affiliations were prevented by the Israeli military authorities from returning to their homes in the West Bank and Gaza Strip. This, too, has deprived Palestinian society of "social capital" (organizational and mobilizing abilities). Some scholars have suggested that this Israeli measure was part of a policy aimed at preventing the emergence of an effective oppositional Palestinian leadership (Migdal 1980, 67).

Extent, Patterns and Features of Palestinian Emigration

Dimensions of class, gender, and "diaspora space" (Brah 1996, 208–10) are all relevant for understanding processes of emigration. Since the second Gulf war and the Oslo accords (i.e., in the 1990s), emigration has become more and more constrained by limited resources as well as the destinations available. Social class is therefore an important determinant of the reasons for and destination of emigration. Daily commuting to the Israeli labor market and emigration, in earlier decades, to Jordan were forms of action that poorer households could afford, although the poorest often could not migrate at all. Communities that come under sustained repression and live under high risk, such as the Palestinian community in Lebanon before 1969 and after 1982,[16] had to seek either collective strategies (as happened between 1969 and 1982, when Palestinians in camps joined the various factions of the PLO) or had to develop their own household strategies such as seeking political asylum in countries that offered it. The latter alternative became the more common strategy after the forced exit of the PLO from Lebanon in 1982. The mass exodus of Palestinians from Kuwait following the Gulf war has had a traumatic ef-

---

16. For a description of the life of Palestinians in camps in Lebanon before and after the arrival of the PLO, see Sayigh 1979.

fect on thousands of Palestinian families who lost their source of livelihood and in many cases their savings.

Levels and Variations

All the communities included in the household survey showed a substantial rate of emigration. As expected, emigration rates varied by type of community and region. However, all nineteen communities in the sample had a significant percentage of households that had one or more emigrants, and this was equally true of towns, villages, and refugee camps across regions (table 4.1). The rates expressed in the survey do not reflect the actual volume of migration that these communities have witnessed within the last five decades; questions were confined to existing households and did not include those that had no members left behind. Hence the survey underestimates the flow of emigration. Emigrants were defined by the survey as "family members who reside outside the West Bank and Gaza Strip and East Jerusalem and who are related to the household head in one of the following ways: father, mother, son, daughter, wife, husband." For the purposes of the survey, to qualify as an emigrant the person had to have spent at least six months outside the West Bank (including East Jerusalem) and Gaza Strip prior to the survey; in other words, to qualify as an emigrant, one had to have crossed an international border and stayed outside for at least six months.[17] That the greatest majority of reported emigrants were married and fell within certain age group ranges is a function of the questions asked. Household heads were asked to name close kin abroad (as defined above), and that meant, in effect, naming mostly emigrants above a certain age; hence the high percentage of those who were reported to be married.

Nearly half of the households surveyed reported having one or more emigrant kin. This is probably an underestimate because the community sample under-represented villages in the West Bank as the task envisaged for the sample was comparative. A Fafo survey conducted in 1995 put the rate of households with emigrants at 57 percent (Pedersen et al. 2001a). Another study

---

17. This is the definition that was adopted in the survey mentioned above. For a detailed discussion of definitions and measurements of migration, see Boyle, Halfacree, and Robinson 1998, chap. 2.

Table 4.1
Community Profile: Households with Emigrants by Community, Sex, Academic Qualifications, and Endogamous Marriages, 1999

Community	Households with emigrants (%)	Emigrants who are males (%)	Emigrants with middle diploma+ (%)	Endogamous marriages[a] (%)	Households surveyed (N)
Jenin (town)	48	50	18	59	65
Jenin (refugee camp)	62	49	21	55.5	66
Tammoun (village)	54	53	20	87.5	70
Zayta (village)	58	58.5	58	75	69
Nablus (town)	65	48	40	79	246
Balata (refugee camp)	65	45	26	70	71
Turmus 'Ayy (village)	88	64	15	76	60
Al-Mazra'a al-Sharqiyya (village)	70	66	8	80	67
Ramallah (town)	65	54	32	57.5	60
Am'ari (refugee camp)	56	53	22	64	68
Husan (village)	48.5	51	16	79	68
Bayt Ummar (village)	35	57	26.5	87	71
Hebron (town)	43	48	27	88	258
Al-Fawwar (refugee camp)	63	45	32	43	70
Bayt Hanoun (village, Gaza)	28	85	58	89	71
Gaza (town)	35.5	59	38	71	599
Nusayrat (camp, Gaza)	39	56	51	66	94
Khuza'a (village, Gaza)	43	59	25	73	67
East Jerusalem	54	53	29	58.5	113
Total	49	54.5	30	72	2253

Source: IWS household survey, 1999

[a] Defined by kinship and community; calculated from marriage partners of females aged fifteen through forty-nine

estimates that the number of Palestinians in the East Bank increased from 70,000 in 1949 to about 1.2 million in 1987, and from several hundred in the Gulf states to about 500,000 for the same period (Gilbar 1997, 24).

Our 1999 survey did reveal wide variations among the communities in this respect.[18] It also revealed that three-quarters (76 percent) of emigrants were brothers or sisters of the head of the surveyed households, and a fifth (20 percent) were sons or daughters. Parents and spouses constituted only a small percentage of emigrants (2 percent and 1 percent, respectively). This pattern indicates that migration is to a large extent family-based, with the elderly staying behind, particularly in the villages. It could also mean that some emigrants choose to return to their villages in their old age, whereas others are forced to do so (as happened to many emigrants to the Gulf region). Generally speaking, as the date of emigration becomes more recent, the percentage of emigrants identified as son/daughter increases, as would be expected for demographic reasons.

Regional variations are evident. The middle region of the West Bank had the highest rates of heads of households with close relatives who were emigrants (69.5 percent), followed by the north of the West Bank (with 60 percent of the resident households having one or more migrant), and Arab Jerusalem (54 percent). The southern region of the West Bank and the Gaza Strip had the lowest rates of household heads with close kin emigrants (46 percent and 36 percent respectively). What is interesting in this pattern is its correspondence with the levels of poverty recorded at the time of the survey (NCPA 1998, 51). The regions with highest levels of poverty (like Gaza Strip and the southern region of the West Bank) recorded the lowest rate of emigration. The middle of the West Bank, which has the lowest rate of poverty, has the highest level of emigration. This pattern also emerges if households are stratified by socioeconomic status.

A putative relationship emerges between what can be termed "class situation" and the existence of one or more emigrants in the household. Very poor households tend to seek emigration more often, it seems, than poor house-

18. Six of the nineteen communities surveyed had a low rate of household emigration (less than 45 percent of households with emigrants). Five communities had a high rate of household emigration (i.e., with 65 percent or more households with emigrants). The remaining eight communities had rates ranging between 45 percent and 64 percent.

Table 4.2
Households With and Without Emigrants by Wealth Index, 1999

| Wealth | Households (%) | | Total |
	With emigrants	Without emigrants	Number
Very poor	51	49	306
Poor	43	57	359
Medium	48	52	745
Upper medium	51.5	48.5	509
Wealthy	51	49	333
Ns	1102	1150	2252

Source: IWS household survey, 1999

holds or those in medium socioeconomic situations, but slightly less than those classified as upper middle class and wealthy (table 4.2). It is likely that more of the very poor have close relatives who have become refugees and dis- placed persons as a result of the 1948 and 1967 wars, and are thus camp resi- dents.[19] This finding does not support the hypothesis that ecological factors determine rates of emigration (Migdal 1980, 58). Although ecological differ- ences exist between the central region of the West Bank with its arid and mar- ginal land and the northern region with its more favorable agricultural conditions, these differences cannot explain the lower rates of emigration in the southern region or, for that matter, in the overcrowded Gaza Strip.

Households whose heads are employers or self-employed are more likely to have emigrants than households whose heads are employees in the private sector. The level of education of household head seems to be relevant to the level of emigration (table 4.3). Households with emigrants tend to have heads with either very high levels of formal education or no education at all.[20]

19. The distribution of wealth by type of community shows (at the time of the survey in 1999) that camps have the highest percentage of the very poor and poor; 44 percent compared to 38 percent in villages, and 22 percent in towns. This is line with the Palestine Poverty Report (NCPA 1998).

20. Data from the survey show the following: 50 percent of the illiterates, 46 percent of those with elementary schooling and preparatory schooling respectively, 48 percent of those with secondary schooling, and 58 percent of those with postsecondary schooling reported one or more migrants in their households. The very uneducated and the well educated have very simi- lar levels of reports of migration (one or more persons in the family).

Table 4.3
Level of Household Head's Education
by the Presence of Emigrants, 1999

| Level of education | Households (%) | | Total |
	With emigrants	Without emigrants	Number
Illiterate	26	26	585
Elementary[a]	20	23	480
Preparatory[b]	18	21	436
Secondary	15	16	347
Higher than secondary	21	15	405
Total	100	100	2253

Source: Data are from the IWS household survey, 1999
[a]Up to grade 6
[b]Up to grade 9

This is more likely to be related to other factors such as the place chosen for emigration and the motive for emigrating, an aspect that I will return to later.

No relationship was revealed between emigration and the refugee or nonrefugee status of the head of the household (defined in coresidential terms), or type of household (nuclear or extended). But female-headed households were found to be more likely to have emigrants than male-headed households. This finding confirms the commonsense observation that emigration is a significant factor (though not the only factor) in the generation of households headed by females. The relationship between female-headed households and significantly higher reports of one or more emigrant abroad remained uniform also by locale (i.e., remained valid for cities, villages, and camps separately) and by region (north, middle, south West Bank, and Gaza Strip).

More than half (56 percent) of emigrants' occupations can be classified as middle-class occupations. These included directors, professionals, teachers, accountants, technicians, and office workers. Fifteen percent of emigrants were in trade, 15.5 percent could be classified as skilled workers, 10 percent were unskilled workers, and the remainder were distributed in various other occupations such as personal services and agriculture.

The percentage of emigrants who acquired middle-class occupations varies according to the country of destination. The Gulf states had the highest percentage employed in such occupations (about 73 percent). The United States and Canada had the lowest ratio (44 percent) in new middle-class occupations. Jordan had a more even spread of occupations, but still a relatively high percentage in middle class occupations (51 percent).

Apart from the almost total absence of employment in agriculture among adult employed emigrants (only six cases of employment in agriculture were registered out of a total of 1,144 cases), the communities studied differed a great deal in the occupational patterns of their emigrants. Thus while an average of 23.5 percent of all emigrants were reported to be employed in jobs as directors or professionals (that is, in upper-middle-class occupations), the percentage varied from one community to another.[21] These variations were found to apply to all middle-class occupations.[22] Employment in trade also showed wide variations among emigrants of the communities studied.[23]

In all major destinations emigrants show a different pattern of occupational structure and stratification than resident nonemigrants. This indicates that emigration has provided an important channel for occupational and social mobility.

What the data on the occupational structure of emigrants show is that emigration has been one of the main mechanisms for Palestinian middle-class formation in general. Some emigrants returned eventually to form part of the Palestinian middle class in the West Bank and Gaza Strip. The fact that "middle class" is a sponge term that includes those who are not employed in "manual" occupations or unskilled or semiskilled jobs or businessmen with sizeable capital explains the wide variations in "middle-class" jobs held according to region and type of community, as well as by period of emigration and country of destination, which determines the contours of opportunities available to immigrants and the cultural space available to them.

21. The variation (in upper-middle-class occupations) starts from hardly any (as in the case of two communities) to rates of over 30 percent (as in the case of three communities, all of which are in the West Bank).

22. Seven of the nineteen communities surveyed reported a high rate (more than 30 percent) of emigrants who engaged in middle-class occupations.

23. Three communities reported a high rate of employment in trade (more than 25 percent of their emigrant employed in trade). Employment of emigrants in skilled and unskilled manual occupations also shows significant variations.

Destinations of Emigrants

The IWS survey results indicate that 20 percent of emigrants left during the period following the *Nakba* and during the Jordanian and Egyptian rule of the West Bank and Gaza Strip (1948–66). Some 17 percent of all migrants left in the wake of the 1967 war. The Israeli occupation forced many families that depended on remittances from emigrant relatives (particularly in Jordan and the Gulf states) and feared losing contact with their relatives to cross the Jordan River. Some 38 percent of migrants left during the first twenty years of Israeli military occupation (1968–87), and 25 percent left within the period between 1988 and 1999. Of the total number of immigrants, some 14 percent were reported to have left the country during 1994–99 alone. This indicates that emigration rates remained significant even after the signing of the Oslo accords, although this period also witnessed a significant rate of immigration to the West Bank and Gaza Strip. The destination pattern of Palestinian emigration has also changed over the years.

Data from the IWS survey (table 4.4) suggest a substantial increase in the number of Palestinian emigrants to the United States and Canada since 1968. A significant and noticeable decline in Palestinian emigration to the Gulf states and other Arab oil-producing states is evident starting in the late 1980s and the early 1990s. This decline is explainable by the repercussions of the Gulf crisis in 1990.

The rise in the share of emigration to North America was accompanied by a corresponding decline in emigration to Jordan. Emigration to Jordan remained significant, however, given the relative ease of moving from the West

Table 4.4
Emigrants by Destination and Period of Emigration (%)

Destination	1948–66	1967	1968–87	1988–93	1994–99
Jordan (East Bank)	60	77	45	23	28
Gulf and other Arab states	19	13	28	23	21
North America	7	1	17	31	27
Other	14	9	10	23	24
Total	100	100	100	100	100

Source: IWS household survey, 1999

Bank to Jordan and the extensive Palestinian family networks that had been established there since the Palestinian *Nakba*. Palestinians born and residing in the West Bank at the time of its annexation by Jordan (1950) were granted Jordanian citizenship, which facilitated movement to Jordan[24] and eased emigration to other Arab states. The effect of that policy is clearly reflected in the bulk of emigrants from the West Bank to Jordan before the Israeli occupation of the former. Emigration to Jordan and other Arab states was propelled by high unemployment in the West Bank, very limited rates of growth in agriculture and manufacture, and the channeling of most foreign aid and public investment toward Jordan (Gilbar 1997, 36–38). Thus both Palestinian labor and capital were attracted to the wider and better opportunities emerging in Jordan and other areas (Hilal 1975, 133–41; Van Arkadie 1977, 24).

The drop in the share of Palestinian emigration to the Gulf and oil-producing Arab states after the first intifada and following the Gulf crisis is related to the decline in oil revenues, the politics of the Gulf crisis following the Iraqi invasion of Kuwait,[25] and the subsequent measures to restrict the presence of Palestinians in the Gulf states. The increase in the number of emigrants to North America probably reflects the better economic opportunities compared to other destinations, the presence of relatives there, and relatively flexible immigration policies by the United States and Canada.

The IWS survey data reveal that half of the emigrants reside in Jordan and a quarter in other Arab countries (mostly Gulf states). Nearly 75 percent of camp emigrants reside in Jordan (table 4.5). Village emigrants seem to be

24. A survey carried out in the first quarter of 1996 by Fafo in Jordan found that 70 percent of those residing in Amman and Zarqa (the two largest cities in the country) and those who were over fifty years of age were born in what has become Israel (Mandate Palestine) or in the West Bank and Gaza Strip (Hanssen-Bauer, Pedersen, and Tiltnes 1998, 87). Because Palestinians moved to the East Bank mostly during the 1950s and 1960s, many who have acquired Jordanian nationality have a substantial number of relatives abroad, often without any emigration having taken place on either side. The United States and Canada are the most important non-Arab destinations for emigrants from Jordan. It is likely that a high percentage of Jordanian emigrants are of Palestinian origin.

25. An accurate figure of Palestinians in Kuwait is not available, because large numbers of Palestinians in Kuwait carry Jordanian passports. It is estimated that some 300,000 Palestinians (mostly from the West Bank and Gaza Strip) were in Kuwait on the eve of the Iraqi invasion of that country in August 1990 (Abu-Bakr 1999, 30).

Table 4.5
Emigrants by Destination and Type of Community (%)

Destination	Town	Camp	Village	Total
Jordan (East Bank)	48	73	37	50
Gulf and other Arab states[a]	35	16	18	26
North America	9	3	34	15
Other	8	8	11	9
Total	100	100	100	100

Source: IWS household survey, 1999
[a] Including North Africa

drawn more to North America. Very few village emigrants are found in Latin America, with hardly any recorded from towns and camps.[26] This is related to a generational pattern of village migration, which paved the way for relatives to be "pulled" out to countries like Chile, Colombia, and Brazil, as well as to North America. The use of the Arabic term *sahaba*—meaning to pull out—to describe the process of individuals abroad providing the necessary documentation and work opportunities for the emigration of a relative—is significant. When work opportunities are available through help provided by kinship networks, then the readiness to work hard rather than to have good qualifications becomes the deciding criterion.

The role of kinship in "pulling out" resident relatives is reflected, often, in "chain emigration," as the following data indicate: the majority of reported emigrants from Jenin town live in Jordan, and only a small number live in the oil-producing states, a pattern similar to that found in Jenin camp, Am'ari camp (near Ramallah), Husan village (near Bethlehem), Bayt Ummar (Hebron district), Hebron city (where a very large majority of emigrants live in Jordan), and the old city of Jerusalem. In Ramallah town only about a quarter of reported emigrants live in Jordan while over a half live in North America; this pattern is similar to that found in the village of Turmus 'Ayya (which lies on

26. More than half of the camp emigrants to Asia (recorded by the household survey designed by the Institute of Women's Studies at Birzeit University) came from one camp (Jenin camp), and more than half of all the town emigrants to Asia come from the adjacent Jenin town and nearly three quarters of village emigrants to Asia come from one village (Zayta). This suggests a selective kin network type of migration. Jenin, Jenin camp, and Zayta are all in the northern part of the West Bank.

the road between Ramallah and Nablus), where three-quarters of its emigrants live in North America, and al-Mazra'a al-Sharqiyya where two-thirds of its emigrants live in North America. In Gaza city nearly two-thirds of emigrants reside in oil-producing Arab countries (including North Africa), a pattern similar to Nusayrat refugee camp in Gaza Strip, where most of its emigrants live in oil-producing countries, and to that of Khuza'a, a village in the southern Gaza Strip.

Looking at emigrants through the lens of level of education and place of residence brings out another feature of Palestinian emigration (table 4.6). Rates of illiteracy and high education vary according to place of residence of emigrants. The highest rates of immigrants with elementary education and less were found in Jordan, followed by the United States, with the lowest rate in the oil-producing Arab states.

Employment opportunities and family networks are major factors in the choice of place of emigration. Jordan could sustain a large percentage of illiterate or barely literate emigrants because of the strength and breadth of family connections, availability of opportunities for semiskilled employment, lack of documentary requirements by West bank residents, and ease of movement to Jordan. Besides, emigration to Jordan was considered, up to 1988 (when Jordan severed its administrative connection with the West Bank), as movement within the same state. That explains why half the emigrants from the West Bank and Gaza Strip in the IWS survey reside in Jordan and constitute two-thirds of those reported as having no more than an elementary education. On the other hand, the oil-producing Arab states attracted a quarter of the emigrants in the IWS survey sample but had a third of those with postgraduate university education.

Certain villages tended to direct some of their emigrants to Latin America where earlier emigrants had managed to establish a foothold; for the same reasons, other villages dispatched their emigrants to North America. This process produced the village or small town emigrant who, with little initial knowledge of the language of the country of destination, invested his energy in hard work in a grocery store or some trade to return later to build a villa in his West Bank village or town (Giacaman and Johnson 2002a, 29–38).

The choice of Jordan for emigration is regionally differentiated; just over 75 percent of emigrants from the southern West Bank went to Jordan, compared to 66 percent from the north and less than 33 percent from the center of

Table 4.6
Emigrants by Country of Destination and Educational Level

| Destination | Level of Education (%) | | | | | Total | |
	Up to 6 years	7–9 years	10–12 years	Up to BA	Postgraduate degree	n	%
Jordan (East Bank)	66	48	39	40	20	1285	49.5
Gulf and other Arab states	16	18	29	41	34	686	26
North America	11	25	18	11	23	391	15
Other	7	9	14	8	23	245	9.5
Total (%)	100	100	100	100	100		100
Total	876	409	505	738	79	2607	

Source: IWS household survey, 1999

the West Bank, whereas only 15 percent of emigrants from the Gaza Strip found their way there. Gazans had much less access to Jordan than West Bankers. Nearly half of Gaza households reported having emigrants in the Gulf, in contrast to 19 percent from the north, 12 percent from the south, 6 percent from the central West Bank, and 17 percent from the Old City of Jerusalem. The United States and Canada attracted emigrants from half of the households in the central West Bank, compared to only 12 percent from Jerusalem, 5 percent from the north, and 3 percent from the southern part of the West Bank and Gaza. This finding confirms the importance of kinship in channeling emigration. However, the scope of employment opportunities and the degree of ease of border crossing into the host countries are also relevant to the type of qualifications needed to maximize chance of stable employment.

The fact that the bulk of emigrants went to places where they have kin and community connections (often stretching two or more generations) is relevant to the explanation of why emigration tended to generate social conservatism. Similarly, the fact that most Palestinian emigrants moved to countries that maintain a strong control over all manifestations of civil society is also relevant to the explanation. Thus the formation of the bulk of the Palestinian middle class through emigration took place within such a political field, regardless of the forces propelling emigration.

Motives, Moments, and Family Networks

Three main motives appear to be associated with emigration from the West Bank and Gaza Strip: work, marriage, and expulsion. Expulsion (as a result of war, invasion, or occupation) is not emigration but could result in the emigration of members of the expellee's household. Less than 11 percent of those interviewed reported pursuit of higher education as a motivator for emigration (table 4.7). Work and marriage alone account for most of all emigrants' motives for crossing the borders of Palestine, and the ratio rises to nearly two-third if those who were born abroad are excluded. If we add expulsion as the reason for being outside Palestine, the percentage jumps to 75 percent (and rises to 81 percent when foreign-born Palestinians are excluded). Work and marriage had equal weight as the reasons for emigration. If we leave out the category of "born abroad," then 54 percent of male emigrants moved outside Palestine for work reasons, compared with only 5 percent of female emigrants. Two-thirds

Table 4.7
Reasons Given by Household Head for Emigration of Close Relative by Community Type and Sex

Reason for emigration	Town (%)	Camp (%)	Village (%)	Total n (%)	Male (%)	Female(%)
Work	28	19	40	800 (30)	50	5
Study	12	7	10	287 (11)	18.5	1
Marriage	30	29	27.5	785 (29)	2.5	61
Accompanying another emigrant	8	10	4.5	200 (7)	2.5	13.5
Expulsion	15	29	11	437 (16)	19.5	12.5
Born abroad	7	6	7	188 (7)	7	7
Total	100	100	100	2697 (100)	100	100

Source: IWS household survey, 1999
Note: Data exclude answers of "don't know" and "no answer"

of females (66 percent) left for reasons of marriage. That means that women's emigration from the West Bank and Gaza Strip is mostly "associational" emigration. Only 2.5 percent of males emigrated for reasons of marriage (i.e., their spouses were already emigrants). Similarly, more males than females left the West Bank and Gaza Strip to study (18.5 percent and 1 percent respectively).

Different types of communities narrated somewhat different clusters of reasons for the emigration of their members. Villages seem to have the highest percentage of emigrants who leave for work or marriage. Towns and camps come second. While the dominant reasons for emigration in all communities surveyed were reported to be work and marriage, each community had its own distinctive emigration profile. This profile relates to its socioeconomic structure, the genealogy of emigrants, the degree of dependence on agriculture, the strength of kinship solidarities,[27] main sources of income, and levels of education, because level of education seems to influence the motive for emigration (table 4.8).

Reasons for living outside the borders of Palestine also varied according to time period. Expulsion was reported as the main reason for the departure of 22 percent of all individuals during the 1948–66 period, 61 percent during the war year of 1967, 5 percent during the period 1968–87, and less than 3 percent during 1988–99. A different pattern emerges for those reported to have emigrated for reasons of marriage. Marriage was responsible for 26 percent of all the emigration during 1948–66, 14 percent for the year 1967, 38 percent for the period 1968–87, and 39.5 percent for the 1988–99 period. If the year 1967 is excluded, the rise in the ratio of emigration for reasons of marriage (i.e., "associational") probably reflects increased arrangements for family reunion or the emigration of nuclear families en masse. The rise in the percentage of those who left for study during the period 1988–99 could be due to the dis-

27. For example, 70 percent of emigrants from Jenin town are outside Palestine for reasons of work and marriage; the rate does not exceed 64 percent for Jenin camp and 60 percent for the village of Tammoun (a village between Nablus and Jenin). All are in the northern region of the West Bank. Tammoun had twice the rate of forced emigrants (expelled) than that of the Jenin camp (20 percent and 10 percent). In al-Mazra'a al-Sharqiyya, near Ramallah town, the percentage of emigrants for reasons of work and marriage amounted to 75 percent, compared to 32 percent in the Am'ari camp (on the outskirts of Ramallah), and to 70 percent in Ramallah town. Reported forced emigration (i.e., expulsion) in the last three mentioned communities, on the other hand, amounted to 4 percent, 58 percent and 14 percent respectively.

Table 4.8
Reasons Given for Emigration by Educational Level of Emigrant (%)

Reason for Emigration	Up to 6 years	7–9 years	Level of education 10–12 years	Up to BA	Postgraduate degree
Work	26	29	29	37	29
Marriage	34	39	29	20	8
Study			15	21	48
Expulsion	25	11	12	11	8
Other	15	21	15	11	7
Total	100	100	100	100	100

Source: IWS household survey, 1999

ruption of higher education during the first intifada and subsequent closures that were imposed by Israel on the West Bank and Gaza Strip.[28]

Results from the IWS survey support the idea that emigrants choose their destination in accordance with the reason for emigration and the family and other connections they have there. The Arab oil-producing states, with their need for skilled and professional labor, provided a "pull" for male emigrants seeking employment opportunities with relatively high wages. After employment was secured in these countries, arrangements were made by the male emigrants to be joined by their families (wives and children), or to start families of their own. Hence work, marriage, and accompaniment were considered by household heads as the dominant motives behind the departure of two-thirds of emigrants to Gulf and other oil-producing Arab states. Expulsion (mostly as a result of the 1948 and 1967 wars) appears as a prominent reason for a quarter of all emigrants to Jordan. The other two main reasons were work and marriage. Work and marriage also figured as the two main driving forces behind Palestinian emigration to North America and Latin America. On the other hand, more than half the emigrants to Europe cited education as a reason (table 4.9).

In sum, the dominant motives for emigration from the West Bank and Gaza Strip have been seeking work and joining (or finding) a spouse, with expulsion being an important factor for a significant portion of Palestinians living outside Palestine during particular periods (the wars of 1948 and 1967). Data show that the three types of communities have experienced varying rates of emigration during one period or another since the *Nakba* of 1948. The continued significance of marriage in promoting emigration (particularly for female migrants) is a factor that reinforces kinship as a determining factor in social relations. This is so because most marriages are conducted between relatives. In this respect, change in class position and country of residence does not, necessarily, involve a change in social attitudes or behavior but could in fact contribute towards adopting highly rigid codes of behavior (in relation to gender, kinship relations, local affiliation, mode of dress, public conduct, cul-

---

28. The IWS survey data show that during the 1988–93 period (i.e., during the first intifada), 32 percent of emigrants left for work, 19 percent left for study, and 43 percent for marriage. As for the period 1994–99 (when the PNA was operational), the survey reveals that 30 percent left for work, 18 percent for study, and 37 percent for marriage.

Table 4.9
Reasons Given for Emigration of Kin by Destination

Place of residence of emigrants	Work (%)	Study (%)	Marriage (%)	Accompaniment (%)	Expelled (%)	Born abroad (%)	Total(%)	Total (n)
Jordan	21	6	33	8	26	6	100	1332
Gulf and Arab world	36	8	26	10	11	9	100	709
U.S. and Canada	46	16	28	5	1.5	3.5	100	393
Europe	23	53	13	3	2	6	100	133
Latin America	75	6	8	0	5.5	5.5	100	52
Other	13	18	52.5	0	5	11.5	100	61
Ns	799	284	781	200	437	179		2680

Source: IWS household survey, 1999

tural matters, and social change in general) if working and living in the emigrant's new country so dictate.

Emigration and Kinship Networks

The traumatic changes experienced by most Palestinians since 1948 have not lessened the importance of kinship obligations in Palestinian communities. The property basis for clan and extended family relations has eroded and in most cases has completely disappeared as a consequence of the privatization of property, the complete transformation of the West Bank and Gaza Strip into market economies, and the dominance of wage or salaried labor as the main source of income. However the vicissitudes of Palestinian life after 1948 did suggest a new relevance for kin relations. In the absence of a national territorial state, extended family relations, in addition to political and professional affiliations, provided the main socioeconomic support system.

Overall, almost three-quarters of emigrants have relatives (other than spouse and children) in their country of destination. Village households reported the highest rate of such connections (81 percent), followed by camps (74 percent) and towns (68 percent). It could be argued that emigrants from villages and camps need kinship networks more than emigrants from towns because they tend to possess fewer personal assets (financial capital and academic and technical qualifications), rather than arguing that kinship networks are weaker in towns. Some indirect support for this idea is provided by the IWS survey results, where urban emigrants were found to have significantly higher levels of education than village and camp emigrants. A quarter (26 percent) of urban emigrants had university degrees, compared to 16 percent of emigrants from villages and 14 percent for camps. Similarly the Gaza Strip reported the lowest regional rate (55 percent) of relatives in the host countries, but had the highest rate (30 percent) of emigrants with university degrees. In other words, Gazans had to rely more on personal assets and less on kinship connections (used as social capital) than the West Bank. Nevertheless, more than half of Gazan emigrants had close kin in their countries of emigration.

As access to emigration increases, particularly for individuals with higher education and professional skills, the need to rely on kinship networks in the country of destination decreases. Data from the survey suggest that emigrants with preparatory-level education or less had the highest rate of relatives in the country of destination, followed (in descending order) by those with secondary education, those with up to a graduate degree, and those with a postgraduate degree. This however should not deflect from the fact that more than half (56 percent) of postgraduate individuals still had close relatives in the countries to which they emigrated.

The rate of females emigrating for work or for study is significantly lower than that of males; the majority of women emigrants are motivated by marriage (see table 4.7). Variations in the reasons given for emigration by region, type of community, country of destination, and level of education (see tables 4.7, 4.8, and 4.9) have to be explained by period of emigration, opportunity (access to jobs and entry and residence requirements in the country of destination), and the availability of assets (including education and marketable skills) and social capital. Kinship networks (as social capital) remain crucial in facilitating the process of emigration.

Tenuous Financial Links with the Homeland

Only 15.5 percent of the resident households with emigrant relatives reported having a regular financial link with the latter. A regular financial link was defined in the survey as involving a transfer of money at least once every three months. In 1999, some 8.5 percent of the households in the West Bank and Gaza Strip were receiving regular financial support from their close relatives abroad, some 6.5 percent of the resident families (with emigrants) were sending money to their relatives abroad, and 0.5 percent were both sending and receiving money, as demanded by the circumstances. The data point to a decrease in financial links with the household members as the date of emigration recedes and new households are established away from home (table 4.10).

The supportive relationship between the emigrant and his close kin at home declines with time as the emigrant establishes a separate household (through marriage and parenthood) and is joined by near kin at home or dies of old age. Some return home in old age or because they are no longer welcome in the country of emigration (as happened to Palestinians in Kuwait during the first Gulf war). Young emigrants (e.g., students or new emigrants who are still searching for work) are more likely to receive regular financial assistance from their resident families than older emigrants.

Table 4.10
Emigrants Who Send or Receive Money Regularly to/from Close Resident Kin

| Age of Emigrant | Sends (%) | Receives (%) | Sends or receives money regularly | | Total n (%) |
			Sends and receives (%)	Neither sends nor receives (%)	
Younger than 30	15.1	19.4	0.2	65.3	412 (100)
30–49	9	4	0	87	1224 (100)
50–59	6	4	0	90	643 (100)
60 years and older	3	4	0	93	384 (100)
Ns	223	171	10	2259	2663

Source: IWS household survey, 1999

Moreover, the place of residence of emigrants is relevant to the financial links they have with their close relatives at home. Emigrants to Jordan have the lowest financial interaction with their close relatives in the West Bank and Gaza Strip. In fact, more households in the West Bank and Gaza Strip sent money regularly to close kin in Jordan than the other way round. One explanation may be that university students from West Bank and Gaza Strip are enrolled in Jordanian universities, and intermarriage between Palestinian families across the Jordan River is a frequent phenomenon.

The IWS survey data reveal very limited regular financial interaction between emigrants in the Arab states (including North Africa) and their relatives in the West Bank and Gaza Strip. Village households with emigrants report the highest rate of receiving regular financial assistance. Twenty percent of village households received such assistance in comparison with less than 4 percent among town households and less than 3 percent among refugee camp households. However, a disaggregation of data reveals that regular financial support from emigrants to close kin at home is concentrated, more or less, in three of the communities surveyed, all of which happen to be villages (two in the West Bank and one in the Gaza Strip).[29]

Only the town of Ramallah, apart from the three villages referred to above, reported more than 10 percent of its households with emigrants receiving regular assistance. Ramallah reported a high rate of emigrants in North America.

The explanation for why the few communities mentioned above have such high rates of regular assistance in contrast to others can be found in the fact that the two West Bank villages (Turmus 'Ayya and al-Mazra'a al-Sharqiyya) have had a very high rate of emigration to North America, and if we add emigrants to South America, the percentage of households with emigrants to these areas rises to over 80 percent in both villages. Moreover the two communities have the highest percentage of emigrants working in trade. A major-

29. These were Turmus 'Ayya (between Nablus and Ramallah) and al-Mazra'a al-Sharqiyya (not far from Ramallah). Both villages reported that 35 percent of all households with emigrants abroad received regular financial transfers from their close relatives abroad. The third community with relatively high regular financial assistance sent by emigrants to close relatives at home is Khuza'a, which is a small village in the south of the Gaza Strip. Khuza'a village reported a rate of 25 percent of households with close emigrants' relatives receiving regular financial assistance.

ity of emigrants from the Gaza Strip village of Khuza'a (the third village with a high rate of regular assistance to relatives at home) were in the Gulf states and other Arab states (mostly in North African oil-producing states).[30] Khuza'a also had a high percentage of emigrants working in trade with high financial transfers to resident close relatives. The linkage between trade and regular money transfers to close relatives in the West Bank and Gaza Strip is possibly due to the better opportunities for accumulating wealth provided by trade.

Not much should be read into the regular assistance made by emigrants to their relatives in Palestine. Where it exists it is almost confined to fairly recent emigrants to rich states (North America and the Gulf states) and to specific localities with high rates of immigrants to these states. After emigrants establish their own families, their financial responsibilities to their relatives staying at home diminish. That does not mean that less regular assistance is not made or that social ties and links are severed. Annual visits and gifts on social and religious occasions remain significant, as does support in times of crisis. Visiting and gift exchanges are maintained, particularly between families in the West Bank and emigrants in Jordan, the Gulf states, and to a lesser degree between those in North America. The celebration of kinship is one way in which Palestinians assert their national belonging (i.e., their connectedness to Palestine as a place and to other Palestinians) in the face of statelessness, dispersion, and colonial occupation.

The Home Communities: Continuity and Change

Social "conservatism" is not simply a consequence of emigration from the West Bank and Gaza Strip. It is also related to Palestinians' subjection to a prolonged colonial-settler occupation. Israeli settler-occupation has been instrumental in the demise of Palestinian agriculture, the dependence of a large percentage of the labor force on employment in Israel, the penetration of the market economy into all aspects of community life in Palestinian areas, and the transformation of these areas into a captive market for Israeli goods. That

30. Two West Bank villages reported a high percentage of emigrants for work and marriage (75 percent for Turmus 'Ayya, and 82 percent al-Mazra'a al-Sharqiyya), whereas Khuza'a reported 49 percent of its emigrant leaving for work and marriage. (However, 21 percent of emigrants were born abroad.)

is in addition to restrictions on the activities and scope of the public sphere. These changes were accompanied by a renewal of the Palestinian national movement in the form of the PLO, which gave priority to liberating the occupied territories and to the establishment of an independent Palestinian state. These developments had a significant impact on the cultural and social life of these areas.

Both the IWS survey and PCBS data reveal the insignificance that agriculture has come to occupy as a source of income for Palestinian households. Less than 2.5 percent of the total labor force of the nineteen communities surveyed was employed in agriculture and fishing (compared to 6 percent as a national average revealed by the PCBS 1997 population census data). The proximity of most villages to towns (almost all within a commuting distance) ensures access to employment in these towns. This, and the limited work opportunities in towns, explain why internal migration has been very small in scale and largely confined to women (who moved into towns for marriage reasons); it has not been unidirectional (that is confined to village-to-town migration) but has also taken place between towns, as the 1997 population census of the West Bank and Gaza Strip has revealed (Malki and Shalabi 2000, 25–27, 49). The pattern of internal migration did not show a pattern of a primate city dominating internal migration. Only after the establishment of the PNA did the twin towns of Ramallah and al-Bira and their district acquire a significant pull, possibly reflecting the increasing prominence of the twin towns as the administrative seat of the PNA government and large NGOs.

The IWS survey results point to a fairly rapid process of integration of camps and villages within the newly established structures of the PNA. In all, a fifth of the labor force in the communities studied was employed by PNA institutions. The figure is in line with the Palestinian national average recorded by national surveys.[31]

In the 1970s and 1980s, Israel provided employment for about a third of the total active labor force of the West Bank and Gaza Strip. Because the

---

31. Ten of the communities recorded a medium range employment in the governmental public sector (i.e., a ration of 10 percent–20 percent of their total active labor force employed by the PNA). Six communities recorded high employment in the governmental public sector (i.e., more than 20 percent of their labor force employed by the PNA). The remaining three communities recorded a rate of less than 10 percent.

workplaces in Israel were within commuting distance for workers from the West Bank and Gaza Strip, and because Israel did not grant residency to Palestinian workers, the majority of Palestinian laborers working in Israel remained commuters rather than becoming migrants. Unlike labor markets in the Gulf states, which attracted predominantly skilled and professional labor, the Israeli labor market required unskilled or semiskilled Palestinian labor. According to the IWS survey results, some 15 percent of the work force in 1999 was employed in Israel or in Israeli settlements (again in line with the national average recorded for that year). The majority of these were employed as building workers or assistants or in various unskilled jobs. Only a very small percentage was employed in professional or semiprofessional occupations (probably Palestinians from East Jerusalem), compared to a fifth of those employed in the West Bank and Gaza Strip (Giacaman and Johnson 2002b, 15).

The establishment of the PNA in 1994 with a fast-expanding governmental sector, the active presence of numerous international and local NGOs, and the expansion in the activities of the private sector, are factors that helped to change the occupational structure in the West Bank and Gaza Strip, which was dominated by an unskilled and semi-skilled labor force.

During the 1990s there was a change in the pattern of emigration that had prevailed in the 1960s, 1970s, and the 1980s, with the "pull" of skilled workers and professionals by the Gulf states. In the 1990s the open gates to these countries, as well as to the Israeli labor market, were closed or narrowed greatly. A wave of repatriation to the West Bank and Gaza Strip followed the Gulf War in 1991 (24 percent of total returnees) and the establishment of the PNA in 1994 (48.5 percent of all returnees). The census data of 1997 show that a significant percentage of returnees had post-secondary education (middle diploma and a university degree).[32] They also show that 37.5 percent of the occupations of West Bank returnees (males and females) before their return can be classified as middle-class occupations. In the Gaza Strip, 68 percent of returnees had white collar jobs (Malki and Shalabi 2000, table 26).

---

32. At the end of 1997, returnees formed about 10.5 percent of the total population of the West Bank and Gaza Strip (54 percent males, and 46.4 percent females). More than a third (36.5 percent) of the returnees came from Jordan, 31 percent from Gulf States, 21.5 percent from other Arab countries, and 5 percent from the United States (Malki and Shalabi 2000, tables 18–20).

In general the number of West Bank and Gaza Strip residents who commuted to work in Israel declined sharply during the 1990s. Prior to September 2000 (the beginning of the second intifada, which brought an end to Palestinian commuting to Israel), the rate had dropped to about half of what it was in the late 1970s and 1980s. Again the communities surveyed varied greatly in the degree of their dependence on employment in Israel.[33]

Employment in the public sector rose sharply in the 1990s, thanks to the establishment of the PNA. Approximately half of the returnees have high levels of education and an urban style of life. With the establishment of the PNA, the reversal of the one-way traffic of emigration and the establishment of an active public sphere with open political debate were new factors that entered the scene in the occupied Palestinian territories. But the collapse of the peace process, which ignited the second intifada and the ensuing systematic destruction of the Palestinian economy, the paralyzing of national institutions, and the fragmentation of society have obstructed the impact of more secular and liberal forces. With the second intifada came a rise in support for the Islamic movement, a factor that strengthened conservatism in the cultural and social fields, and the more urban and secular style of life remained confined to the twin cities of Ramallah and al-Bira.

Outlining a Sociological Story of Palestinian Emigration

Nearly half of all the households surveyed in the West Bank and Gaza Strip reported at least one emigrant who is a close relative of the head of the household.[34] This finding remains an underestimation because it only reports on emigrants who are close relatives of resident household heads. Emigration has

33. In five communities, between 10 percent to 20 percent of the active labor force commuted to work to Israel and its colonies; in eight communities, more than 20 percent of the active labor force was so employed; and in six communities, less than 5 percent was.

34. As can be expected, the number of relatives living abroad increased significantly with the increase in the age of the male head of household; among those who were 20–29 years old, 28 percent reported having family abroad; the percentages were 41 percent for 30–39 year olds, 52 percent for 40–49 year olds, 56 percent for 50–59 year olds, 63 percent for 60–64 year olds, and a high of 66 percent for those who were 65 year olds or older. As the age of the head of the household increases, he or she is more likely to have close kin living abroad for various reasons (work, marriage, study, expulsion, etc.).

been and continues to be, since 1948, a significant and persistent feature of all the types of Palestinian communities, particularly in the West Bank and Gaza Strip. Emigration from Palestine was known before 1948, but it never acquired the scale and significance it did after that. Emigrant labor abroad has entailed processes of deconstruction of households in the communities of the West Bank and Gaza Strip and the construction of new households in the country of destination. Labor commuting to Israel—which started in 1968 and continued until the beginning of the second intifada in September 2000—did not entail such deconstruction and reconstruction of households, but it nevertheless had an impact on household arrangements by promoting, through the supremacy of wage labor, the primacy of the conjugal bond emphasized by the increased dependence of women on men's wage income particularly with the marginalization of agriculture since the beginning of the Israeli occupation in 1967 (Moors 1995).

Emigration and labor commuting went hand in hand with other processes that affected Palestinian communities. These processes included the spread of secular education (both at the basic and higher levels), the marginalization of agriculture as a source of employment and livelihood, and the dominance of wage labor as the sole or main source of income.

Differences between communities are reflected in where migrants went, the kind of relations they kept with resident relatives, the types of occupations they found, and the degree to which they depended on relatives in the country of destination to facilitate their entry, residence, and work. An important part of the variations between the communities can be explained in terms of the history of emigration itself, as earlier successful emigrants tended to draw others from home communities to where they happened to settle. Other variations can be explained in terms of the economy of the community itself, the role of agriculture in its economy, and the impact of wider processes (such as the spread of education) on the resources that each household could mobilize. The limitations imposed by arid agriculture, the confiscation of land for building Israeli colonial settlements, the restrictions imposed on industrial and economic growth, the high rates of unemployment (including among college and university students), the accessibility (or lack thereof) of commuting labor in Israel and the kind of labor available there are all factors that explain overall high rates of emigration and differential rates among communities.

Kinship (as a basic organizational directive), social class (as a basic determinant of life chances), and gender (as reflected in decision making within the household as well as a determinant of life chances) are all pertinent in explaining the dynamics and patterns of emigration. But they acquire their specific explanatory power only when placed in the context of the political economy of the West Bank and Gaza Strip, particularly those aspects of it related to the absence of an independent Palestinian state and the subjection of the West Bank and Gaza Strip to external rule (up to 1967) and to colonial-settler occupation since June 1967.

Social class appears to be relevant for the understanding of emigration, but not in a simple and unidirectional way. The highest rates of emigration were found to exist among the "well off" and the very poor. Both had strong motives to secure or improve their life chances. Households headed by employers or the self-employed are much more likely to have emigrants than employees in the private sector (mostly in informal employment). Furthermore, households headed by public-sector employees (those employed by the PNA and UNRWA) tend to have a higher ratio of emigrants than private sector employees.

In the IWS survey, households with close relatives abroad scored better than other households on the possession of a number of amenities such as washing machine, dishwasher, microwave oven, phone, computer, private car, satellite dish, and heating. However, a Fafo study found no correlation between ownership of household durable goods and having close relatives abroad (Pedersen et al. 2001a, 160), indicating a need for further investigation of the complex relations between class situation and the changes that emigration brings in the production and reproduction of systems of inequality in gender and class relations, and in terms of the production and reproduction of identities (local, national, ethnic, religious).

Emigration has been the strategy of those who seek to improve their (and their family's) life chances and those seeking to move out of the zone of vulnerability, poverty, and deprivation. Emigration is related to social class in two ways: first, those in upper social classes use their class resources to select places and jobs that reproduce their class position and possibly augment their assets. Second, those in lower social-class positions use emigration as a means for social mobility and sometimes (especially for those working in the Gulf states) show the change in their class position by the kind of houses they build, the investments they make, and the presents they bring when they visit the home communities.

The relationship between class and emigration is, therefore, much more complex than statements positing that households with close relatives abroad are better off because of remittances they receive. Only a small portion of households (and they are mostly located in a small number of communities) receive regular remittances from abroad. Better-off households are better equipped to emigrate and to find better income-generating employment or enterprises. They also can better afford to send family members to study abroad (a portion of whom do not return). This is particularly true of emigration to North America, Europe, and the Gulf states, but it does not necessarily apply to emigrants to Jordan, and it certainly is not true of commuters to Israel.

Kinship networks remain important in certain fields of social action despite the changes in property relations and ownership and in the patterns of occupational structures prevailing in West Bank and Gaza Strip communities. Most households are of the nuclear type, and joint ownership of property is not known for the overwhelming number of households related by kinship. Kinship has been a factor in emigration processes in more than one way. It has worked to create a "chain" as earlier successful emigrants took it upon themselves to "pull" relatives from the communities of the West Bank and Gaza Strip to new destinations.[35]

It could be argued that the mobilizing of resources in the emigration process is helped by kin marriage. Data show that marriages to close relatives (of the first degree) in Palestinian communities remain high. Such marriages totaled 28 percent of all marriages in the year 2000, just over 26 percent in the West Bank, and just over 31 percent in the Gaza Strip (PCBS 2000b).[36] A survey carried out by Fafo in 1995 in the West Bank and Gaza Strip found that nearly 27 percent of all marriages of women born between 1940 and 1949 were to first cousins, and the percentages for women born between 1949 and

35. For the concept of "chain migration," see Boyle, Halfacree, and Robinson 1998, 36.

36. The PCBS demographic survey of 1995 gives slightly higher figures for the frequency of close marriage, 27 percent for the West Bank and 32 percent for the Gaza Strip. However the period between the two surveys is too short to warrant the inference of a decrease in the ratio of close marriage. Marriages to other relatives showed a slight decline in the West Bank (from 20 percent to 19 percent) and a slight rise in the Gaza Strip (from 20.2 percent to 21.5 percent).

1969 was just over 28 percent (Pedersen et al. 2001a, 82). Our survey (based on a sample of communities rather than a national sample and confined to marriages of women between the ages of fifteen and forty-nine in the year 1999) found that 27 percent of women in the nineteen communities were married to their male cousins, and nearly 18 percent were married to other relatives. In all about 44.5 percent of marriages were to relatives of various degrees. The rates remained high in all three types of communities, including towns.[37]

Communities that reported high rates of households with emigrants did not have lower or higher rates of endogamous marriages than found in other communities.[38] In other words emigration and endogamous marriages are not alternative mechanisms for managing risk and highly precarious situations. They have been going hand in hand for decades, and given the specifics of the political economy of the West Bank and Gaza Strip, social conservatism was one of the major unintended consequences.

The low participation of women in the formal sector of the West Bank and Gaza Strip economy, and the existence of the same conditions in many of the countries chosen as destinations for Palestinian emigrants (Jordan and the Gulf states, all with strong patriarchal culture that had also developed strong radical Islamic movements), could only help to enforce conservative attitudes. Women's emigration has remained dependent on their menfolk as fathers or husbands.

Emigration has, objectively speaking, helped to reproduce social conservatism in more than one way, apart from the exclusion of most women from

37. Villages recorded the highest rate of cousin marriages (28.5 percent) and camps the lowest (24 percent); towns fell in the middle position (27 percent). However, households with no emigrants show a higher rate of marriages to relatives in all three types of communities and overall than households with emigrants. Twenty-four percent of women reported having married their first cousins in households with emigrants, compared to 30 percent among those who reported no migrants from the household. Villages showed a higher rate of community endogamy (other than marriages to kin) than camps and towns (28 percent for city, 20 percent for camp, and 30 percent for village). The rates remain high in all three types of communities, including towns.

38. Seventy-two percent of all female marriages (of women between the ages of fifteen and forty-nine) in the communities surveyed were endogamous (kinship and community).

participation in paid employment and their segregation from the public sphere. First, emigration deprived Palestinian communities of social and cultural capital (i.e., from whose with high education and skills who had to emigrate) and put many of them in places where they were marginalized socially, culturally and politically and subjected them, along with other labor emigrants, to strict social control. This dynamic involved, at some stages, leaving wives and children behind for a while with a consequence of reinforcing patriarchal relations for those remaining at home.

Second, the fact that a large percentage of emigrants found work and residence in Jordan and the Gulf states (particularly in the Emirates, Kuwait, and Saudi Arabia, where large numbers of Palestinians found work) required most emigrants and their families to adjust to the largely "conservative" culture of the host countries. The state in these countries controlled the mass media and civil society organizations (where they attempted to exist), and some financed regional Arabic newspapers and television stations that propagated a (politically, culturally, and socially) conservative ideology and financed movements that oppose liberal, secular, and socialist movements and outlooks. Most of these countries witnessed, in the 1980s and 1990s, the emergence of political movements with ideologies phrased in religious language and symbols, which made them difficult to challenge. This religious ideology was transmitted back home through regular visits or upon final return.

Third, Palestinian employment in Israel created commuters who met Israelis simply as employers (without any formal contract), and Palestinian contact with Israelis in the West Bank and Gaza Strip was restricted to contact between the occupied and the occupiers and colonial settlers. That is, Palestinians were excluded from the liberal-democratic aspect of Israeli life, which has been largely reserved for Jews. In fact, this face-to-face contact with the culture of an occupying, repressive, and in many aspects racist force may well have given conservatism a nationalistic or religious dimension.

Fourth, there is the absence of an independent Palestinian state and the continued Israeli domination and colonial presence that has kept a tight control over all trends that might lead to urban construction, cultural dynamism, and an active public sphere. This domination was achieved through control of urban planning, land allocation, political repression, and the blocking of economic activity and investment by Palestinians. It is no accident that the overwhelming majority of privately owned economic enterprises in the West Bank and Gaza Strip are made up of tiny (employing less than five individuals) family-owned and run businesses.[39]

This should not lead to the conclusion that Palestinian society in the West Bank and Gaza Strip is static or stagnant. It is a society where different social forces with different agendas (liberal, secular, Islamist, populist, nationalist, socialist) are at work. It is also a society that is fighting to overthrow a colonial-settler occupation, and is undergoing various processes, some of which are outlined in this chapter. There is, however, a need to study processes that have been triggered by education, expatriate capital investment, changes in both the national and Islamist movement, the establishment of a central territorial authority represented by the PNA, and many other forces. These trends and processes need to be observed and their ramifications studied.

39. The results of the December 1997 census showed that 76,962 establishments in the West Bank and Gaza Strip employed 191,361 persons, that is, an average of 2.5 persons per establishment (PCBS 1997a, table 34).

5

THE PARADOX OF WOMEN'S WORK

Coping, Crisis, and Family Survival

Eileen Kuttab

The Israeli-Palestinian Declaration of Principles (Oslo agreement) of September 1993, signed by the Palestine Liberation Organization and Israel, resulted in a peace agreement that committed both parties to a series of actions and interim measures including partial Israeli territorial withdrawal and limited Palestinian self-government. This agreement created a political environment of euphoria and optimism among the Palestinian people, who had suffered a long colonial occupation by Israeli forces of more than thirty-five years. Moreover, a new mind-set was promoted whereby people felt less pressured by the daily presence of the occupiers and more responsible for their own affairs. The Palestinian National Authority (PNA) was expected to have the power and will to control the future of the country under the assumption that there would be more opportunities for self-reliance through expansion of the labor market and that the Palestinian economy would be liberated from full dependence on the Israeli economy, especially the Israeli labor market.

This state of euphoria did not last long, as the situation changed drastically after a period of about seven years. The al-Aqsa intifada erupted in September 2000 as an expression of protest against Palestinian acceptance of a political agreement with no viability and against Israeli intransigence in the implementation of agreed-upon measures.

The post-Oslo optimism was reflected in the way social movements and nongovernmental organizations altered their agendas by defining the period as a stage in state building or as a postconflict situation, as though the major conflict with Israel had been resolved. The pending issues (withdrawal from the settlements, status of Jerusalem, and right to return) were postponed or left to the final stage negotiations. In this context, social and developmental issues became important, and the women's movement felt that it was the right time to address women's rights and concerns as priority issues, hence raising gender inequality as an important and visible issue (Hammami and Kuttab 1998).

Throughout the 1980s, the Palestine Liberation Organization or national movement had worked to mobilize different sectors of society around issues of value to democratic transformation.[1] Women's activism on issues of gender and class were actively promoted on the political, social, and national levels. This accumulated democratic experience successfully empowered women to play an important role in the first intifada in 1987. After Oslo, the PNA as well as the international donor community interpreted the situation as a postconflict situation. Formal government institutions were being formed, and the political and legal systems, the economy, and education became important spheres of intensive work. This on one hand marginalized women's mass-based political activity but on the other it prompted them to play a role in the making of the quasi-state. Hence, the state-building activity turned to be a catalyst for the women's movement; stimulated by the magical words of good governance, legal reform, and economic opportunity, it set its mind on an agenda that would make women's rights and women's concerns part of the process. This process brought in sharper relief the gender inequality that had always existed but that had taken a back seat to the liberation struggle.

Now the period that opened with the optimism generated by the signing of the Oslo agreement is ending on a far different note: massive poverty, unemployment, and human insecurity for many Palestinians, brought about by Israel's policy of closure and siege and its use of brutal force against the Palestinian population. How Palestinian women and their families have made this journey from resistance to state building and into survival through coping, and what their role has been in the process are some of the major questions under investigation. Moreover, I explore some of the continuities in patterns of women's work in relation to enduring macroeconomic and political features that underlie both the so-called postconflict era of the Oslo agreement and the prolonged conflict of the intifada years, and consider the role and place of women's work in coping strategies during this protracted and unequal

1. See Taraki 1991; Jad 2000b; Kuttab 1993 on Palestinian mass based organizations and democratization and on the transformation of the Palestinian national movement that occurred in the late 1970s.

conflict. I argue that the unusually low formal labor force participation of Palestinian women constitutes a paradox when compared to the historic legacy of women's activism combined with flexible and creative adaptation to various roles and pressures through the prolonged conflict. Such a paradox can only be explained by understanding how "other" economic activities—what I term "resistance economies" located in the household—function as means of steadfastness. Income-generating projects developed by mass-based organizations, and "coping strategies" for survival in the second intifada, have enhanced and prolonged the life of the Palestinian household and absorbed the different levels of conflict and pressure.

One should be reminded that during the 1970s and 1980s, the democratic, mass-based organizations enhanced the developmental process in order to support resistance strategies more creatively and dynamically. Although these organizations were political expressions, they became developmental tools, basing their authority on popular accountability and legitimacy through the services they promoted.

These organizations were more inclined to express the priorities of low-income groups in general and adopted income-generating projects, especially in the mid-1980s, when the strategy of resistance also integrated the idea of "liberation." Their objectives were twofold: to integrate women into the development process and to activate their role in the national economy following the Women in Development (WID) approach promoted by the donor community. The second objective was to create a new kind of social organization, more productive and efficient in nature as well as responsive to people's needs and a tool for social and political mobilization. This was a goal that responded to the new political agenda of "democratization" that aimed at expanding the base of these institutions by reaching the villages and refugee camps. At that time, and in a parallel approach, the national movement emphasized economic independence as a necessary dimension of the political and national struggle. Nationalist groups encouraged the mushrooming of these projects especially during the first intifada, when slogans such as self-reliance and boycotts of the Israeli market were promoted as national goals.

Palestinian women's low formal labor force participation—averaging around 10 percent since 1967—constitutes another dimension of the paradox in light of relatively high levels of female education and relatively high levels of support for women's work outside the home (see Johnson's essay in this volume) and also in light of increased need. Although participation did rise in the more stable environment of the Oslo years, I will examine structural constraints both in labor markets and in the overarching dynamic of colonial rule to which everyday practices of resistance respond. Some of these constraints are located in women's work in the informal economy, but it is also true that most female labor remains firmly anchored in household economies. In a 2000 time-use survey, the Palestinian Central Bureau of Statistics (PCBS) found that while women aged twenty-five to forty-four worked over eight hours per day (every day of the week), only 6 percent of women's work was paid (PCBS 2001, 17). Likewise, in this chapter I explore the features of this paid work. Nevertheless, it is essential to keep in mind the wider canvas of women's work and the salience of household economies, to which I return in my discussion of household production and coping strategies during the second intifada. Abu Nahleh's ethnographic look at Palestinian families during this period complements my contextual review.

Post-Oslo Dynamics

The political environment after the Oslo agreement elevated the expectations of women in relation to economic opportunities, access to education, and political representation. Examining the implication of these expectations for the labor markets, which is one focus of this chapter, I argue that although the political changes affected women's employment opportunities to some extent through the expansion of the public sector (mainly the health and education sectors) and the service sector (PCBS 2002b), this expansion did not dramatically change the structurally segregated labor market. Most of the jobs that the PNA generated were related to the building of institutions—ministries, security services, infrastructure, and construction. These new jobs were mainly male-oriented and did not accommodate women except in clerical jobs and in the services sector, where employment generation was limited. Some token positions were also intended for women in policy-making positions within the PNA.

In this chapter, I will also analyze how women, whose participation rate in the labor market has never exceeded 12 percent since the Israeli occupation of 1967 (Pedersen et al. 2001b; PCBS 2000d), have played an important role in the survival of the Palestinian family in times of crisis. The first part of the chapter will address the structural imbalances of the Palestinian gendered labor market that prohibit or discourage women from entering the labor market. It has been claimed that cultural factors have been the main obstacle to women's entry into the labor market. The analysis that follows sheds light on other factors that may explain the low rate of women's participation in the labor force.

In the last section I will explore specific coping strategies that women and households use to survive in times of crisis. During the second intifada, families have faced continuous aggression leading to loss of economic resources and income, deprivation, uprooting, and displacement. These factors have all compromised and threatened Palestinian family survival. Yet families still manage and are able to cope with the barest requirements of livelihood. Coping with daily pressures has become a way of life and a mode of resistance. Coping strategies have relevance to gender dynamics, as women are often the main agents in promoting such strategies. Domestic production and the selling of women's gold or trousseaux were used during the 1948 and 1967 Arab-Israeli wars and have become part of the resistance heritage. These strategies have become the only available means of survival, given high unemployment exceeding 50 percent of the labor force in the West Bank and Gaza Strip (World Bank 2003), and poverty levels of over 60 percent of households (World Bank 2003). As the Israeli forces continue to kill and injure civilians, imprison breadwinners, demolish homes, and deport and separate families, a siege-and-closure policy is surrounding all these acts.

I will also explore the reverse side of resistance and steadfastness strategies, namely, the limitations of these coping strategies. Although families and in particular women have been coping for the last half century, the ferocity of aggression and the high level of impoverishment and deprivation have become intolerable. As days go by without a drastic change in the political status quo, and as the Israeli policy of deprivation is ratcheted without limit, Palestinian families may reach the limits of their ability to cope. It has become clearer through personal testimonies[2] that women are feeling helpless in the face of mounting misery. Thus, if the Israeli aggression continues, women's

2. The Institute of Women's Studies at Birzeit University was commissioned by UNIFEM to conduct a study on the impact of political violence on women; the data and interviews support this analysis (Kuttab and Barghouti 2002).

degree of tolerance will decrease. This inevitably will have negative repercussions on families and on women's physical and mental health. Moreover, ties of solidarity that are forged in times of crisis among the community members and relatives may fray and disintegrate. Women play an important role in creating and maintaining such ties, and losing the capacity to do so can affect the whole community.

Methodological Issues: Occupation, Gender, and Labor Markets

Defining labor trends in a unique setting such as the Palestinian one calls for a nuanced approach that is often lacking in mainstream economic analysis. An analysis of labor trends in Palestine must take into account the conditions wrought by the thirty-five-year history of Israeli colonial aggression and occupation, accompanied by continuous political instability. It must also take into account not only the ongoing and prolonged relation of dependence between the Israeli and Palestinian economies, but also, and more significantly, the volatile fluctuations and changes that have characterized this dependent relationship over time. Volatility has not only been caused by political and economic factors affecting Israel and the region (such as recessions, wars, and changes in Gulf labor markets) concerning their ability or willingness to absorb Palestinian labor, but is also very much tied in with the dynamics of the structural relationship between colonizer and colonized. More specifically, not only broad labor trends and, in particular, gender imbalances and occupational segregation must be understood within this colonial framework. The gendered nature of labor markets where women are mostly active in the domestic domain cannot be explained only by reference to issues of choice, cultural practices and preferences, or features of the economy. Nor can they be understood without looking at the global and regional context where labor trends have undergone drastic changes through globalization.

After the Oslo accords, Israel remained in control of most natural resources and borders and roads: those connecting villages and cities and those linking the West Bank with the Gaza Strip and the occupied territories with surrounding regions (MOPIC, UNDP, and DFID 2002). Hence, because of dependency on Israel's goodwill, the opportunity to stabilize the economy and make it functional in order to generate employment opportunities remained limited. Since the eruption of the al-Aqsa intifada in September 2000, even this economic process has been brought to a halt. The current reality is characterized by intensive structural distortion and pressure caused by the closure policy imposed by the Israeli occupying forces, and restrictions on the mobility of labor, commodities, and capital (UNSCO 2001). These restrictions have caused tremendous infrastructural imbalances, restricted the potential of economic growth, and denied Palestinians any functional role in running their economic institutions. All these factors have an impact on gender relations and women's position in the economy as a whole. These conditions further damaged a Palestinian economy that (since Israel's occupation in 1967) had been structurally distorted, has not been permitted to grow, and was fully dependent on Israel. This is not to say that prior to this period the economy was stable and viable. The colonial nature of the Israeli occupation since 1967 has imprisoned the Palestinian economy, forced major structural distortions, and prohibited its growth, forcing a situation of full dependence on the Israeli economy in general and the Israeli labor market in particular.

Bearing in mind that the Palestinian economy is a "resistance economy" where women play a crucial role, one can see that the Israeli occupation has regenerated and strengthened the traditional gendered division of labor that existed under Jordanian rule, where women were occupationally segregated, concentrated in agriculture and services, marginally treated as reserves in times of need, and employed only in jobs that were compatible with their reproductive roles, roles that were considered to be an extension of their traditional domestic roles.

The decline in the role of agriculture in the Palestinian economy since 1967, and the obstruction of the industrial sector, has undermined the Palestinian employment sectors. The labor force was reoriented to serve the labor intensive areas of the Israeli economy. Hence, women's labor activities cannot be understood separate from this larger context. It is clear that the Palestinian workforce has been geared to specific sectors of the Israeli labor market, and the obstacles put on the manufacturing activities had specific implications for the integration of women into wage work. Additionally, the declining role of agriculture has meant a growing reliance on marginal and underpaid or nonpaid labor, which had a great significance for women (Hammami 1997, 7). In short, this kind of economy has maintained gender segregated labor markets, and women have been pushed to more informal and subsistence activities that have further cemented the patriarchal nature of the labor market and the division of labor within the household.

Labor Market Trends: Global and Regional

Globalization has coincided with higher unemployment among less skilled workers, widening income inequality. One of the important trends in labor markets in the advanced economies has been a steady shift in demand away from less skilled toward more skilled occupations (Anker 1998). This trend has produced dramatic rises in wage and income inequality between the more and the less skilled in some countries and has increased unemployment among the less skilled in other countries. It is important to bear in mind that these changes are not devoid of gender implications. Differences in wages and employment across countries can be explained by the differences in labor market structures (Lechner and Coli 2000, 177–79). Economic restructuring has led to an increase in flexibility and insecurity in labor markets, informalization and downsizing of the industrial workforce, and income polarization, all of which have affected both high- and low-income countries. These changes have resulted in social polarization and increased poverty for those who become unemployed and lack the necessary skills required by labor markets. Again these processes have specific gender dimensions, including higher levels of female as opposed to male unemployment, informalization of work often performed by women, and increased participation of women in the informal sector (Beneria and Bisnath 2001, 172). Labor markets are gender segregated; most women are employed in only a few areas, such as light manufacturing or services industries, unskilled or clerical occupations, and informal activities. The patterns of female employment such as household work indicate that women continue to be less active in the industrial sector, away from agriculture and into the service sector (World Bank 2004).

Available data on the Arab region, however, indicate that female labor force participation rates have generally been on the increase particularly during the last two decades, a growth that is linked to globalization (UNDESA 1999). Yet by 2000 the average female labor force participation in the Arab region was still the lowest among developing regions (ILO 2000). These rates are lower than expected when considering the region's fertility rates, its educational levels, and the age structure of the female population (World Bank 2004). Some economists have indicated that women in the Arab region have been entering the labor force in record numbers, but much of the increase has come from the informal sector. The significance of this sector for women's employment is widely cited but difficult to document and analyze in the absence of relevant statistics. When data are available they suggest that many new female entrants to the informal sector tend to be less educated, young, and belong to households that have migrated from rural areas (Zafiris et al. 2003, 66). Informal sector employment has traditionally been widespread in agriculture, although that is changing with increasing urbanization in most countries of the Arab region. On the other hand, the urban informal sector is a significant employer of women, especially for the self-employed, unpaid family laborers, part-time workers, and domestic workers (Zafiris et al. 2003, 67).

For instance, 85.6 percent of women in Gulf states worked in the service sector in 1990, compared to 9 percent in industry and 5.4 percent in agriculture. The question that must be raised here is whether these workers are migrant female workers or locals. In contrast, in the least developed countries such as Yemen or Sudan, 82.5 percent of employed women worked in the agriculture sector in 1990, compared to 13.3 percent in the service sector and 4.2 percent in industry. Were these differences due to considerably fewer female migrant workers in Yemen and Sudan? Between these two extremes, 37 percent of working women in the Maghrib and 46.7 percent in the Mashriq were economically active in the service sector in 1990, compared to 47.4 percent for the Maghrib and 40.3 percent for the Mashriq in agriculture, and 15.5 percent for the Maghrib and 13 percent for the Mashriq in industry (UNWISTAT 1999; CAWTAR 2001). Thus, patterns and sectors of women's employment in the Arab world vary significantly.

Some researchers have assumed that Arab culture and traditions have been mainly responsible for the gender gap in the labor market. Moghadam explains this gap as being caused by the "patriarchal gender contract," where a set of relationships between men and women are based upon the male breadwinner/female homemaker roles in which the male has direct access to wage employment, or control over the means of production, and the female is largely economically dependent upon male members of her family. The result of this division of labor is occupational segregation (2000, 242).

In 2000 the labor participation rate for women aged fifteen through sixty-five in the Arab region was 35.6 percent, compared to 45.2 percent for Latin America, 62 percent for Asia, and 57.4 percent for Africa (CAWTAR 2001). This is a result of a vicious cycle reflected in the low female labor force participation rates in the region and the concentration of women in sectors that became feminized. Hence, gender segregation is a very significant issue for the Arab region. However, more data are needed to understand its origins and implications for education and training, wage determination mechanisms, and the interaction between work and household choices on the one hand, and family formation on the other (Zafiris et al. 2003, 70).

The Arab region has undergone economic structural changes in line with global trends, with a rise in employment in the service sector and a reduction in employment in the agricultural sector. Although the proportion of working women in the Arab region has risen over time, regional disparities and occupational distribution are evident and are determined by the nature of the economic diversity and the global structural requirements (UNDESA 1999; CAWTAR 2001).

The data indicate important variations in women's economic activity in the Arab region that seem to be associated with the type of economy within the region, or the extent to which the region has moved away from agriculture and into the service sector, that is, the extent to which the regional economy has been globalized. The less globalized the economy, the greater the involvement of women in agricultural economic activities, the more globalized the higher incorporation into the service sector, a pattern that is similar to the patterns of change over time in men's employment as well in this region. Consequently, women's employment in the Arab world seems to be highly influenced by the structural changes taking place within the global and regional economies and by the availability of employment opportunities. This second factor undermines the argument that culture and traditional division of labor are the main determinants of gendered segregated labor markets (UNDESA 1999; CAWTAR 2001).

In summary, changes in labor trends in the Arab world indicate the important influence of globalization on women's economic activity in the region, expressed in declining economic activity of women in agriculture and the expansion of the service sector that is in turn and in varying degrees apparently dependent on the stage of incorporation into the global market.

Context: Uniqueness or Similarity?

Has the Palestinian occupied territory experienced similar changes in the labor market, or has the Israeli occupation prevented even the adoption and replication of these global and regional trends? The prolonged Israeli domination over the West Bank and Gaza Strip and the systematic policy to change the social-economic structure of the occupied areas to meet Israeli political and economic goals have continued to have drastic and destabilizing effects on Palestinian society. The highly industrialized and technologically advanced Israeli economy still possesses the power to deprive Palestinians of the efficient use of their economic resources by restructuring the local economy for its political goals. It has also expanded its sovereignty through prioritizing integration over separation and dispossession over exploitation (Roy 1995, 117). Even with the Oslo-Cairo agreements concluded in 1993, Palestinians still have no control over economic resources, sectoral development, and political expression. The term "dependent development," often used to characterize the dependency of developing countries' economies on the global market, cannot fully explain the unique economy of the occupied territories. One cannot talk about normal economic viability or stable labor markets when over 60 percent of Palestinian households have fallen under the poverty line, when over 50 percent of the labor force were unemployed in 2002 (World Bank 2003), and when the material infrastructure and political, social, and cultural institutions that managed the everyday life of the Palestinian people have been destroyed.

Sara Roy has remarked on the inadequacy of prevailing theories of dependency and underdevelopment in understanding the uniqueness of the Palestinian situation:

> How would existing theories explain the political repression of the Palestinians, the harassment of educational institutions, the discriminatory application of economic policy, the denial of legal protections, the destruction of personal property, the deportation of the Palestinian leadership, the arbitrary

use of power, the endemic conflict between Israelis and Arabs and racism? Whereas development theories identify dominance, inequality and exploitation as reasons for underdevelopment, they fail to account for dispossession and destruction of production resources as the principle reason for underdevelopment. (1995, 120)

Roy continues to say that underdevelopment no longer is motivated just by economic imperatives, but by political and ideological ones, too (125–26).

These political conditions have further aggravated and expanded the already existing process of underdevelopment. Comparison of the periods before and during the second intifada reveals changes in labor trends and explains the impact of the severity of the political conditions on the labor market and the effect of these conditions (if any) on gender relations.

Gendered Trends: Women's Employment, 1993–2000

Pre-Oslo Profile

According to the Palestinian Central Bureau of Statistics, women's formal labor-force participation in Palestine has been historically very low, a feature that is shared by other countries of the region. The population of the West Bank and Gaza Strip is young, with 46.5 percent younger than fifteen years. The mean household size is about seven persons[3] (PCBS 1999e). The high dependency ratio of the Palestinian households, the lack of social safety nets and services, and limited employment opportunities are strong explanatory factors for the low labor-force participation of women. In 1991, only one out of every four persons in the occupied territories was in the labor force. This statistical fact however, disguises major regional differences (Heiberg and Ovensen 1993, 185). The low ratio of women compared to men in the labor force in the West Bank and Gaza Strip extends to the whole region; female

---

3. The total fertility rate for those with less than a secondary education is 6.32, for those with secondary education the rate is 5.57, and for those with more than secondary the rate is 4.52. On average, a married Palestinian woman has 4.79 children, of which 0.30 did not survive (PCBS 1999e).

participation in the labor force is the lowest in Gaza (Heiberg and Ovensen 1993, 186).

There are relatively small regional differences in the composition of the labor force by gender, age, and education. The Gaza labor force is slightly more male dominated and younger than the one in the West Bank and Arab Jerusalem. The labor force in Arab Jerusalem comprises more women who are older and more educated than does the average total for the occupied territories (Heiberg and Ovensen 1993). In general, Palestinian women did not constitute more than roughly 10 percent of the labor force in the early 1990s according to Fafo; PCBS puts their rates at 6.2 percent in 1993 and 11.2 percent in 1995 (PCBS 1995).

These percentages are among the lowest in the Arab world. Furthermore, the invisibility of various female informal economic activities raises questions regarding exclusion from social protection, long hours in labor-intensive work, and hazardous conditions, which have implications for women's physical, mental, and reproductive health (ILO 2003). These concerns do exist in the Palestinian occupied territories as more and more women are entering informal employment as a coping strategy because of limited access to formal labor opportunities. According to the ILO, there is a decrease in wage employment mostly but not exclusively in Israel, compensated by a considerable increase in self-employment and to a lesser extent in unpaid family work, where women are concentrated. Some 56,000 wage employment positions were lost and replaced by over 47,400 self-employment positions. It can be safely assumed that self-employment is mostly in subsistence agriculture, petty trade, and personal services. The net aggregate change is a decline of 6,000 jobs over three years (ILO 2004, 25).

Since the last half of the twentieth century, the Palestinian territories have not experienced any political or economic independence, which in turn has resulted in structural distortion of the economy. In both periods, when the West Bank was under Jordanian rule from 1948 to 1967 and then under the Israeli occupation from 1967 to date, state policies did not give any real opportunity for developing the productive sectors of the economy. Israeli rule has marginalized the industrial sector; focused on semiskilled labor in either light manufacturing or construction, which were mainly male sectors; maintained the subsistence economy in agriculture or primitive agriculture to remove them as a basis for any compatible competition; and enlarged the service sector. These features have been intensified continually and structurally implanted through legal and regulatory means (Dakkak 1988).

Historically, female labor opportunities in the Palestinian economy have been provided in five labor market areas: the agricultural sector, the nonagricultural sector, the Israeli labor market, the informal economy, and the domestic economy. The domestic economy, which is mainly a female sector, is the only one that does not offer wages; thus it is not considered to be part of the economic sectors (Hammami 2001).

Oslo Stage

During the 1990s, Palestinian women seem to have been mostly absorbed in the informal and domestic economies, with 55.6 percent of West Bank working women and 60.6 percent of Gaza working women found in the informal economy, and 83.6 percent of West Bank women and 85.7 percent of Gaza women active in the domestic economy (Ovensen 1994). PCBS labor force and formal employment figures reveal that by 2000, women's labor force participation was still low; women age twenty years and older accounted for 10.4 percent of the labor force. Furthermore, women were overrepresented in the agriculture and service sectors and underrepresented in industry; 34.6 percent of employed women were absorbed in the agriculture, hunting, forestry, and fishing sectors and 45.9 percent in the service sector (PCBS 2000d). Hence, during this period, women tended to be concentrated in the nonformal and domestic sectors; this suggests that when women are not able to find jobs in the formal labor market, they create employment possibilities for themselves in the informal sector (Hammami 2001).

PCBS data for 1992 and 1999 reveal interesting time trends in women's labor-force participation. A main change is the increase in the percentage of women absorbed in the formal labor market, especially in the Gaza Strip. This increase seems to be the direct result of the expansion of the public sector after the formation of the PNA, which has expanded opportunities for women to enter the labor force on a larger scale. In addition, the creation and expansion of the public sector has also affected positively the private sector, which has also expanded women's opportunities of absorption in the formal labor force. PCBS data show that in 1992 women were 10 percent of the formal labor force in the West Bank, and by 1999 they were 14.1 percent, whereas in the Gaza Strip women's participation rate in 1992 was 1.7 percent and increased to 8.8 percent in 1999 (PCBS 1995; 1999e; 2000d).

As shown in table 5.1, the creation and expansion of the public sector was accompanied by an increased opportunity for women to join the labor force in the private sector as well. The data demonstrate a sharper change in the service sectors and other branches from 35.5 percent in 1992 rising to 46.2 percent in 1999, followed by a rise in mining and manufacturing from 8.1 percent in 1992 to 12.9 percent in 1999. Conversely, women's employment in the agriculture, hunting and fishing sectors came down from 51.9 percent in 1992 to 31.8 percent in 1999. It appears that opportunities for women's employment in the private and public sectors increased during the post-Oslo period at the expense of agriculture. These data confirm that one of the main employers of women is the service sector, absorbing the highest percentage of

Table 5.1
Distribution of Employed Persons in the Palestinian Territory by Economic Activity and Sex, 1992, 1999 (%)

Economic activity and sex	1992[a]	1999	Change
MALES			
Agriculture, hunting, fishing	16.7	9.3	-44.3
Mining, quarrying, manufacturing	12.5	16.0	28.0
Construction	37.5	25.8	-31.2
Commerce, hotels, restaurants	14.5	18.6	28.3
Transportation, storage, communication	5.7	5.4	-5.3
Services and other branches	13.1	24.9	90.1
Total	100	100	
FEMALES			
Agriculture, hunting, fishing	51.9	31.8	-38.7
Mining, quarrying, manufacturing	8.1	12.9	59.3
Construction	0.9	0.8	-11.1
Commerce, hotels, restaurants	3.0	7.4	146.7
Transportation, storage, communication	1.6	0.9	-43.8
Services and other branches	35.5	46.2	30.1
Total	101	100	

Sources: PCBS 2000d, 1999e; Israel Central Bureau of Statistics 1993
[a]Excluding East Jerusalem

formally employed women, which includes both the private and the public sectors. This is a feature of women's employment trends in the region as well. (PCBS 1995; 1999e; 2000c).

Table 5.2 shows an important rise in the participation rate of women in the formal employment sector and a change in the type of work. The data indicate that the expansion of the PNA structures led to the opening of work opportunities in clerical jobs and other occupational categories. Although women's employment in the agricultural sector remains central, it has declined owing to the devaluation of agricultural land and agricultural produce in the face of Israeli competitive policies and confiscation of land and water resources. Of interest here is the rise in women's employment in elementary occupations, which reveals a new trend of women's employment. Clearly, further research is needed to elaborate changes in women's patterns of employment over time, including more intensive research in the area of elementary

Table 5.2
Employment in the Palestinian Territory
by Occupation and Sex, 1992, 1999

Occupation and sex	1992[a]	1999	Change (%)
No. of employed males (1,000)	289.8	502	73.2
Scientific and professional workers, managers, administration and clerical workers (%)	8.7	18.8	116.1
Service, shop, market workers (%)	16.1	7.4	-54.0
Skilled agricultural and fishery workers (%)	16.6	6.6	-60.2
Skilled workers (%)	31.7	34.2	7.9
Elementary occupations (%)	26.8	32.9	22.8
No. of employed females (1,000)	29.4	86	192.5
Scientific and professional workers, managers, administration and clerical workers (%)	33.1	44.2	33.5
Service, shop, market workers (%)	5.2	2.8	-46.2
Skilled agricultural and fishery workers (%)	52.9	31.0	-41.4
Skilled workers (%)	7.1	11.4	60.6
Elementary occupations (%)	1.6	10.6	562.5

Sources: PCBS 2000d, 1999e; Israel Central Bureau of Statistics 1993
[a]Excluding East Jerusalem

occupations and occupations within the informal sector. Table 5.2 supports the notion that the expansion of the public and private sectors has contributed to increasing women's incorporation into the labor force.

Agriculture was the second largest employer of women in the occupied territories for the year 1999. Women are mainly unpaid family laborers and not wage workers; some are tenant farmers. For women living in the Gaza Strip agriculture provides two-fifths of the employment. In Gaza, there is a feminization of agricultural work as men have been leaving agriculture for better-paying jobs in other sectors. The share of men's employment in Gaza agriculture in 1999 is only 11.5 percent compared to 41.2 percent for women. In Israel and Israeli settlements Palestinian women are seasonal agricultural laborers; women have for different factors been marginal in the Israeli labor market (Esim and Kuttab 2002; Hammami, 2001).

Women's Employment: Occupational Segregation

The formal labor markets provide limited employment opportunities for Palestinian women. According to the 1999 labor force survey, employed women made up 12.3 percent of the labor force (PCBS 1999e). Most of them were in the service sector (scientific and professional workers and administrative and clerical workers), followed by agriculture and manufacturing. Within each economic activity, women are "crowded" into a small number of sectors and secure only a small range of jobs within those sectors such as teaching, nursing and public sector employment (Hammami 1997).

Services have employed the highest percentage of women from 1992 to 1999. In services more than half of the employed women are working in education, health, social, and public services (MAS 2000). Since the creation of the PNA and its ministries, the total number of jobs in the public services has been increasing. Although these jobs are filled mainly by men, the public services have created some opportunities for women. In Israel and within Israeli settlements, Palestinian women are in lower paying and unskilled jobs such as cleaning services (Esim and Kuttab 2002).

The agricultural sector is shrinking because of the Israeli policy of land confiscation, settlement building, and (more recently) the building of the Separation Wall, which has expropriated huge quantities of agricultural land and water resources. In addition, the limited support of both the Palestinian

Authority and donor community to the agricultural sector has resulted in a gradual shrinking of rural women's economic activities (Esim and Kuttab 2002).

The manufacturing sector employed 15.2 percent of Palestinian women in the West Bank in 1999 and 11.3 percent in Israel and Israeli settlements. These are mostly semiskilled and lower skilled jobs in factories and workshops, mainly in the garment, leather, and footwear industries. However, only 5.2 percent of working women in Gaza worked in manufacturing in 1999. It is likely that women's home-based work and subcontracting work in these industries are not being counted by the official statistics. Hence, women's employment in manufacturing is likely to be much higher in the Gaza Strip if these informally employed women were counted (Esim and Kuttab 2002).

An Economy under Siege: 2000–2003

The organic link between the political and the colonial impact of the Israeli occupation and the viability of the labor market and changes in occupational trends is more clearly reflected in the al-Aqsa intifada period since September 2000. It has been shown that the economic well-being of a society cannot possibly be realized under a colonial occupation that has the economic ability and the political will to destroy the basis for a society's survival. An ILO report on the situation of workers in the occupied territories in 2002 has noted that the economic and social situation has been deteriorating since 2000; rising levels of poverty and unemployment have led to a humanitarian crisis (ILO 2003, 2). Severe restrictions on the movement of persons and goods within the Palestinian occupied territories and between these territories and Israel have resulted in a dramatic decline in consumption, income, and employment. In 2002, an estimated 60 percent of the population in the occupied territories lived on an income of less than US$2.15 per day. The economy has suffered a massive shock resulting from the closures and restrictions that translated into a decline in per capita income. The drop in real per capita gross national income is unprecedented. In 2002, the economy registered its third consecutive year of decline. The cumulative drop in per capita income in 2002 is staggering; it stood at 47.7 percent of the 1999 level. The decline seems to have deepened, with 2002 marking the sharpest annual drop, estimated at 26.4 percent (PCBS 2003; World Bank 2003).

Within the regional context, the GDP of the occupied territories between 1990 and 2001 was 1.8 percent lower than the regional average. All neighboring countries had an average annual GDP growth of 4.9 percent. Although there is a similarity between regional and local Palestinian labor market trends, this gap is indicative of the specificities of the colonial situation and its critical impact on the overall economy.

Indicators of the labor market point to deterioration in participation and employment levels in 2002 compared to 2001. The labor force participation rate declined by 1.6 percent (to 38.2 percent), and employment contracted by 4.3 percent not counting a 5.5 percent increase in the number of newcomers to the labor force. Unemployment rose to 38 percent in Gaza and 28.0 percent in the West Bank. Also the number of persons of working age outside the labor force increased, suggesting a discouraged worker effect. According to the ILO Director-General's report, Palestinian unemployment between 2000 and 2002 was higher than in other countries facing political instability (ILO 2003, 11). This supports the argument that the Israeli colonial impact on the labor markets is more severe and deeper than conditions afflicting other countries suffering from political instability because of its colonial nature.

Table 5.3 summarizes the shifts and changes that have taken place in employment by sector and sex since 2000. The table shows that the rate of participation of both men and women fifteen years of age and older in the labor force declined in 2001. However, this downward trend for both men and women seems to have reversed in 2003, although not reaching the previous 2000 levels of labor force participation of 70.1 percent. We note a reversal of the downward trend in women's participation as well. The table also shows that the percentage of unemployed women has risen since 2000. This may indicate that a higher proportion of women began to seek work as a means of coping with impoverishment and emergency, especially as their rate of participation in the labor force in the first quarter of 2004 surpassed the rate for 2000. Adding up employed and unemployed, we find that a high of 32 percent of women were registered in the labor force in the first quarter of 2004, compared to 25 percent for the year 2000. In other words, while female employment in the first two years of the intifada declined by 2.3 percent for 2001 and 2002, the rate of unemployed women rose disproportionately, figures that can be explained not only in terms of both the initial decline and then rise in the rate of participation of women in the labor force, but also in the entry of new

Table 5.3
Main Indicators in Labor Force Participation by Sex, 2000–2004

Indicator			Year		
Labor force[a]	2000	2001	2002	2003	Q1-2004[b]
Participation rate of women	12.7	10.4	10.4	12.8	13.2
Participation rate of men	70.1	66.8	65.5	67.6	66.6
Employed women in agriculture, hunting, forestry	34.6	26.3	29.9	33.6	29.6
Employed men in agriculture, hunting, forestry	9.8	9.4	11.9	11.9	11.3
Employed women in services and other branches	45.9	54.2	54.3	29.3	52.2
Employed men in services and other branches	27.0	31.0	32.0	50.1	31.0
Unemployed women	12.3	14.1	17.2	18.6	18.8
Unemployed men	14.4	27.3	33.5	26.9	27.7

Source: PCBS 2004a, http://www.pcbs.org/english/gender/indicator.htm
[a]Includes men and women aged fifteen and older
[b]First quarter of 2004

women seeking employment but not able to find it. Perhaps this is another indication of the limitations of the gendered labor markets and the ways women tend to cope with emergency and crisis.

Summarizing the findings of PCBS annual reports from 1999 to 2002, we note that one of the important issues in the labor force is the further marginalization of women. The decline in the rate of participation in the labor force after the eruption of the intifada is much higher for women than for men. This may be explained by two main factors. The first is the political insecurity that has discouraged women to go to work and undergo the daily difficulties imposed by the closure policy. A second factor may be that as a defense mechanism, women may have reverted to being housewives after a long period of unsuccessful job searching and dealing with society's attitude toward women's work as secondary in relation to men. According to the relaxed definition,[4] there has been no change in the participation rate of women in the labor force in the West Bank between 1999 and 2002, yet the percentage of women in the

4. The "relaxed definition" includes the number of unemployed persons plus "discouraged workers" outside the labor force.

labor force in the Gaza Strip has decreased. It is natural that fewer women compared to men are listed as unemployed during the period under review. Even if we use the relaxed definition of unemployment, the data show that there is a negative impact on the rate of women's participation in the labor force. Hence, one of the coping strategies for women under these circumstances may have been a negative trend, one which is expressed by their withdrawal from the labor market and identifying themselves as housewives, whereas for men, who are defined as the main breadwinners, the numbers reflect actual high unemployment.

It is worth observing that the labor market picked up in the first three quarters of 2003, both in the West Bank and Gaza, reflecting higher levels of economic activity. Overall employment increased by 21.3 percent compared to its low level in 2002. However, the last quarter of 2003 registered deterioration, pointing again to the fragility of the overall trend (ILO 2004, 21). Close to 290,000 persons (89 percent of whom are men) were unemployed, according to the ILO definition, or unemployed and discouraged from looking for work. This means that the unemployment rate is 35.5 percent, and the number can go higher if women confined to their homes by necessity and not by choice are included (ILO 2004, 23).

The Israeli closure policies and the denial of work permits have meant that Palestinian workers are unable to work in Israel or Israeli settlements. Most of the workers in Israel come from East Jerusalem. The actual number of Palestinians from the West Bank and Gaza (excluding Jerusalem) who work in Israel is highly dependent on the continuously changing restrictions on the movement of persons within the occupied territories and into Israel. According to a report by the Coordinator of Government Activities in the Territories (COAT 2004), only 4.2 percent of Palestinians who had valid permits to work in Israel, in Israeli-controlled industrial zones, and in settlements within the occupied territories were women. Employment of Palestinian women in the territories is essentially in agriculture, industrial estates, and domestic work (ILO 2004, 10). A valid work permit is no guarantee of actual employment, particularly for those workers who have to enter Israel to work (ILO 2004).

The labor market has undergone declines in terms of participation of workers in Israel and Israeli settlements from the West Bank and Gaza Strip. This decline, a result of the closure policy, has been sharper in the Gaza Strip because closures have been enforced in a more draconian manner there

(PCBS 2000d). In terms of women's participation in labor in Israel and settlements, it should be noted that the rate was low even before the Intifada, yet the new conditions have affected further the participation of women in Israel, and the PCBS data show that the percentage of women working in this sector did not exceed 0.1 percent (PCBS 2000d). It is very obvious from data indicated in table 5.4 that income from wages seems to be the most stable income for the household, and it seems that the private sector is more able to play a role in sustaining the families than the public sector.

On the other hand, PCBS data as shown in table 5.2 indicate that occupations are still segregated according to gender. Agriculture remains an important provider of employment for women, although declining since 2000, from 34.6 percent to 33.6 percent in 2003 and 29.6 percent in the first quarter of 2004. This is likely an underestimation, owing to under-reporting of women's work in agriculture. Women's highest levels of absorption remain in the service sector, with rates fluctuating from 45.9 percent in 2000 to 54.2 percent in 2001 and a low of 29.3 percent in 2003, yet up to 52.2 percent in the first quarter of 2004, perhaps indicating the presence of fluctuating market conditions.

Thus, it is clear that women's work is still concentrated in the agriculture and service sectors, and this trend has been more pronounced since 2000 but still compliant with the prevailing trend since the 1960s. Most of the women are working in the service sector, which is the only sector that actually hired a higher percentage of women workers. Other sectors (including agriculture) experienced a decline in women's participation, although not in 2003 and 2004 (PCBS 2004a). The labor market picked up somewhat in the first three

Table 5.4
Distribution of Households by Main Source of Income,
West Bank and Gaza, January–March 2004 (%)

Wage from private sector	31.8
Household projects	12.1
Wage from public sector	18.5
Work in farming or breeding livestock	5.8
Wage from Israeli work sector	7.9
Remittances	3.4
Financial assistance	19.2

Source: PCBS 2004a, 15

quarters of 2003 both in the West Bank and Gaza Strip, reflecting the higher level of economic activity because of the easing of the closure policy. Overall employment increased by 21.3 percent compared to its low level in 2002. Employment both in Israel and the territories showed a positive trend. However, the deteriorating performance of the last quarter of 2003 highlighted the fragility of the overall trend (ILO 2004, 21).

Employment trends for males have also changed, owing first to a decline in the industrial and construction sectors and second to an increase in both agriculture and service sectors. Construction is especially important for Palestinians working in Israel, which is consistent with the pattern of low-skilled labor exports. The decline in construction employment for Palestinians is a result of the closure of the Israeli labor market and relatively low level of manufacturing. Males have also lost their employment in the private sector in both industry and crafts as well as the local construction sector. Yet, there seems to be an increase in employment-generation schemes in 2003–4. Employment in the public sector (government institutions and local councils) has maintained its stability, particularly in keeping the same number of employees and even increasing the numbers in certain institutions. This appears to be a PNA policy to support Palestinian households. So far, the public sector maintains its importance as a sector in generating employment for women as noted earlier in the Human Development Report of 2003 (UNDP 2003).

Occupational Segregation in the Occupied Territories

The PCBS data show that the closure policies have enlarged the gender gap within occupations in both the West Bank and Gaza Strip between 1999 and 2002. The occupation has not only maintained the same gendered labor markets but has deepened the structural occupational segregation based on gender through its closure policy reaffirming the patriarchal labor market that has further marginalized women through limiting their opportunities and destroying or closing these informal income generating projects (Kuttab 1989).

Cultural limitations have prohibited women's mobility under siege, and the closure policy has again reproduced the male breadwinner as the only model for economic production challenging the post-Oslo new pattern of women's participation in wage labor. For instance, mobility restrictions entail different consequences for men and women; they affect female teachers and pupils more than their male counterparts, owing to the difficulties and dangers they face in traveling to and from schools. Female teachers are more likely to stop going to work when they have to walk long distances in isolated areas to avoid checkpoints and settlers (ILO 2004, 5). There is an increase in the value of certain occupations, including professional, clerical, service, and retail work. In contrast, the weight of clerical work, services, and market workers has been strengthened while elementary occupations and crafts have lost their weight. This conforms to the overall changes that occurred in the labor force, namely, the loss of employment in Israel and the weakening of both the industrial and construction sectors, sectors where most prevailing jobs are in elementary occupations, or in both crafts and occupations (PCBS 2002b). Between 2000 and 2003, jobs have been lost in the productive sectors of the economy and gained in the low-productivity sectors. The bulk of net job creation over the three years has taken place in services, commerce, and agriculture. Conversely, net job losses are registered in manufacturing and in construction (in the West Bank only). This loss indicates that the economy in the occupied territories has been shifting toward lower productivity activities generating less value added and hence less income (ILO 2000, 23).

Gender and Employment Status

Changes in employment status differ by gender. The overall number of self-employed men and unpaid family members has increased (although the percentage is small), and there is a decline in the numbers of wage workers and employers. The data for women show a decrease in the self-employed and employer categories, a fact with deeper negative implications for women's economic activity. In addition, we see an increase in the percentage of women wage employees. Although there is a decline in the rate of women versus men in relation to work as unpaid family members, 30 percent of workers in this category are women (PCBS 2002b).

As indicated in table 5.3, workers who lost their jobs have moved either to the service sector because it is the most stable, or to self-employment, as shown in table 5.5, where the increase for men is up from 19.5 percent in 1999 to 30.2 percent in 2002. Given the downward trend in wage employment, the only option that remains for unemployed wage workers is to create their own employment through self-employment schemes. For women, wage

Table 5.5
Employed Persons in the Palestinian Territory
by Employment Status and Sex, 1999–2002

Indicator	1999	2000	2001	2002
Males (1,000s)	502	504	430	407
Employer (%)	6.2	5.4	5.3	4.4
Self-employed (%)	19.5	21.4	26.7	30.2
Wage employee (%)	69.7	67.9	61.9	58.7
Unpaid family member (%)	4.6	5.4	6.0	6.6
Females (1,000s)	86	93	78	79
Employer (%)	1.2	1.1	1.3	0.0
Self-employed (%)	14.0	9.7	7.7	8.9
Wage employee (%)	57.0	55.9	64.1	62.0
Unpaid family member (%)	27.9	33.3	26.9	29.1
RATIO OF FEMALES TO MALES				
Employer (%)	3.2	3.7	4.3	0.0
Self-employed (%)	12.2	8.3	5.2	5.7
Wage employee (%)	14.0	15.2	18.8	20.5
Unpaid family member (%)	103.9	113.8	81.3	85.6

Source: PCBS 2000d; 2002b

employment in fact increased over time, up from 57 percent in 1999 to 62 percent in 2002.

Recent PCBS data indicate that unemployment rates have gone up during the intifada years, with only 14.1 percent unemployment rate for both sexes in 2000, up to 25.5 percent for 2001, to 31.3 percent for 2002, but down to 25.6 percent for 2003. A PCBS press release (PCBS 2004a), published in May 2004, states that the unemployment rate in 2003 went down to previous levels, and disaggregated data indicate a drop of unemployment to 26.9 percent among men and 18.6 percent among women.

Table 5.6 reveals changes in sectors of employment but unfortunately not by sex. For instance, there seems to be no question that employment in agriculture has risen slightly, perhaps indicating a rising trend. Employment in the construction sector, on the other hand, seems to have declined over time, suggesting that this reduction is a result of the closure policy that has prohibited Palestinian workers from reaching work sites and due to the policy of replacing Palestinian workers with other foreign workers coming from

Table 5.6
Basic Changes in Labor Force Indicators in the Occupied Territories, 1995–2003 (ILO Standards)

Variable	1995	1996	1997	1998	1999	2000	2001	2002	2003
Labor force participation (%)	39.0	40.0	40.5	41.4	41.6	41.5	38.7	38.1	40.4
Full employment (%)	60.7	64.3	70.4	79.1	82.8	80.9	70.5	64.4	68.2
Underemployment (%)	21.1	11.9	9.3	6.5	5.4	5.0	4.0	4.3	6.2
Unemployment (%)	18.2	23.8	20.3	14.4	11.8	14.1	25.5	31.3	25.6
Employed in agriculture (%)	12.7	14.2	13.1	12.1	12.6	13.7	12.0	14.8	15.7
Employed in construction (%)	19.2	16.8	18.4	22.0	22.1	19.7	14.6	10.9	13.1
Employed in manufacturing (%)	18.0	16.8	16.4	15.9	15.5	14.3	14.0	12.9	12.5
Employed in services (%)	25.6	29.2	28.2	27.1	28.1	29.9	34.5	36.9	32.9
Elementary occupation workers (%)	18.3	28.7	28.9	31.0	29.7	21.1	16.1	14.2	14.3
Craft and related trade workers (%)	27.5	24.0	24.6	24.7	22.7	22.0	19.0	17.5	18.6
Employed in Israel and settlements (%)	16.2	14.1	17.1	21.7	23.0	19.6	13.7	10.3	9.7
Employers (%)	6.9	5.5	5.3	5.8	5.5	4.6	4.7	3.7	3.5
Self-employed (%)	21.2	22.3	22.9	21.0	18.7	19.6	23.9	26.8	27.8
Wage employees (%)	61.7	61.4	62.0	65.3	67.8	66.1	62.2	59.2	57.3
Unpaid family members (%)	10.2	10.8	9.8	7.9	8.0	9.7	9.2	10.3	11.4
Average monthly work days[a]	21.0	22.0	22.0	23.0	22.6	23.2	23.1	23.0	23.3
Average weekly work hours[a]	42.1	43.5	44.0	45.0	44.2	43.1	42.2	41.1	41.7
Median daily net wage (NIS)[a]	46.3	46.2	50.0	57.7	69.2	69.2	61.5	60.0	55.8

Source: PCBS 2003

[a]Workers in Israel and settlements are included

European countries such as Romania or other Middle Eastern countries, such as Turkey. Employment in the manufacturing sector dropped. Services take the reverse pattern: 29.9 percent of those employed in 2000 worked in this sector, but by 2003 the rate was 32.9 percent. The table suggests that the economy is quite unstable, that we cannot make definitive statements about employment as the trends are not consistent in one way or the other, but that agriculture and services seem to have compensated for the loss of work in the manufacturing and construction sectors.

Women's Coping Strategies: Informal Employment and Home Production

In this section, I argue that although women have not found work opportunities in the formal labor market, they are determined to work, and have created their own opportunities by either working in the informal sector or by creating their own household space to produce items for home consumption, or for the local market. One of the main reasons for women of large families to take on production of food or services at home is to respond to daily life needs and to decrease expenditures. This represents a coping strategy that is adopted intensively as a strategy specifically when households are facing financial pressures or crises triggered perhaps by the breadwinner's unemployment, imprisonment, or death. In times of economic crisis, when the family's livelihood is threatened, such activities are categorized as economic coping strategies. In times of national or political crisis, such activities can be seen also as modes of resistance undertaken by women in particular in response to the family's imminent impoverishment or collapse.

General global trends regarding the informal sector clearly indicate that for different reasons, the impact of the market economy and of global restructuring is generally not generating wage employment in sufficient volumes to facilitate the absorption of labor surplus. Evidence suggests that the globalization process tends to have an adverse impact in different ways on economies that are not sufficiently diversified, creating winners and losers. Earning a living in the informal sector appears to be the only option for losers, and this option has gender implications. Moreover, evidence suggests that female labor in this sector is relatively overrepresented in most world regions (Sethuraman 2000).

In the context of the West Bank and Gaza Strip, the PCBS has concluded through labor force surveys that informal work represents both unpaid work within the family and self-employment. According to the 1999–2000 time-use survey, 30.2 percent of working women and 5.6 percent of working men worked in the family unpaid labor sector in 2000. For the Gaza Strip, the rate is 43.8 percent for women and 4.4 percent for men. Hence women in both the West Bank and Gaza represent the majority of the informal sector. For the self-employed category, 9.4 percent of the women workers in the West Bank and 11.6 percent of women in Gaza are self-employed. The assumption here is that women professionals are rare, and hence these percentages represent workers in the informal sector (PCBS 2001).

Local Trends: Informal Employment

In the occupied territories, informal employment as a category has not been incorporated in labor force surveys, yet categories of secondary work, employer, and self-employed have been assumed to give some idea of the informal employment. In addition, categories of casual wage-workers and subcontract workers, which are part of the labor force surveys, do indicate the concentration of women, especially in the last category (Heiberg and Ovensen 1993). Informal employment has been growing in Palestine as a result of a number of factors; these can be explained in the context of integration of the Palestinian economy in the global and regional economic trends. However, other unique historical and political factors represent the more fundamental reasons regarding Palestine (Esim and Kuttab 2002). Informal employment was either the only option to women or could be considered coping forms of survival especially in the context of national crisis, as in the first and second intifada.

The results of the 1993 Fafo survey shows that women constitute 62.5 percent of all individuals engaged in informal sector work in the Gaza Strip and 55.5 percent of those in the West Bank in refugee camps, which indicates that almost more than half of the informal sector workers in Palestine are women.[5] (Ovensen 1994; Esim and Kuttab 2002).

5. The category "informal economy" was not sufficiently defined in the survey; thus, this percentage should be treated with caution.

Agriculture is the second largest employer of women in the occupied territories, where women work mainly as unpaid family labor or as tenant farmers. In Gaza, feminization of agricultural work has become a phenomenon as men have been leaving agriculture for better-paying jobs in other sectors. When looking at the share of men's employment in agriculture in Gaza, the rate is 11.5 percent compared to 41.2 percent for women (Esim and Kuttab 2002). Women also do two types of home-based work: traditional income-generating production, which includes food processing, carpet weaving, and handicrafts; and industrial subcontracting in the production of garments, apparel, leather, and footwear (Esim and Kuttab 2002).

Traditional methods of labor force measurement do not adequately capture women's economic activity. Both the Fafo 1993 survey and Ovensen (1994) attribute this discrepancy to measurement methods and definitions of work. The question arises because of the apparent contradiction between the recorded low rate of women's participation in the labor force and women's high education level and qualifications to enter the labor market. The possible involuntary or unpaid nature of women's labor may result in the undervaluation of their employment; this should not, however, be confused with underemployment or underutilization of labor among women. On the contrary, the results for women's time use show that women on average spend almost sixty hours a week on housework and income-generating activities (Heiberg and Ovensen 1993, PCBS, 2001b). For women with higher skills, the informal sector may also be an alternative when formal opportunities are closed to them or are exploitative. Issues like poor wages and exploitation were cited in different studies as reasons women prefer home-based work. In addition, given the age structure of women in the informal sector (mainly in peddling), this sector plays the role of a "second career" option in post-childbearing years. Women in the different sectors of informal employment complain of the seasonal and erratic nature of their work and cite instability and low wages (Hammami 2001).

"Need Is the Mother of Innovation": Income-Generating Projects

The Israeli occupation has transformed most Palestinian employment in certain periods of the national struggle into informal employment. Because the formal sector is unstable as a result of political instability, informal employment has become an everyday culture and living style. According to the ILO, there is a close correlation between the economic situation and military occupation that plots fatal Palestinian intifada casualties as a proxy for the intensity of the conflict and compares it with unemployment in the occupied territories. This co-linearity between the two trends supports the view that a higher degree of conflict leads to a lower level of economic activity, which in turn translates into higher rate of unemployment. Although statistically the evidence is still not clear, the unemployment rate for the last quarter of 2003 shows a rate of 20.7 percent in the West Bank and 31.9 percent in Gaza. More important than the rate is the high number of both unemployed persons and discouraged workers (PCBS 2003). According to PCBS, the self-employed category for men has increased from 19.5 percent in 1999 to 30.2 percent in 2002, which is another indicator that men are slipping into the informal sector. Palestinian women's informal employment is widespread because opportunities in the formal labor market are limited. Women are seen both as victims of crisis and as repositories of knowledge about coping mechanisms. To be able to minimize costs and raise profits, women follow strategies such as small-scale processing and time reallocation (Singerman 1998).

Data from a relatively small survey of three hundred women conducted in June 2001 by the Institute of Women's Studies at Birzeit University confirm that women in the occupied Palestinian territories engage in informal employment because of the limited opportunities available in the labor market. The sample consisted of women who were involved in income-generating projects based on informal employment in the West Bank and Gaza Strip. The survey found that these women are mainly unskilled and that their production is an extension of their traditional roles in housework and does not generate high income. The breakdown by age is as follows: 42 percent are between thirty and forty years of age, 37.5 percent are older than forty, and 20.5 percent are younger than thirty, which is similar to the overall profile existing in other studies.[6] Most of the women in the sample were married with an av-

6. Other studies like the PCBS time use survey of 2000, UNSCO economic reports, the Falcot survey, MAS (who conducted sixty-four in-depth interviews with owners of small enterprises both women and men in 2001), and UNIFEM (who studied micro-enterprise projects in dairy and handicrafts in Gaza Strip) have agreed that there are major obstacles facing women's micro-enterprises.

erage of 4.8 children, 60 percent had children younger than seven, and most of the women were found mainly in informal work in services and commerce. Yet the largest number of women, almost half of the sample, had secondary education (Esim and Kuttab 2002).

Domestic Economy: Home-Based Work

Household-based economic activity has traditionally played an important role in maintaining households, mostly in terms of the production of food for consumption, but also for sale. This economy is largely the domain of women. However, the rapid socioeconomic changes taking place during the years of occupation, and the increasing incorporation of workers into the Israeli labor market, land fragmentation and expropriation, and control of water sources must have affected the position and importance of the domestic economy. Over the years, a change in consumption patterns of food, away from locally and home-grown products to ready-made processed items, has been evident. These changes raise questions about the survival of the domestic economy as a household coping strategy in the face of these important socioeconomic changes. The IWS survey of 1999 sought to investigate whether domestic production continued to be a feature of household survival strategies in the late 1990s and identified food production, minor agricultural activities, and livestock raising as areas for the possible survival of a gender-based domestic economy, perhaps in modified forms.

Initial analysis of the responses of 2,222 women revealed that food processing at home is alive and well, with 80 percent of women reporting that they make pastries, 75 percent make preserves, 63 percent still bake bread, and 24 percent process dairy products. That is, contrary to expectations, this particular aspect of the domestic economy continues and is very much part of women's unpaid work in the studied communities. In contrast, only 14 percent of women reported that they engaged in minor agricultural activities such as maintaining a kitchen garden and collecting herbs in season, 10 percent raised poultry, 3 percent livestock, and 0.4 percent bees, all an indication of the overall decline in agricultural production as a way of life over the years.

Adding up responses to home production activities in these three categories, a domestic production index was developed, and it revealed that overall, 11 percent of respondents engaged in none of these activities, 24 percent engaged in one activity, 38 percent in two, and 30 percent in three and up to eight activities. The data also revealed a pattern of increasing domestic production by increasing age, but not by education, with 39 percent of women twenty to twenty-nine years old engaging in two and 24 percent in three activities, 42 percent engaging in two and 29 percent in three activities for those thirty to thirty-nine years old, and 41 percent engaging in two and 30 percent in three activities for those forty to forty-nine years old. This peak age of activity begins to decline at fifty years or more with 24 percent of this group reporting engaging in two activities and 25 percent in three or more. Thus it appears that domestic production is a function of age not as merely a biological category, but as a stage in a woman's life cycle, home production being at its peak during the middle year's of a woman's life cycle, probably after she had completed her family size, but when the children are still at home, requiring additional work and income.

The other interesting finding of the IWS survey is the negative relationship between domestic production and wage labor. With 8 percent of women respondents describing themselves as working for wages, it was found that 41 percent of those working women reported no or minimal (only one type of production) involvement in food production, minimal agricultural activity, and animal husbandry, compared to 35 percent among those who are not working, and 59 percent of those working engaging in two to eight activities compared to 65 percent among those not in the labor market. That is, although the level of engagement of working women in home domestic production is high, women nevertheless tend to do so at a significantly lower level than those working only at home.

Urban-rural differences were also important, as one would expect, with 58 percent of urban women engaging in two to eight activities, compared to 65 percent for camps and a high of 81 percent for villages. That is, rural women are significantly more engaged in domestic production than camp women, followed by city women. The availability of land and space, combined with the rural agricultural or semiagricultural way of life, is a determinant. What is of interest here is that camp women seem to be more active in home production than city women. This may relate to financial need and large family sizes, compared to city women. Interestingly, Gaza women seem to engage more actively in domestic production, with 70 percent of Gaza women engaging in two to eight types of production, compared to 66 percent for the center (rural bias), 65 percent for the south, 63 percent for the north, and an all-time low of 32 percent for Jerusalem. This makes sense if we think of home production as essentially a support of immediate needs, given the higher levels of poverty in Gaza. With the exception of Jerusalem, the other regions have similar rates.

Overall then, a substantial proportion of women engage in domestic production, but to varying degrees, depending on the stage in the life cycle, the presence of growing children, whether women are active in the labor force, and locale. In other words, the domestic economy continues to form an important component of women's work, even when working for wages outside the home, and it appears to be an important family coping strategy in the face of limited incomes and relatively large family sizes.

In the IWS survey the women were also asked to explain why they engaged in home production. Of all women engaged in home production, 22 percent listed financial reasons, that is, to subsidize the family income; 45 percent listed other factors, such as the food being tastier, better, healthier, and cleaner; and 33 percent listed both. In total, 55 percent of the women reported engaging in domestic production as a supplement to family income. Interestingly, only 2 percent of those who reported that they engaged in domestic production also reported that they produced for sale.

The survey findings reveal that the domestic economy is still substantial. Although higher domestic production is mainly for consumption and not for trade, this strategy eases the pressure of declining wages and incomes (IWS,2001).

Coping in National Crisis: Resistance Through Steadfastness, Disengagement, and Adaptation

Palestinians have learned to adapt economically since the 1967 occupation, when the value of agricultural land and subsistence economy began to decline and weaken in the face of competition with Israeli agriculture. The proletarianization of the Palestinian peasantry and the introduction of a cash economy have gradually changed consumption patterns, bringing them more in line with market oriented consumption. In this context, the household then also began to shift from being a productive unit to a consumption unit. Challenges or economic crises caused by political instability can have an outlet constructed around returning to traditional consumption patterns where the household economy has been a coping strategy. In all the different situations of political and economic hardship, the Palestinian household becomes the unit of decision making, and in situations where the household faces danger and threat to its existence and continuity, a strategy combining different coping options is used. It becomes possible to assemble a combination of income sources and expenditures where pooling of resources becomes a basic principle. Much of that is rooted deeply in the culture of informal solidarity. Although not much research has been conducted in this area, it is reasonable to make this assumption based on our knowledge of the community.

During the first intifada, "development" practice took on a more comprehensive approach, where gender and class issues became more politicized as they were tied to the future vision of the Palestinian state, a state that has been defined as democratic and able to promote equal opportunities between the sexes. In this context, women adopted a strategy of positive resistance either in the form of collective production of marketable items in one household or in a neighborhood, or a productive cooperative in an independent space, in order to boycott Israeli goods and generate income to support their families (Kuttab 1989). Moreover, different Palestinian grassroots organizations were created to take over the development process. Their main objective was to meet the vital needs of the resistance policy that the united leadership of the intifada promoted by addressing basic needs of the different sectors of the society. They dealt with a broad spectrum of social categories in towns, rural areas, and refugee camps, using a decentralized approach that made them more sensitive to the priorities and needs of the people. They were committed to introducing a change in the quality of the life of the people and to empowering them politically to help them face the policies and practices of the occupying forces and to respond to the political agenda of the national movement. These organizations played a significant role in revolutionizing the existing policies of "steadfastness" and "survival" into a more dynamic strategy of resistance and disengagement. (Kuttab 1989).

Although these grassroots organizations were an extension of the national movement, they undertook economic activities like income-generating projects as part of the political program to challenge the Israeli occupation. However they combined other noneconomic principles like social liberation (at least rhetorically) as an integral part of national and economic liberation.

Their strategy of resistance was to establish efficient productive institutions that would enhance the Palestinian economy and decrease the degree of dependency on the Israeli market. The ultimate goal was to transform Palestinian society from a consumer and passive receiver of Israeli goods and foreign aid to a productive active economy that is able to respond to community needs and priorities. Meanwhile, they provide an acceptable level of services and support for the people as a condition for steadfastness (Kuttab 1989). Although these strategies were restricted to the intifada, some of them continue to exist, and testimonies of women in the UNIFEM study on the impact of political violence signals the continuation of these strategies at a neighborhood level, especially in times of long curfews and siege (Kuttab and Barghouti 2002).

Coping for Survival: the Al-Aqsa intifada

Coping strategies can take different forms. They can be based on one or several activities that are parallel to each other depending on the intensity and depth of the insecurities that the household faces. They can be short term or long term depending on the nature and the time frame of the crisis. Any crisis does require adjustment of some kind, but when a crisis persists over a long time and exceeds a reasonable time and scope, it becomes a struggle for survival. What we are witnessing today in Palestine is a one-sided struggle for survival that involves Palestinian households and families using different combinations of survival strategies to cope with the most inhumane conditions. The family's survival has been undermined and threatened by the Israeli forces through a continuous state-sponsored program of destruction of economic, social, political and cultural systems and structures, social networks, and material infrastructure. Through this programmed violence, the majority of Palestinian households have lost their everyday basis for human survival.

Adjusting and coping with different kinds of challenges are positive acts that have become a lifestyle. In general, the living conditions of people have continued to deteriorate since the beginning of the occupation in 1967, even when positive changes that occurred under the occupation such as short-term open labor markets and certain improvements in health indicators are factored in. These improvements proved to be temporary and superficial when compared to the programmed destruction that has devastated the majority of people's lives. Equally revealing is the people's creativity in promoting coping mechanisms as a symbol of determination because they believe that they have a just cause.

In the current conditions, especially in the last five years of the intifada, the situation has worsened and the challenges have expanded and become so complicated that people have expressed helplessness and anxiety more than in other periods. The state of anxiety has been especially acute because neither the time limit for such a situation nor the scope of violation and destruction by the Israelis can be projected. This feeling of uncertainty and anxious insecurity has put the family on continuous alert and on an emergency footing. Although the material rewards are not very high within the current economic crisis, coping mechanisms are of great value, not in terms of abstract monetary gain but of human survival. Moreover, when we compare the different coping strategies that Palestinian households have deployed in the different stages of the political struggle, we realize that there has always been a correlation between the intensity of the challenge and the nature of the coping strategy or combination of strategies chosen.

The World Bank has noted that Palestinian women have historically served as shock absorbers in national crises (World Bank 1993; 2002a). Yet it is worth mentioning that although women have been the backbone of the household's continuity and resistance during the past stages of the political struggle, the situation has never reached the present level of despair, and it is unlikely that they can continue to cope with the same tools they have used before. The depth of deterioration of the overall living conditions of the Palestinian family, including unemployment, poverty, and the mass demolition of houses as in Jenin and Rafah camps, foretells a major disaster. Although some families are better equipped to cope than others, the most vulnerable are the poor, particularly female-headed households, large households with limited income, families with fixed medical expenses, families with elderly, and families that lack labor to work on the land; hence, families require a combination of coping strategies to make life salvageable.

In general, when evaluating these strategies one can categorize them within broad themes. They are formed and affected by regional variations, socioeconomic factors, rural versus urban differences, and intensity of the need. The choice of a strategy or a combination of strategies depends on the particular situation and the level of physical, social and economic damage that has been inflicted. It also can take different forms and can vary from reducing or postponing consumption to selling assets, or depending on remittances and aid from outside the family, or living on credit or income-generating activity at the level of household, or combining formal work that generates a modest fixed income with another informal employment that can add to the income of the family without any formal obligations to the state. Pooling resources, using savings, or reallocating resources has been used in different stages. The construction of an informal social network of solidarity, which is based on the "idiom of kinship" has become a functional mode of social relations. Households that cannot depend on kinship networks for survival extend the definition of kinship to include friends and neighbors. This is one of many coping strategies (discussed below) that have been promoted in crisis situations rooted in the culture.

Consumption-Reduction or Substitution

Most goods and services are still available in the Palestinian market because of the aggressive Israeli marketing policy and the unhindered mobility of Israeli goods, whereas Palestinian goods have to go through various administrative and military obstacles, notably the checkpoints erected all over the occupied territories. The purchasing power of the majority of people has declined. Closure has meant living with less of everything—money, food, and space (O'Brien and Pickup 2002, 11). Hence the only way to survive is to use whatever resources are available to the family itself. It has been noted that practical contributions to survival are based on knowledge accumulated throughout their daily routines in managing their daily living.

In this strategy, there are different mechanisms that the family may use. They can use their savings to cover daily basic needs especially when the breadwinner is unemployed and the family is large. The World Bank notes that the average income has declined by almost half, and average consumption by one third. Savings can maintain a reasonable consumption level for seventeen months (World Bank 2003, 34). Oxfam findings revealed that by summer 2002 (beginning September 2000), villagers in the West Bank would had exhausted their savings so they have to find other ways to get by (O'Brien and Pickup 2002). Their strategy may take different forms like cutting consumption, reallocating resources, and selling household assets. Although these strategies may be successful in the short run, they can also carry serious threats to the health and social well being of the family members (O'Brien and Pickup 2002). Another strategy used by village households is the use of food items that they have preserved and stored in season, to be strategically used in times of crisis or need (O'Brien and Pickup 2002).

The use of such strategies can have negative implications because they undermine the capacity for future recovery through their impact on health, education, and physical assets. In particular when we are talking about cutting consumption, the main actor in this context would be the women who are responsible for running the daily household activities. They can economize on a range of products, including essential basic products like food and water. A PCBS survey found that 51 percent of households reduced the quantity of food consumed, and 63 percent reduced the quality of their food (PCBS 2002). This strategy, which is among the most popular and widely used strategies, can vary and can take two forms; one is serious as it can result in malnutrition, and the other is social, limiting hospitality, an important cultural component of informal social networking. According to a study conducted jointly by Johns Hopkins University, al-Quds University, and CARE International between May and July 2002, there was an increase in acute malnutrition and chronic malnutrition among children ages 6–59 months in the West Bank, which they assume is a result of mainly economic factors rather than access (Johns Hopkins University 2002).

Another important issue that should not be neglected is the fact that reduction in consumption or choosing another consumption pattern has an intrahousehold allocation factor that is gendered and culturally rooted. Many research findings[7] have indicated that women in poor families, especially in the villages, who prepare food have less of it in terms of quality and quantity as they prefer to offer it first to men as breadwinners and children (especially males) as an act of sacrifice and motherhood. Obviously this has a hazardous

---

7. The Institute of Community and Public Health at Birzeit University conducted a survey in 1999 on consumption patterns; findings have indicated that there is a gendered pattern of consumption in the Palestinian household where women eat less protein, as they leave it to the men, who are considered the breadwinners.

impact on women's health. It should be noted, however, that the age structure and the blood relation among women themselves can play a negative and reversed role. Women who are in-laws and are not of the same *hamula* (clan), or are younger single women, will be undermined in the patriarchal system, which will affect their access to quantity and quality of food, especially in the village environment. On the other hand, it is also a fact that this pattern of reduction of consumption has decreased the demand for luxury goods, either expressed as not buying any goods or substituting fresh goods with canned or frozen ones, which is culturally not desirable.

In nonfood areas, consumption of goods and services may be cancelled entirely. This applies to furniture, clothes, or other consumer goods whose purchase can be scrapped or postponed. For instance, weddings may be either postponed or limited in expenses. According to PCBS (2004a, 31), there were 24,847 marriages in the West Bank and Gaza Strip in 1999, 23,890 in 2000, and 24,635 in 2001. These figures may not indicate that there has been a drastic change in the number of marriages during the intifada; nevertheless, many newlyweds who would normally have moved into a separate home or set of rooms may be compelled to continue living with their parents. These arrangements may introduce potential tensions and problems to the household, but they do facilitate the pooling of resources.

Other more modest coping strategies that are secondary involve decreasing the allowance for children, or even having them walk to school, or limiting participation in social events like weddings and gift giving. In some schemes, women have created collectives where they contribute a sum of money periodically that is organized as a revolving loan used each week by one woman to manage the house expenditures. These loans can ease the frustration and solve the family's problem for a period of time (Esim and Kuttab 2002).

Selling Resources and Assets

Selling assets like land, livestock, and gold has been the most frequently used method for meeting immediate emergencies when other sources of support are exhausted (O'Brien and Pickup 2002, 13). One of the problems of selling such assets is that their value could decline in situations of economic crisis.

However, using this option is sometimes unavoidable not only to buy food, but to pay off mounting debts. The first thing sold is usually the wife's gold, as corroborated by the PCBS figures. This has been a historical cultural component for sustaining the family before resorting to selling the family's strategic or productive assets. Here also such an act can have a gender dimension, as the family may start with selling the wife's gold before considering selling land or the car. It indicates that women's personal assets are easily transformed in times of emergency for collective use.

Living on Credit: "Life on Account"

Another option in time of crisis is to postpone payments for goods and services such as electricity and water. This is corroborated by PCBS statistics for the first quarter of 2004, indicating that the crisis is ongoing. A PCBS survey reveals that most households cannot pay utility bills and that on average households have three outstanding bills (PCBS 2004a, 34).

It is a common strategy to stop paying for water and electricity as well as municipal fees when income is reduced. Because these services are provided through the PNA, it is generally expected that it is unlikely that electricity or water will be denied, given the severe conditions that most of the families experience. It is assumed in Palestine that the PNA institutions have made an informal decision not to enforce any punitive measures in these cases. In other situations however, where the electricity comes from a nearby Israeli settlement, and where the municipality is responsible for paying the bill for the entire village, the municipality will disconnect service to households that do not pay their bills. It should be noted that credit lines are threatened when the Israelis are involved either directly or indirectly, which makes the situation all the harder for Palestinian families (Pedersen et al. 2001b).

Buying goods on credit at local stores has proven to be the most important way of keeping households afloat. This is feasible in a community where all residents and shopkeepers have either kinship relations or are neighbors or friends. The main risk here is the threat of denial of credit as a result of the delay in payments. That is why sometimes debtors have to make partial payments to keep their credit line viable.

Income-Generating Projects

"A day's catch in fishing can be sold for NIS3,000, but the expenses of getting this catch leave me with only 500 shekels," said a Gazan fisherman. Because this may be a seasonal catch, or a lucky one (eluding Israeli patrols that stop Gaza fishermen and force them back to the shore), the earnings of Gaza fishermen are undependable and cannot be used as a coping strategy. For workers who lost their jobs in the Israeli labor market, very few were able to find jobs that were adequate in terms of income. Hence, they end up either accepting any job by using informal relations and networks, or start a clothing stall on sidewalks that can generate about NIS20 or 30 per day (Gilen et al. 1994).

Remittances and Interhousehold Redistribution

One of the important safety nets for Palestinian households has been the extended family network. It is found to be an important redistributive mechanism, differentiated along the lines of the individual household, the strength of the family network, and the resources available to the other families in the network (Sletten and Pedersen 2003, 45). Interhousehold redistribution takes place when brothers support each other in paying bills or buying food or other goods. Another form of support that is more continuous is when households merge and pool their resources. These forms only happen when family relations are very close. Other forms of financial support are given on certain occasions when there is a social event or when a man dies and the widow is kept with the family to raise her children. Many families even make a decision where one of the brothers marries the widow to become a father to his brother's children and thus maintain the family's property. This has been a coping strategy especially in cases of martyrdom, where women have to compromise their grief over the loss of their husbands and adapt to the brother to survive and maintain the support of the family (Giacaman and Johnson 2002a).

Remittances from abroad have often been important for Palestinians, even during the first intifada. Yet according to a Fafo report (Pedersen et al.

2001b, 47),[8] it seems that there is little indication that remittances from abroad now play a large role in the financing of Palestinian households. People who were in the Gulf and who moved to Jordan as a result of the Gulf War in the early 1990s have lost their income and wealth and can no longer remit funds to Palestinians in the occupied territories. Overall, this source of support is not a very important one. A PCBS survey on family income in 2004 reports that remittances represent only 3.4 percent of income. Yet some families have family members who are living abroad and have the capacity to send small amounts as monetary gifts, which can make a little difference for some families (Pedersen et al. 2001b, 47).

Social Welfare, Aid, and Emergency Job Creation

According to an Oxfam study (O'Brien and Pickup 2002), people seem to deprecate the value of most forms of social welfare and aid, the main complaint being that assistance comes only once or twice and so it has little value in terms of long-term coping. Families allege that the one-time cash payments from ministries like the Ministry of Labor or the infrequent UNRWA food packages, which last some twenty days only, are not enough. That kind of aid cannot solve a structural problem; a more consistent welfare distribution policy like that practiced by Islamic welfare committees (Zakat committees), the Ministry of Social Affairs, and UNRWA to the chronically poor and to social hardship cases is more effective. The formal and informal welfare systems do not appear to have come to grips with the "new poor" who were created by the closure policy. It seems that the only way the new poor can cope effectively is to earn an income.

Donor assistance to the occupied territories has increased sharply since 2000, and much of it has been directed to emergency assistance. Part of this assistance was channeled into employment projects, often in the form of infrastructure investments to repair roads and other assets destroyed by the Israeli army in its repeated incursions in the territories. Between September 2000 and January 2002, donors disbursed US$105 million, leading to the creation

---

8. The report also talks about remittances going out of the West Bank and Gaza Strip, as part of a rent for a house that belongs to a family who has relatives in Jordan, or about sending olives and olive oil to relatives abroad. This practice has not stopped in the intifada.

of some eight thousand full-year equivalent jobs, which represent a small fraction (5.6 percent) of the jobs lost in the intifada crisis (ILO 2004). Food aid programs seem to be much more cost efficient in the short term in delivering benefits than job creation programs, owing to the high cost of intermediary inputs in the latter. However, employment generation rather than food aid is identified by Palestinians as a major need and a preferred method of assistance. Clearly, the employment programs should be continued, but the content and the target group should be more gender specific, although this assistance can only partially alleviate the crisis caused by the military occupation (ILO 2004, 29).

Conclusion

The enormous difficulties that Palestinian households face under the Israeli colonial occupation have been somewhat ameliorated by women's work. Although the participation rate of women in the labor force has been limited, their informal work and economic, social, and organizational skills have made a great difference in sustaining their families during this ongoing national and economic crisis.

The chapter has focused on three different yet interrelated themes. One issue is the impact of colonial occupation and recent aggression on the labor market, which has been one of structural imbalances by maintaining its gendered segregated nature and even by marginalizing women in formal labor in certain sectors and imposing exploitive conditions of work in the informal sector. One manifestation of these imbalances is the low rate of participation of Palestinian women in the labor force. Although colonization, war, and instability have an important impact on labor markets in general, women are more vulnerable. The data suggest that there are more women seeking work these days, perhaps to compensate for the unemployment of men. It has been observed that when the family's existence is threatened, women are pushed to work to generate income, especially when the breadwinner is not able to meet the basic needs of the family.

Although the conditions of the Palestinian people are unique, the gendered markets and the occupational segmentation and segregation of employment in the occupied territories are similar to regional patterns in that employed women are mostly absorbed in the service and agricultural sectors.

Thus, in order to give more access and opportunities to women, a rebuilding or restructuring of the internal labor markets should be made in a gender-sensitive way such that equal opportunities are given to qualified women.

Data on employment before and during the intifada show that conflict and aggression have negatively impacted the labor markets and have pushed women and men to find alternative employment in the informal labor market as a strategy for survival in an environment of high unemployment, low participation of women in the labor force, and poverty reaching 62 percent.

An additional issue that has been emphasized in this chapter is that Palestinian women in the occupied territories have been economically active, although their contribution has not been reflected in formal statistics, because the bulk of their economic activity lies in the informal and domestic economies. In addition to formal labor, their economic activity includes informal employment for wages, home production for consumption, and efforts to cope with the overall crisis of Palestinian society perpetrated by occupation policies. It is important to realize that women's activities have been expressions of resistance as much as they have been an effort to survive the Israeli colonial onslaught. Collectively and individually, women have been providing social security, care for the wounded, and psychological support for those grieving loss of life. Although women engage in some of these activities to protect their own families, one can also view them as resistance strategies.

Lastly, with all the positive contributions that women make to maintain the family and cope with the crisis, these efforts may still be insufficient to withstand the type of aggression to which Palestinians are being subjected, including mass house demolitions, internal displacement, and mass impoverishment by design. These policies will eventually take their toll on households and especially on women. The scope of destruction and intensity of violence seem unpredictable, and there will be a time when families and in particular women cannot cope, and there is already evidence that some households and communities are not able to adapt. Indeed, occupation policies are not only affecting the material base but the social and psychological ones as well, and these kinds of stress are affecting not only individuals but also the social networks and relations that in times of crisis promote solidarity and sustain the community.

WORKS CITED
INDEX

WORKS CITED

Abu-Bakr, T. 1999. *Palestinians in Kuwait and the Gulf Crisis* (in Arabic). Amman, Jordan: Jenin Centre for Strategic Studies.

Abu-Lughod, L. 1989. "Zones of Theory in the Anthropology of the Arab World." *Review of Anthropology* 18:267–306.

Abu Nahleh, L. 2002a. "Preferences for Male and Female Children in Marriage: Who Should Girls and Boys Marry and Why." In *Inside Palestinian Households*, edited by R. Giacaman and P. Johnson, Birzeit, West Bank: Birzeit Univ.

———. 2002b. "Preferences for Employment: Contrasts Between Daughters and Daughters in Law." In *Inside Palestinian Households*, edited by R. Giacaman and P. Johnson. Birzeit, West Bank: Birzeit Univ.

Abu Nahleh, L., and P. Johnson. 2002. "Education: Choices, Preferences, and Aspirations for Male and Female Children." In *Inside Palestinian Households*, edited by R. Giacaman and P. Johnson. Birzeit, West Bank: Birzeit Univ., Institute of Women Studies and Institute for Community and Public Health.

———. 2003. "The Impact of Occupation, Wars, and Armed Conflicts on the Arab Family: The Case of Palestine." Unpublished paper presented at the ESCWA conference on the Arab Family, 7–9 Oct. Beirut, Lebanon.

Abu-Rayya, K. n.d. *Ramallah: Ancient and Modern*. American Federation of Ramallah, Palestine.

Abu Shukr, A. 1990. *External Migration from the West Bank and Gaza Strip, and Its Economic and Social Impact* (in Arabic). Jerusalem: Arab Thought Forum.

Agarwal, B. 1997. "Bargaining and Gender Relations Within and Beyond the Household." *Feminist Economist* 3, no. 1:1–39.

Ahmad, Aijaz. 1995. "The Politics of Literary Postcoloniality." *Race and Class* 36, no. 3:2–20.

Altorki, Soraya, and H. Zurayk. 1995. "Changes in Values in the Arab Family" (in Arabic). *Al-Mustaqbal al-Arabi* 200:76–113.

Amiry, S. 2003. *Throne Village Architecture: Palestinian Rural Mansions in the Eighteenth and Nineteenth Centuries* (in Arabic). Ramallah: Riwaq.

Ammons, L. 1979. "West Bank Arab Villages: The Influence of National and International Politics in Village Life." Ph.D. diss., Harvard Univ.

277

Amr, Y. 1985. *Arab Khalil al-Rahman: A City with a History* (in Arabic). Ramallah: Dar al-Qalam.

Anker, R. 1998. *Gender and Jobs: Sex Segregation of Occupations in the World.* Geneva: ILO.

Appadurai, A. 1997. *Modernity at Large: Cultural Dimensions of Globalization.* Delhi: Oxford Univ. Press.

Asad, T. 1975. "Anthropological Texts and Ideological Problems: An Analysis of Cohen on Arab Villages." *Review of Middle East Studies* 1:1–32.

Assad, R. 1997. "The Effects of Public Sector Hiring and Compensation Policies on the Egyptian Labor Market." *World Bank Economic Review,* Jan. 11.

Ata, I. W. 1986. *The West Bank Palestinian Family.* London, New York, Sydney, and Henley: KPI.

Barakat, H. 1993. *The Arab World: Society, Culture and State.* Berkeley: Univ. of California Press.

Barghuthi, M. 1998. *I Saw Ramallah* (in Arabic). Casablanca: Arab Cultural Center.

Ben-Arieh, Y. 1975. "The Population of the Large Towns in Palestine During the First Eighty Years of the Nineteenth Century, According to Western Sources." In *Studies on Palestine During the Ottoman Period,* edited by M. Ma'oz. Jerusalem: Magnes Press, 49–69.

Beneria, L., and S. Bisnath. 2001. "Gender and Poverty: An Analysis for Action." In *The Globalization Reader,* edited by F. Lechner and J. Coli. London: Blackwell.

Bishara, A. 1998. *Ruptured Political Discourse and Other Studies* (in Arabic). Ramallah, West Bank: Palestinian Institute for the Study of Democracy.

Bornstein, A. 2002. *Crossing the Green Line Between the West Bank and Israel.* Philadelphia: Univ. of Pennsylvania Press.

Bourdieu, P. 1990. *The Logic of Practice.* Stanford: Stanford Univ. Press.

——. 1993. *The Field of Cultural Production.* Cambridge: Polity Press.

——. 1994. "Social Space and Symbolic Power." In *The Polity Reader in Social Theory.* Cambridge: Polity Press: 111–20.

——. 1998. *Pascalian Mediations.* Cambridge: Cambridge Univ. Press.

——. 2001. *Masculine Domination.* Stanford: Stanford Univ. Press.

Bowman, G. 1999. "The Exilic Imagination: The Construction of the Landscape of Palestine from Its Outside." In *The Landscape of Palestine: Equivocal Poetry,* edited by I. Abu Lughod, R. Heacock, and K. Nashef. Birzeit, West Bank: Birzeit Univ.

Boyle, P., K. Halfacree, and V. Robinson 1998. *Exploring Contemporary Migration.* Harlow: Longman.

Brah, A. 1996. *Cartographies of Diaspora.* London: Routledge.

Calhoun, C. 1995. *Critical Social Theory: Culture, History, and the Challenge of Difference.* Oxford: Blackwell.

CAWTAR. 2001. *Globalization and Gender: Economic Participation of Arab Women.* Tunis: CAWTAR.

Cohen, A. 1965. *Arab Border Villages in Israel.* Manchester: Manchester Univ. Press.

Connor, S. 1996. "Cultural Sociology and Cultural Sciences." In *The Blackwell Companion to Social Theory,* edited by B. Turner. Oxford: Blackwell.

Cook, C., A. Hanieh, and A. Kay. 2004. *Stolen Youth: The Politics of Israel's Detention of Palestinian Children.* London: Pluto Press in Association with Defence for Children International, Palestine section.

Coordinator of Government Activities in the Territories (COGAT). 2004. Presentation to the ILO Committee.

Dajani, A. 1993. *The Twin Cities of Ramallah and al-Bireh and Their Surroundings.* N.p.

Dakkak, I. 1988. "Development from Within: A Strategy for Survival." In *The Palestinian Economy: Studies in Development under Prolonged Occupation,* edited by G. Abed. London: Routledge.

Davis, R. 2002. "Ottoman Jerusalem: The Growth of the City Outside the Walls." In *Jerusalem 1948: The Arab Neighborhoods and Their Fate in the War,* edited by S. Tamari, 2d ed. Jerusalem: Institute of Jerusalem Studies and Badil Resource Center.

De Certeau, M. 1988. *The Practice of Everyday Life.* Berkeley: Univ. of California Press.

Development Studies Program, Birzeit Univ. (DSP). 2002. http://home.birzeit .edu/dsp.

Doumani, B. 1995. *Rediscovering Palestine: Merchants and Peasants in Jabal Nablus, 1700–1900.* Berkeley: Univ. of California Press.

———. 2003. "Introduction." In *Family History in the Middle East: Household, Property, and Gender,* edited by Beshara Doumani. Albany: State Univ. of New York Press.

Economic Policy Research Institute (MAS). 2000. *Economic Monitor.* No. 7. Ramallah, West Bank: Economic Policy Research Institute.

ESCWA Center for Women. 2003. *Arab Preparatory Meeting for the Ten Year Review of the International Year of the Family (IYF) 1994+10—Beirut.* http://www .escwa.org.lb/ecw/ev_details.asp?ID=16.

Esim, S., and E. Kuttab. 2002. *Women's Informal Employment in Palestine: Securing a Livelihood Against All Odds.* ERF Working Papers Series, Paper 0213.

Fargues, Philippe. 2003. "Family and Household in Mid-Nineteenth-Century Cairo."

In *Family History in the Middle East: Household, Property, and Gender,* edited by B. Doumani. Albany: State Univ. of New York Press: 23–50.

Farsoun, S. 1970. "Family Structure and Society in Modern Lebanon." In *Peoples and Cultures of the Middle East: An Anthropological Reader,* edited by L. Sweet. Vol. 2. Garden City: Natural History Press.

Fleischmann, E. 2003. *The Nation and Its "New" Women: The Palestinian Women's Movement 1920–1948.* Berkeley: Univ. of California Press.

Frisch, H. 1997. "Modern Absolutist or Neopatriarchal State Building? Customary Law, Extended Families, and the Palestinian Authority." *International Journal Middle East Studies* 29:341–58.

Geertz, H. 1979. "The Meaning of Family Ties." In *Meaning and Order in Moroccan Society: Three Essays in Cultural Analysis,* edited by H. Geertz, C. Geertz, and L. Rosen. Cambridge: Cambridge Univ. Press.

Gerber, H. 1987. *The Social Origins of the Modern Middle East.* Boulder, Colo.: Lynne Rienner.

Ghabra, S. 1988. "Palestinians in Kuwait: The Family and the Politics of Survival." *Journal of Palestine Studies* 17, no. 2:62–83.

Giacaman, R. 1997. "Population and Fertility: Population Policies, Women's Rights and Sustainable Development." In *Palestinian Women: A Status Report,* no. 2. Birzeit, West Bank: Birzeit Univ.

Giacaman, R., and P. Johnson. 2002a. "Characteristics of Heads of Households, Household Composition, and Household Labor Patterns." In *Inside Palestinian Households,* edited by R. Giacaman and P. Johnson. Birzeit, West Bank: Birzeit Univ., Institute of Women Studies and Institute for Community and Public Health.

———, eds. 2002b. *Inside Palestinian Households: Initial Analysis of a Community-Based Household Survey.* Vol. 1. Birzeit, West Bank: Birzeit Univ.

Giacaman, R., A. Abdullah, R. Abu Safieh, and L. Shamieh. 2002. *Schooling at Gunpoint: Palestinian Children's Learning Environment in Warlike Conditions: The Ramallah/al-Bireh/Beitunia Urban Center.* Birzeit: West Bank: Birzeit Univ., Institute of Community and Public Health.

Giacaman, R., H. Saab, V. Nguyen-Gillham, A. Abdullah, and G. Naser. 2004a. *Palestinian Adolescents Coping with Trauma. Initial Findings.* Birzeit: Institute of Community and Public Health, Birzeit Univ.

Giacaman, R., A. Mataria, V. Nguyen-Gillham, R. Abu Safieh, A. Stephanini, S. Chattery. 2006. "Quality of Life in the Palestinian Context: An Inquiry in War-Like Conditions." Birzeit: Institute of Community and Public Health, Birzeit Univ.; Gaza Community Mental Health Programme; World Health Organization, Jerusalem.

Gieryn, T. 2000. "A Space for Place in Sociology." *Annual Review of Sociology* 26:463–96.

Gilbar, G. G. 1997. *Population Dilemmas in the Middle East.* London: Frank Cass.

Gilen, Signe, et al. *Finding Ways: Palestinian Coping Strategies in Changing Environments.* Fafo report 177. Oslo: Fafo Institute of Applied International Studies.

Glavanis, K., and P. Glavanis. 1989. *The Rural Middle East.* London: Zed Books.

Graham-Brown, S. 1982. "The Political Economy of the Jabal Nablus, 1920–48." In *Studies in the Economic and Social History of Palestine in the Nineteenth and Twentieth Centuries*, edited by R. Owen. London: Macmillan, 88–176.

———. 1989. "Impact on the Social Structure of Palestinian Society." In *Occupation: Israel over Palestine*, edited by N. Aruri. Belmont: AAUG Press.

Granqvist, H. 1931. *Marriage Conditions in a Palestinian Village.* Vol. 1. Finland: Helsingfors.

Hammami, R. 1993. "Women in Palestinian Society." In *Palestinian Society in Gaza, West Bank, and Arab Jerusalem: A Survey of Living Conditions*, edited by M. Heiberg and G. Ovensen. Oslo: Fafo Institute for Applied International Studies.

———. 1997. *Labor and Economy: Gender Segmentation in Palestinian Economic Life.* Birzeit, West Bank: Women's Studies Program, Birzeit Univ.

———. 1998. "The Cultural Construction of Gender Work and Culture: Palestinian Rural Women's Work Experience in the Pre-Nakba." In *Women's Time and Alternative Memory*, edited by H. Sadda et al., 299–313. Cairo: Women and Memory Forum.

———. 2001. "Gender Segmentation in the West Bank and Gaza Strip: Explaining the Absence of Palestinian Women from the Formal Labor Force." In *The Economics of Women and Work in the Middle East and North Africa*, edited by M. Cinar. Amsterdam: JAI Press.

———. 2004a. "On the Importance of Thugs: The Moral Economy of a Checkpoint." *Middle East Report* 34, no. 231/32:26–34.

———. 2004b. "Attitudes Towards Legal Reform of Personal Status Law in Palestine." In *Women's Rights and Islamic Family Law: Perspectives on Reform*, edited by L. Welchman. London: Zed Press.

Hammami, R., and E. Kuttab. 1998. "Towards New Strategies for the Women's Movement, Democratic Transformation and Independence." In *After the Crisis: Structural Changes in Palestinian Political Life* (in Arabic). Ramallah: Muwatin, the Palestinian Institute for the Study of Democracy.

Hanssen-Bauer, J., J. Pedersen, and A. A. Tiltnes, eds. 1998. *Jordanian Society: Living Conditions in the Hashemite Kingdom of Jordan.* Fafo report 253. Oslo: Fafo Institute of Applied International Studies.

Harvey, D. 2001. *Spaces of Capital: Towards a Critical Geography*. London: Routledge.

Hass, A. 2003. *Reporting from Ramallah*. Cambridge, Mass.: MIT Press.

Heiberg, M., and G. Ovensen, eds. 1993. *Palestinian Society in Gaza, West Bank, and Arab Jerusalem: A Survey of Living Conditions*. Fafo report 151. Oslo: Fafo Institute for Applied International Studies.

Hilal, J. 1970. "Father's Brother's Daughter Marriage in Arab Communities: A Problem for Sociological Explanation." *Middle East Forum* 46, no. 2:73–84.

———. 1975. *West Bank: Economic and Social Structure 1948–1974* (in Arabic). Beirut: Research Center.

———. 1998. *The Palestinian Political System after Oslo: An Analytical and Critical Study* (in Arabic). Beirut and Ramallah: Institute for Palestine Studies and the Palestinian Institute for the Study of Democracy.

———. 1999. *Palestinian Society and the Problematic of Democracy* (in Arabic). Nablus, West Bank: Center for Palestinian Research and Studies.

———. 2002. *The Formation of the Palestinian Elite* (in Arabic). Ramallah, West Bank: Muwatin, Palestinian Institute for the Study of Democracy; Amman, Jordan: Al-Urdun al-Jadid Research Center.

Hobsbawm, E., and T. Ranger. 1983. *The Invention of Tradition*. Cambridge: Cambridge Univ. Press.

Holy, L. 1989. *Kinship, Honor, and Solidarity: Cousin Marriage in the Middle East*. Manchester: Manchester Univ. Press.

Hoodfar, H. 1997. *Between Marriage and the Market: Intimate Politics and Survival in Cairo*. Berkeley: Univ. of California Press.

Hopkins, N., ed. 2003. *The New Arab Family*. Cairo: American Univ. of Cairo.

Hovedenak, A., J. Pedersen, D. H. Tuastad, and E. Zureik. 1997. *Constructing Order: Palestinian Adaptation to Refugee Life*. Fafo report no. 236. Oslo: Fafo Institute for Applied International Studies.

al-Hut, B. 1984. *Political Leaders and Institutions in Palestine 1917–1948* (in Arabic). 'Akka: Dar al-Aswar and Institute for Palestine Studies.

Institute of Community and Public Health, Birzeit Univ. (ICPH). 2002. Emergency 2002 Reports. http://icph.birzeit.edu/emergency_reports.htm.

Institute of Women's Studies (IWS). 2001. "Women's Income Generating Projects Survey." Unpublished report.

International Labor Office (ILO). 2000. *World Labor Report*. Geneva: ILO.

———. 2003. *The Situation of Workers of the Occupied Territories*. Report of the Director-General. Geneva: ILO.

———. 2004. *The Situation of Workers of the Occupied Territories*. Report of the Director General. Geneva: ILO.

Jad, I., et al. 2000a. "Transit Citizens: Gender and Citizenship under the Palestinian Authority." In *Gender and Citizenship in the Middle East*, edited by S. Joseph. Syracuse: Syracuse Univ. Press.

———. 2000b. *Women and Politics* (in Arabic). Birzeit, West Bank: Institute of Women's Studies, Birzeit Univ.

Jean-Klein, Iris. 2000. "Mothercraft, Statecraft, and Subjectivity in the Palestinian Intifada." *American Ethnologist* 27, no. 1:100–127.

———. 2001. "Nationalism and Resistance: The Two Faces of Everyday Activism in Palestine During the Intifada." *Cultural Anthropology* 16, no. 1:83–126.

Johns Hopkins Univ. et al. 2002. *Health Sector Bi-weekly Report*, No. 1. Jerusalem.

Johnson, P. 2002. "Perceptions of the Costs and Benefits of Children." In *Inside Palestinian Households*, edited by R. Giacaman and P. Johnson. Birzeit, West Bank: Birzeit Univ., Institute of Women Studies and Institute for Community and Public Health.

Johnson, P., and E. Kuttab. 2001. "Where Have All the Women (and Men) Gone? Reflections on Gender and the Second Palestinian Intifada." *Feminist Review* 69:21–43.

Joseph, S. 2004. "Conceiving Family Relationships in Postwar Lebanon." *Journal of Comparative Family Studies* 35, no. 2:271–93.

Ju'beh, N. 2003. Interviewed by Lisa Taraki, Ramallah, West Bank, Nov.

Ju'beh, N., and K. Bishara. 2002. *Ramallah, Architecture and History* (in Arabic). Ramallah, West Bank: Riwaq and Institute for Jerusalem Studies.

Kandiyoti, D. 1988. "Bargaining with Patriarchy." *Gender and Society* 2, no. 3:282–89.

Kark, R. 1989. "Transportation in Nineteenth-Century Palestine: Reintroduction of the Wheel." In *The Land That Became Israel: Studies in Historical Geography*, edited by R. Kark. New Haven and Jerusalem: Yale Univ. Press and Magnes Press, Hebrew Univ. of Jerusalem, 57–76.

Karmi, G. 2002. *In Search of Fatima: A Palestinian Story*. London and New York: Verso.

Karmon, Y. 1975. "Changes in the Urban Geography of Hebron During the Nineteenth Century." In *Studies on Palestine During the Ottoman Period*, edited by M. Ma'oz. Jerusalem: Magnes Press, 70–86.

Katz, E. 1997. "The Intra-Household Relations of Voice and Exit." *Feminist Economist* 3, no. 3:25–46.

Khalidi, R. 1997. *Palestinian Identity: The Construction of Modern National Consciousness*. New York: Columbia Univ. Press.

Khater, A. F. 2001. *Inventing Home: Emigration, Gender, and the Middle Class in Lebanon 1870–1920*. Berkeley: Univ. of California Press.

Khuri, F. 1970. "Parallel Cousin Marriage Reconsidered: A Middle Eastern Practice

That Nullifies the Effects of Marriage on the Intensity of Family Relationships." *Man,* new ser., 5, no. 4 (1970): 597–618.

Kimmerling, B., and J. Migdal. 2003. *The Palestinian People: A History.* Cambridge, Mass.: Harvard Univ. Press.

Kushner, D. 1997. "Zealous Towns in Nineteenth-Century Palestine." *Middle Eastern Studies* 33, no. 3:597–612.

Kuttab, E. 1989. "Community Development under Occupation: An Alternative Strategy." *Journal of Refugee Studies* 2, no. 1:131–38.

——. 1993. "Palestinian Women in the Intifada: Fighting on Two Fronts." *Arab Studies Quarterly* 15, no. 2:69–85.

Kuttab, E., and R. Barghouti. 2002. "The Impact of Political Violence on Palestinian Women." Unpublished report prepared for UNIFEM.

Labadi, F. 2004. "Is a Woman Half a Man? Diya and the Utilization of Principles of Shari'a in Public and Customary Legal Processes." In *Women's Rights and Islamic Family Law: Perspectives on Reform,* edited by Lynn Welchman. London: Zed Press.

Lechner, Frank, and J. Coli. 2000. *The Globalization Reader.* London: Blackwell.

Levi-Strauss, C. 1968. *The Elementary Structures of Kinship.* Boston: Beacon Press.

Lutfiyya, A. M. 1961. "Baytin, a Jordanian Village: A Study of Social Institutions and Social Change in Folk Society." Ph.D. thesis, Univ. of Michigan.

Lutfiyya, A. M. 1966. *Baytin, a Jordanian Village: A Study of Social Institutions and Social Change in a Folk Society.* The Hague: Mouton.

Malki, M., and K. Shalabi. 1993. *Socioeconomic Changes in Three Palestinian Villages* (in Arabic). Ramallah, West Bank: Ma'an.

——. 2000. *Internal Migration and Palestinian Returnees in West Bank and Gaza Strip.* Ramallah, West Bank: Palestine Economic Policy Research Institute.

Manna', A. 1999. *The History of Palestine in the Late Ottoman Period 1700–1918: A New Reading* (in Arabic). Beirut: Institute of Palestine Studies.

Masri, M. 1997. *Nablusiyyat* (in Arabic). Nablus: Khalid Bin Walid and Najah Presses.

McCann, L. 1993. *Patrilineal Co-residential Units (PCUs) in Al-Barha: Dual Household Structure in a Provincial Town in Jordan.* Amman, Jordan: UNICEF.

Migdal, J. 1980. *Palestinian Society and Politics.* Princeton, N.J.: Princeton Univ. Press.

Ministry of Planning and International Cooperation (MOPIC), UNDP, and DFID. 2002. *National Report on Participatory Poverty Assessment (Voice of the Palestinian Poor).* Ramallah, West Bank: Ministry of Planning and International Cooperation, UNDP, and DFID.

Mogannam, M. 1937. *The Arab Woman and the Palestine Problem.* London: Herbert Joseph.

Moghadam, V. 2000. "Enhancing Women's Economic Participation in the Arab Region." Paper prepared for the Mediterranean Development Forum (MDF) conference, Cairo.

Moors, A. 1995. *Women, Property, and Islam: Palestinian Experiences 1920–1990.* Cambridge: Cambridge Univ. Press.

Muhammad, Z. 2002. *On Palestinian Culture* (in Arabic). Ramallah, West Bank: Palestinian Institute for the Study of Democracy.

Mundy, M. 1995. *Domestic Government: Kinship, Community, and Polity in North Yemen.* London: I. B. Taurus.

Musallam, A. 2003. *The Diaries of Khalil Sakakini: New York, Sultana, Al-quds 1907–1912* (in Arabic). Jerusalem: Institute of Jerusalem Studies and Khalil Sakakini Cultural Center.

National Commission for Poverty Alleviation (NCPA). 1998. *Palestine Poverty Report 1998.* Ramallah, West Bank: Palestinian National Authority.

Nicholson, L. 1997. "The Myth of the Traditional Family." In *Feminism and Families,* edited by H. Nelson. London: Routledge.

O'Brien, L., and F. Pickup. 2002. *Forgotten Villages: Struggling to Survive under Closure in the West Bank.* Oxfam Briefing Paper no. 28. New York: Oxfam.

Ovensen, G. 1994. *Responding to Change: Trends in Palestinian Household Economy.* Oslo: Fafo Institute for Applied International Studies.

Paasi, A. 2002. "Place and Region: Regional Worlds and Words." *Progress in Human Geography* 26, no. 6:802–11.

Palestine Monitor. 2004. Statistics for the Palestinian Intifada, 28 Sept. 2000–1 Mar. 2004. http://www.palestinemonitor.org/nueva_web/facts_sheets/intifada.htm (2004).

Palestine Red Crescent. 2005. http://www.palestinercs.org/Presentation%20Power-Point%20Curfew%20Tracking%20July%202002_files/frame.htm.

Palestinian Central Bureau of Statistics (PCBS). 1995. *Labor Force Survey, Annual Reports.* Ramallah, West Bank: Palestinian Central Bureau of Statistics.

———. 1997a. *Demographic Survey of the West Bank and Gaza Strip; Final Results.* Ramallah, West Bank: Palestinian Central Bureau of Statistics.

———. 1997b. *The Health Survey in the West Bank and Gaza Strip: Main Findings.* Ramallah, West Bank: Palestinian Central Bureau of Statistics.

———. 1997c. *District by District Comparative Results. The Demographic Survey in the West Bank and Gaza Strip, District Report Series,* no. 10. Ramallah, West Bank: Palestinian Central Bureau of Statistics.

——. 1999a. *Population, Housing and Establishment Census—1997.* Ramallah, West Bank: Palestinian Central Bureau of Statistics (city and region-specific data sets).

——. 1999b. *Final Results, Population Report: Nablus Governorate: Second Part.* Ramallah, West Bank: Palestinian Central Bureau of Statistics.

——. 1999c. *Final Results, Population Report: Jenin Governorate: Second Part.* Ramallah, West Bank: Palestinian Central Bureau of Statistics.

——. 1999d. *Final Results, Population Report: Hebron Governorate: Second Part.* Ramallah, West Bank: Palestinian Central Bureau of Statistics.

——. 1999e. *Labor Force Survey, Annual Reports.* Ramallah, West Bank: Palestinian Central Bureau of Statistics.

——. 1999f. *Population Report, Palestinian Territory, Final Results.* Part 1. Ramallah, West Bank: Palestinian Central Bureau of Statistics.

——. 2000a. *Population, Housing, and Establishment Census, Final Results: Ramallah City.* City Reports Series 005. Ramallah, West Bank: Palestinian Central Bureau of Statistics.

——. 2000b. *Health Survey 2000; Basic Results.* Ramallah, West Bank: Palestinian Central Bureau of Statistics.

——. 2000c. *Labor Force Survey—1999,* original data set. Ramallah, West Bank: Palestinian Central Bureau of Statistics.

——. 2000d. *Labor Force Survey, Annual Report 1997–2000.* Ramallah, West Bank: Palestinian Central Bureau of Statistics.

——. 2001. *Time Use Survey 1999/2000: Time Use in the Palestinian Territory.* Ramallah, West Bank: Palestinian Central Bureau of Statistics.

——. 2002a. *Family Formation in the Palestinian Territory.* Ramallah, West Bank: Palestinian Central Bureau of Statistics.

——. 2002b. *Labor Force Survey, Main Findings (Jan.-Mar. 2001 and round June 2002).* Labor force reports nos. 20–25. Ramallah, West Bank: Palestinian Central Bureau of Statistics.

——. 2003. *The Labor Force 2003 Annual Report.* Press Release. Ramallah, West Bank: Palestinian Central Bureau of Statistics.

——. 2004a. *Impact of the Israeli Measures on the Economic Conditions of the Palestinian Households (8th Round: Jan.-Mar. 2004).* Press conference on the survey results, May 2004.

——. 2004b. *Health Survey 2004: Summary of Main Indicators.* Ramallah, West Bank: Palestinian Central Bureau of Statistics.

Palestinian NGO Emergency Initiative in Jerusalem. 2002a. "Destruction of Palestinian Nongovernmental Organizations in Ramallah." Unpublished report circulated on the Internet.

———. 2002b. "Report on Destruction of Palestinian Governmental Institutions in Ramallah." Unpublished report circulated on the Internet.

Parmenter, B. M. 1994. *Giving Voice to Stones: Place and Identity in Palestinian Literature.* Austin: Univ. of Texas Press.

Pedersen, J. 1997. *West Bank and Gaza Strip Living Conditions: Are Refugees Different?* Oslo: Fafo Institute for Applied International Studies.

Pedersen, J., et al. 2001a. *Growing Fast: The Palestinian Population in the West Bank and Gaza Strip.* Fafo report no. 353. Oslo: Fafo Institute for Applied International Studies.

Pedersen, J., et al. 2001b. *Paying a Price: Coping with Closure in Two Palestinian Villages.* Fafo report 371. Oslo: Fafo Institute for Applied International Studies.

Peteet, J. 1991. *Gender in Crisis: Women and the Palestinian Resistance Movement.* New York: Columbia Univ. Press.

———. 1994. "Male Gender and Rituals of Resistance in the Palestinian Intifada: A Cultural Politics of Violence." *American Ethnologist* 21, no. 1:31–49.

———. 1997. "Icons and Militants: Mothering in the Danger Zone." *Signs* 23, no. 1:103–29.

Qaddura, Y. 1999. *The History of the City of Ramallah* (in Arabic). Ramallah, West Bank: Rafidi Printers.

Qura, N., ed. 2002. *Ramallah the Dream, Ramallah the Place* (in Arabic). Ramallah, West Bank: Ramallah Public Library.

Rashad, H., and Magued Osman. 2003. "Nuptiality in Arab Countries: Changes and Implications." In *The New Arab Family,* edited by Nicholas Hopkins. Cairo Papers in Social Sciences. Cairo: American Univ. of Cairo Press.

Rosenfeld, H. 1976. "Social and Economic Factors in Explanation of the Increased Rate of Patrilineal Endogamy in the Arab Villages in Israel." In *Mediterranean Family Structures,* edited by J. G. Peristiany. Cambridge: Cambridge Univ. Press.

Rosenfeld, M. 2004. *Confronting the Occupation.* Stanford: Stanford Univ. Press.

Rothenberg, C. E. 1998/1999. "A Review of the Anthropological Literature in English on the Palestinian Hamula and the Status of Women." *Journal of Arabic and Islamic Studies* 2:24–48.

Roy, S. 1987. "The Gaza Strip: A Case of Economic De-development." *Journal of Palestine Studies* 17:56–88.

———. 1995. *The Gaza Strip: The Political Economy of De-development.* London: Institute of Palestine Studies, I. B. Tauris.

———. 2002. "Why Peace Failed: An Oslo Autopsy." *Current History* 101, no. 651:8–16.

Rubinstein, D. 2002. "The Rumors about Palestinian Democracy Were Premature." *Haaretz,* 18 Sept.

Russell, S. S. 1995. *Policy Dimensions of Female Migrants to the Arab Countries of Western Asia: International Migration Policies and the Status of the Female Migrant*. New York: United Nations, Department for Economic and Social Information and Policy Analysis, Population Division.

Ryan, C. 2005. "Reform Retreats amid Jordan's Political Storms." *Middle East Report Online*. 10 June. http://www.merip.org/mero/mero061005.html.

Said, E. 1999. *Out of Place: A Memoir*. New York: Knopf.

Sakakini, H. 1987. *Jerusalem and I: A Personal Record*. Jerusalem: Habash Press.

Salah, Y. n.d. *Pages from the Palestinian Memory: Recollections of Yusra Salah* (in Arabic). Birzeit, West Bank: Birzeit Univ.

Sayigh, R. 1979. *Palestinians from Peasants to Revolutionaries*. London: Zed Books.

———. 1981. "Roles and Functions of Arab Women: A Reappraisal." *Arab Studies Quarterly*, 3, no. 3 (1981): 258–74.

———. 1989. "Encounters with Palestinian Women under Occupation." In *Occupation: Israel over Palestine*, edited by N. Aruri, 465–90. Belmont: AAUG.

Scholch, A. 1993. *Palestine in Transformation 1856–1882*. Washington, D.C.: Institute for Palestine Studies.

Seikaly, M. 1995. *Haifa: Transformation of an Arab Society, 1918–1939*. London: I. B. Tauris.

Sen, Amartya. 1990. "Gender and Cooperative Conflicts." In *Persistent Inequalities: Women and World Development*, edited by Irene Tinker. Oxford: Oxford Univ. Press.

Sethuraman, S. V. 2000. *Gender, Informality, and Poverty: A Global Review: Gender Bias in Female Informal Employment and Incomes in Developing Countries*. Draft study of the World Bank and WIEGO.

Shaheen, A. 1982. *Ramallah, Its History and Its Genealogies*. Birzeit: Birzeit Univ.

Shaheen, N. 1992. *A Pictorial History of Ramallah*. Beirut: Arab Institute for Research and Publishing.

Shami, S. 1996. "Gender, Domestic Space, and Urban Upgrading: A Case Study from Amman." *Gender and Development* 4, no. 1:17–23.

Sharabi, H. n.d. *Embers and Ashes: Memoirs of an Arab Intellectual* (in Arabic). Ibn Rushd Press.

Shehadeh, R. 1985. *Occupier's Law: Israel and the West Bank*. Washington, D.C.: Institute for Palestine Studies.

Sholkamy, Hania. 2003. "Rationales for Kin Marriages in Rural Upper Egypt." In *The New Arab Family*, edited by Nicholas Hopkins. Cairo: American Univ. of Cairo Press, 62–79.

Singerman, D., and H. Hoodfar. 1996. *Development, Change, and Gender in Cairo: A View from the Household*. Bloomington: Indiana Univ. Press.

——. 1998. "Engaging Informality: Women, Work, and Politics in Cairo." In *Middle Eastern Women and the Invisible Economy*, edited by R. Lobban, Jr. Gainesville: Univ. Press of Florida.

Sletten, P., and J. Pedersen. 2003. *Coping with Conflict: Palestinian Communities Two Years into the Intifada*. Fafo report 408. Oslo: Fafo Institute for Applied International Studies.

Stack, C. 2003. "Frameworks for Studying Families in the Twenty-First Century." In *The New Arab Family*, edited by Nicholas Hopkins. Cairo: American Univ. of Cairo Press.

Stacul, J. 2003. *The Bounded Field: Localism and Local Identity in an Italian Alpine Valley*. Berghahn Books.

Stokke, L. 2002. "Marriage Patterns." In *Growing Up Fast: The Palestinian Population in the West Bank and Gaza Strip*, edited by J. Pederson, S. Randal, and M. Khawaja. Fafo Report 353. Oslo: Fafo Institute for Applied International Studies.

Stone, L. 1997. *Kinship and Gender: An Introduction*. Boulder: Westview Press.

Tamari, S. 1981. "Building Other People's Homes." *Journal of Palestine Studies* 11–12, no. 1:31–66.

——. 1982. "Factionalism and Class Formation in Recent Palestinian History." In *Studies in the Economic and Social History of Palestine in the Nineteenth and Twentieth Centuries*, edited by R. Owen, 177–202. London: Macmillan.

——. 1983. "The Dislocation and Re-constitution of a Peasantry: The Social Economy of Agrarian Palestine in the Central Highlands and Jordan Valley, 1960–1980." Ph.D. diss., Faculty of Economic and Social Studies, Univ. of Manchester.

——. 1989. "Israel's Search for a Native Pillar: The Village Leagues." In *Occupation: Israel over Palestine*, edited by Nasser Aruri. Belmont, Mass.: Association of Arab-American University Graduates.

——. 1993. "The Transformation of Palestinian Society: Fragmentation and Occupation." In *Palestinian Society in Gaza, West Bank, and Arab Jerusalem: A Survey of Living Conditions*. Fafo report 151. Oslo: Fafo Institute for Applied International Studies.

——. 1995. "D'Ema Bovary a Hasan al-Banna: dynamiques culturelles des petites villes en mediterranee orientale." *Peuples Mediterranees* 72–73:271–300.

——. 2001. "Jerusalem: Subordination and Governance in a Sacred Geography." In *Capital Cities: Ethnographies of Urban Governance in the Middle East*, edited by S. Shami, 175–98. Toronto: Centre for Urban and Community Studies, Univ. of Toronto.

——, ed. 2002a. *Jerusalem 1948: The Arab Neighbourhoods and Their Fate in the War*. Jerusalem: Institute of Jerusalem Studies and Badil Resource Center.

——. 2002b. "Bourgeois Nostalgia and the Abandoned City." Unpublished paper.

Tamari, S., and I. Nassar, eds. 2003. *Ottoman Jerusalem in the Jawhariyeh Memoirs* (in Arabic). Jerusalem: Institute for Jerusalem Studies.

Taraki, L. 1991. "The Development of Political Consciousness among Palestinians in the Occupied Territories, 1967–1987." In *Intifada, Palestine at the Crossroads*, edited by J. Nassar and R. Heacock. New York: Praeger.

——. 1999. "On the Importance of Having Kin." Unpublished paper, Institute of Women's Studies household survey project.

Tawil, R. 1979. *My Home, My Prison*. New York: Holt, Rinehart and Winston.

Taylor, C. 2002. "Modern Social Imaginaries." *Public Culture* 14, no. 1:91–124.

Tillon, G. 1966. *The Republic of Cousins: Women's Oppression in Mediterranean Society*. London: al Saqi Books.

Tuastad, D. 1997. "The Organization of Camp Life: The Palestinian Camp of Bureij, Gaza." In *Constructing Order: Palestinian Adaptations to Refugee Life*, edited by A. Hovenednak, J. Pederson, D. Tuastad, and E. Zureik. Fafo report 236. Oslo: Fafo Institute for Applied International Studies.

Tuqan, F. n.d. *Difficult Journey, Mountainous Journey* (in Arabic). 'Akka: Dar al-Aswar.

United Nations Department of Economics and Social Affairs (UNDESA). 1999. *World Survey on the Role of Women in Development: Globalization, Gender, and Work. Report of the Secretary General to the Fifty-fourth Session: Sustainable Development and International Economic Cooperation: Women in Development.* New York, UNDESA.

United Nations Development Program (UNDP). 2003. Human Development Report. Oxford: Oxford Univ. Press.

——. 2005. *Arab Human Development Report: Towards Freedom in the Arab World.* New York: United Nations Development Programme.

United Nations Office of the Special Coordinator in the Occupied Territories (UNSCO). 2001. *The Impact on the Palestinian Economy of the Recent Confrontations, Mobility Restrictions, and Border Closures, 28 Sept.–26 Nov.* Gaza: UNSCO.

United Nations Relief and Works Agency (UNRWA). 2003. UNRWA emergency appeal 2003. Gaza: UNRWA Headquarters Gaza, Department of International Relations (www.unrwa.org).

United Nations Women's Indicators and Statistics Database (UNWISTAT). 1999. CD ROM, version 4.

Usher, G. 2003. "Facing Defeat: The Intifada Two Years On." *Journal of Palestine Studies* 32, no. 2:21–40.

Van Arkadie, B. 1977. *Benefits and Burdens: A Report on the West Bank and Gaza Strip*

Economies since 1967. Washington, D.C.: Carnegie Endowment for International Peace.

Welchman, L. 1992. "The Islamic Law of Marriage and Divorce in the Occupied West Bank: Theory and Practice." Ph.D. diss., Department of Law, School of Oriental and African Studies, London Univ.

"The Workers of the Strip. . . . All Ways Are Blocked, There Is No Answer to the Pleas of Their Children." 2002. *Al-Ayyam*, 3 July.

World Bank. 1993. *Developing the Occupied Territories: An Investment in Peace.* Vol. 1. Washington, D.C: World Bank.

——. 2002a. *Long-Term Policy Options for the Palestinian Economy.* Jerusalem: World Bank.

——. 2002b. *Fifteen Months—Intifada, Closures and Palestinian Economic Crisis—An Assessment.* Washington, D.C.: World Bank. 2002.

——. 2003. *Two Years of Intifada, Closures, and Economic Crisis: An Assessment.* Washington, D.C: World Bank.

——. 2004. *MENA Development Report: Gender and Development in the Middle East and North Africa: Women in the Public Sphere.* Washington, D.C: World Bank.

Yunis, I., et al. 1991. *The Transformation of an Urban Community: Studies in Social Morphology, Ruralization, and the Informal Sector in the City of Ramallah.* Occasional Paper No. 4, Afaq Filistiniyya Series (in Arabic), Birzeit, West Bank.

Zafiris, et al. 2003. "Women in the Mena Labor Market: An Eclectic Survey." In *Women and Globalization in the Arab Middle East: Gender, Economy, and Society,* edited by E. Doumato and M. Posusney. Boulder: Lynne Rienner.

Zureik, Elia. 2003. "Demography and Transfer: Israel's Road to Nowhere." *Third World Quarterly* 24, no. 4:619–30.

INDEX